The Heart
of the Matter

The Heart
of the Matter
Pastoral Ministry in
Anabaptist Perspective

Erick Sawatzky
Editor

Publishing House
the new name of Pandora Press U.S.
Telford, Pennsylvania

copublished with
Herald Press
Scottdale, Pennsylvania

Cascadia Publishing House orders, information, reprint permissions
contact@CascadiaPublishingHouse.com
1-215-723-9125
126 Klingerman Road, Telford PA 18969
www.CascadiaPublishingHouse.com

The Heart of the Matter

Copublished with Herald Press, Scottdale PA 15683

Published in association with Institute of Mennonite Studies
Associated Mennonite Biblical Seminary
3003 Benham Avenue
Elkhart IN 46517-1999

Library of Congress Catalog Number: 2003026789
ISBN: 1-931038-22-8
Printed in the United States of America by Evangel Press, Nappanee, Indiana
Book and cover design by Gwen Miller
Cover graphic by David Fast

Unless otherwise noted, Bible quotations are from the New Revised Standard
Version (NRSV), copyright 1989, by the Division of Christian Education of
the National Council of Churches of Christ in the USA. Other versions cited
include the King James Version (KJV), the New American Bible (NAB), and the
New International Version (NIV).

Library of Congress Cataloging-in-Publication Data
The heart of the matter : pastoral ministry in Anabaptist perspective /
Erick Sawatzky, editor.
    p. cm.
Includes bibliographical references and indexes.
    ISBN 1-931038-22-8 (pbk. : alk. paper)
    1. Anabaptists—Doctrines. 2. Pastoral theology—Anabaptists.
I. Sawatzky, Erick. II. Title.
BX4931.3.H43 2004
253'.088'2897—dc22

                        2003026789

Contents

Preface   vii
Erick Sawatzky

Contributors   ix

Introduction   1
Loren L. Johns

1 **"That some would be pastors"**   15
Ross T. Bender

2 **Worldly preachers and true shepherds**   24
Anabaptist anticlericalism in the Lower Rhine
Karl Koop

3 **Mennonite ministry and Christian history**   39
Walter Sawatsky

4 **Ecclesiology, authority, and ministry**   60
An Anabaptist-Mennonite perspective
Gayle Gerber Koontz

5 **The pastor as teacher**   74
Perry B. Yoder

6 **A New Testament model for ministry and leadership**   85
Jacob W. Elias

7 ***Ordination* in the King James Version of the Bible**   105
Loren L. Johns

8 **The pastor as prophet**   118
Ben C. Ollenburger

9 **Pastors and the church's witness in society**   129
Ted Koontz

10 **"For God so loved"**   138
Mary H. Schertz

11 **The pastor as healer**   149
Willard M. Swartley

12 **The pastor as spiritual orienteer**   162
A pastoral theology approach
Arthur Paul Boers

13 **Paying attention**   176
The minister as listener
June Alliman Yoder

14 **Pastoral ministry as improvisatory art**   186
Rebecca Slough

15 **The pastor as caregiving sage**   198
Daniel S. Schipani

16 **Power and authority**   213
Helping the church face problems and adapt to change
J. Nelson Kraybill

17 **What is at the heart of pastoral ministry?**   228
Erick Sawatzky

Introduction to appendixes   238

Appendix 1   239
*Ministerial formation and theological education
in Mennonite perspective*

Appendix 2   257
Theological education and curricular design at AMBS

Index of Scripture references   263

Subject index   266

Preface

Throughout my professional life, issues of pastoral ministry and leadership have been for me a special focus of theological reflection. I have been privileged with opportunities to serve in diverse settings, which have afforded opportunity to consider fundamental issues and questions—what I have come to consider the heart of the matter in pastoral ministry—from several points of view. I am grateful for manifold, rich experiences I enjoyed as a congregational pastor, as a prison chaplain, and as field education director and teacher involved in the ministerial formation of seminary students for many years. Those experiences have nurtured my Christian faith and shaped my ministerial vocation.

It was in the light of such praxis that I envisioned the project culminating in this book. I mean *praxis* in the sense of practice that we reflect on, experience that in turn validates our thought. In fact, during my years of teaching at Associated Mennonite Biblical Seminary I held that practical experience in ministry and formal thought need each other in education for ministry. Without careful reflection, the church loses its vision, its focus. Without experiences of life in the church, formal theological thought loses its context, its locus.

My philosophy of field education centers on an action-reflection model of learning and growth. At Associated Mennonite Biblical Seminary we seek to provide ministry students with opportunities for integrating formal and practical education, for refining their ministerial skills, for learning to reflect theologically on ministry, and for developing pastoral identity. It is my hope and my prayer that this book will generate further reflection, dialogue, and collaboration for the sake of faithful and fruitful pastoral ministry in our increasingly global society and postmodern culture.

I am grateful to the AMBS teaching faculty for their participation in this project and for the excellent essays they have contributed to this collection. Special thanks go to President Nelson Kraybill, Dean Loren Johns, and my colleague Daniel Schipani, for their encouragement and support. A grant from the Fund for Peoplehood Education of Mennonite Education Agency made possible two substantial, structured faculty conversations around the project. Active participation and a wonderful, collegial spirit characterized these gatherings. A committee including Keith Harder, Heidi Regier Kreider, Jane Thorley Roeschley, and Anne Stuckey provided valuable counsel along the way.

I also owe a debt of gratitude to the congregations where I have been a member, as well as to the institutions and programs to which I have related in various capacities. I think particularly of several hundred students who allowed me to have a part in their ministerial formation. I am thankful for so many pastoral leaders and theologians who touched my life and stimulated my theological vision in significant ways. Thanks especially to John A. Esau, who served as Director of Ministerial Leadership Services for the General Conference Mennonite Church, for his tireless attention to vital issues of pastoral ministry and authority.

My thanks also go to those who provided assistance during the final phase of this project, especially at Institute of Mennonite Studies. I received invaluable help from IMS director Mary Schertz and from Barbara Nelson Gingerich, who prepared the manuscript for publication. Michael A. King was graciously accommodating as publisher at Cascadia Publishing House.

Last, but certainly not least, I thank Beverley, my wife, God's gift of companionship in life and ministry.

ERICK SAWATZKY

Contributors

Ross T. Bender is Dean Emeritus of Associated Mennonite Biblical Seminary, where he also served as Professor of Christian Education. His writings include *Education for Peoplehood: Essays on the Teaching Ministry of the Church* (Institute of Mennonite Studies, 1997), and *The People of God: A Mennonite Interpretation of the Free Church Tradition* (Herald Press, 1971).

Arthur Paul Boers is Assistant Professor of Pastoral Theology and Coordinator of the Spiritual Formation Program at Associated Mennonite Biblical Seminary. He is author of many articles and books, including, most recently, *The Rhythm of God's Grace* (Paraclete, 2003).

Jacob W. Elias is Professor of New Testament at Associated Mennonite Biblical Seminary. He is also copastor, along with his wife Lillian, of Parkview Mennonite Church, Kokomo, Indiana. Elias is the author of *1 and 2 Thessalonians,* Believers Church Bible Commentary (Herald Press, 1995).

Loren L. Johns is Dean and Associate Professor of New Testament at Associated Mennonite Biblical Seminary. He has written and edited numerous works, including, most recently, *The Lamb Christology of the Apocalypse of John: An Investigation into Its Origins and Rhetorical Force* (Mohr Siebeck, 2003).

Gayle Gerber Koontz is Professor of Theology and Ethics at Associated Mennonite Biblical Seminary. She has written numerous articles and is coeditor of *A Mind Patient and Untamed: Assessing John Howard Yoder's Contribution to Theology, Ethics, and Peacemaking* (Cascadia Publishing House, 2004).

Ted Koontz is Professor of Ethics and Peace Studies at Associated Mennonite Biblical Seminary. His published work includes *Godward: Personal Stories of Grace* (Herald Press, 1996), which he edited.

Karl Koop is Associate Professor of Historical Theology at Canadian Mennonite University, and Adjunct Professor at Associated Mennonite Biblical Seminary, where he taught theology and Anabaptist-Mennonite studies for five years. He coedited, with Mary Schertz, *Without Spot or Wrinkle: Reflecting Theologically on the Nature of the Church* (Institute of Mennonite Studies, 2000). A version of his essay was printed in *Mennonite Quarterly Review* 76 (October 2002): 399-412.

J. Nelson Kraybill is President of Associated Mennonite Biblical Seminary. He has authored several books, including *On the Pilgrim's Way: Conversations on Christian Discipleship during a Twelve-Day Walk across England* (Herald Press, 1998).

Ben C. Ollenburger is Professor of Biblical Theology at Associated Mennonite Biblical Seminary, Elkhart, Indiana. Among his publications are the commentary on Zechariah in the New Interpreter's Bible (Abingdon Press, 1996), and *Old Testament Theology: Flowering and Future* (Eisenbrauns, 2004).

Walter Sawatsky is Professor of Church History and Mission at Associated Mennonite Biblical Seminary, where he serves as director of the Mission Studies Center. He is editor of *Mission Focus: Annual Review,* and *Religion in Eastern Europe.*

Erick Sawatzky is Associate Professor Emeritus of Pastoral Ministry at Associated Mennonite Biblical Seminary, where he was also Director of Field Education. He has served as pastor of congregations in Canada and the U.S., as a pastoral counselor, and as a prison chaplain.

Mary H. Schertz is Professor of New Testament at Associated Mennonite Biblical Seminary. She also serves as director of the Institute of Mennonite Studies and AMBS editor of *Vision: A Journal for Church and Theology.* She is a coauthor of *Seeing the Text: Exegesis for Students of Greek and Hebrew* (Abingdon Press, 2001), and editor of several books, including (with Ivan Friesen) *Beautiful upon the Mountains: Biblical*

Essays on Mission, Peace, and the Reign of God (Institute of Mennonite Studies, 2003).

Daniel S. Schipani is Professor of Pastoral Care and Counseling at Associated Mennonite Biblical Seminary. He lectures widely and is the author or editor of twenty books on pastoral and practical theology and education, including, most recently, *The Way of Wisdom in Pastoral Counseling* (Institute of Mennonite Studies, 2003).

Rebecca Slough is Associate Professor of Worship and the Arts and Director of Field Education at Associated Mennonite Biblical Seminary. She served as managing editor for *Hymnal: A Worship Book* (Faith & Life Press, Brethren Press, Mennonite Publishing House, 1992).

Willard M. Swartley is Professor of New Testament at Associated Mennonite Biblical Seminary. He has edited numerous books, including *Violence Renounced: René Girard, Biblical Studies, and Peacemaking* (Pandora Press, 2000), and has authored many articles and five books, including, most recently, *Homosexuality: Biblical Interpretation and Moral Discernment* (Herald Press, 2003).

June Alliman Yoder is Associate Professor of Communication and Preaching at Associated Mennonite Biblical Seminary. She edited *The Work Is Thine, O Christ: In Honor of Erland Waltner* (Institute of Mennonite Studies, 2002).

Perry B. Yoder is Professor of Old Testament at Associated Mennonite Biblical Seminary. His most recent book, with coauthor Mary Schertz, is *Seeing the Text: Exegesis for Students of Greek and Hebrew* (Abingdon Press, 2001).

Introduction

Loren L. Johns

At the heart of the mission of Associated Mennonite Biblical Seminary is the task of preparing faithful and effective leaders for the church. Beyond the practical, goal-oriented benefits of preparing for ministry, the opportunity simply to dedicate an extended period of time to study of Scriptures, the history and theology of the church, and the art and skills of ministry represents a precious gift for those who take it. The chance to sit with the gifted scholars and teachers of the church and to discuss the issues that matter most in life—such an opportunity is something sacred, exciting, and much to be desired.

It is with such a sense of awe and excitement that I sit with the gifted scholars and teachers of the church represented in this volume. In this book one finds some of the most important conversations and issues facing the church today. Here we find the story of debates and discussions among scholars and teachers over the last forty years or so regarding the nature and authority of pastoral ministry. They write of attempts to articulate and understand the respective traditions, values, and perspectives important to our sense of heritage and identity, whether in the Old Mennonite tradition, the General Conference Mennonite tradition, or in conversation with other theological traditions. Although the subtitle is "Pastoral Ministry in Anabaptist Perspective," the authors represent just a portion of the contemporary Anabaptist family. This is not intended as a comprehensive treatment of pastoral ministry in Anabaptist perspective.

Here we find explanations for puzzling comments about pastoral ministry as we come to understand the historical and theological journeys behind them. Here we find constructive practical theology—attempts to articulate for this time and place what God calls us to as pastors. Here we find bold proposals for rethinking some of the church's answers in the past, even as we are encouraged to take that

1

past seriously. Here we find critical reflection on how we participate in God's mission in the world—not only as disciples, but also as ministers, as representatives of God to others. Here we come to the heart of the matter.

The Anabaptist-Mennonite tradition is at its best when it understands its own history within its broader historical and theological context and when it values the contributions of that history without fossilizing it—perpetuating it for its own sake—or devaluing the history and contributions of the broader church of which it is a part. Tradition has value only insofar as it remains in a living, dynamic relationship with the changing realities of life. Perhaps the only thing worse than maintaining a tradition simply because it is there is abandoning a tradition because one never learned it or understood it or appreciated its dynamic tension with alternative traditions.

This book is a picture, expression, reappropriation, and extension of that tradition, both in its attempts to rethink and critically assess that theological heritage and in its articulation and reappropriation of that heritage for a new era. This book is an exercise in doing what Jesus said scribes trained for the reign of God do; we bring out of our treasure both what is new and what is old (Matt. 13:52).

Ross Bender, dean of AMBS from 1964 to 1979, introduces the subject matter with the story of the Dean's Seminar, an extended series of conversations among AMBS faculty about the New Testament theology of ministry and its implications for the church today. At the heart of these conversations were debates between "functionalism" and "office"; between the supposed early Paul and the late Paul; between ministry understood as the task of all God's people, who are individually gifted as equal members of Christ's one body, and ministry understood as vested in a special way in the office of the pastor as a seminary-trained professional. Were the advocates of the functional view really taking the "early Paul" more seriously, or were they unconsciously and illegitimately led to privilege functionalism under the influence of the egalitarian antiauthoritarianism of the 1960s? Is not the "late Paul" canonical too—and perhaps even more relevant for an age when ministry requires tending to the maintenance of institutions?

The conversations in the Dean's Seminar were passionate. In the end, the seminar concluded that "the Christian ministry is present in all its theological fullness wherever the people of God is gathered and its members are obedient in the exercise of their gifts" (see pages 17-18 below). This essentially functionalist perspective did not enjoy universal support, however, and other voices in the church—including those of John Esau, Henry Poettcker, Rod Sawatsky, and Erick Sawatzky—continued to raise serious questions about the adequacy of this conclusion. They saw a disempowered pastorate, ineffective leadership, and the prospect of a church adrift without authority vested in designated leaders. How many times has the church, in the name of the priesthood of all believers or of the diverse giftedness of the Spirit, actually succeeded only in disempowering its leadership?

In his essay, Ross Bender explores the potential common ground between these seemingly opposed views of pastoral ministry. Bender suggests that one fruit of these continued conversations was the 1992 document written and adopted by the AMBS faculty, *Ministerial Formation and Theological Education in Mennonite Perspective,* which is reproduced as Appendix 1 in this volume. (For an articulation of how this understanding of ministerial formation and theological education has informed AMBS's approach, see Appendix 2: "Theological Education and Curricular Design at AMBS.")

Despite the varying perspectives of twentieth-century Mennonite scholarship about the continued validity or helpfulness of the concept of the priesthood of all believers, there was a broad consensus that sixteenth-century Anabaptists were innovators in this area and broadly practiced the concept. In his essay on anticlericalism and pastoral identity among Anabaptists of the Lower Rhine, Karl Koop questions the basis of this consensus. Citing the work of Marlin Miller, John D. Roth, and others, Koop notes that appeals to the priesthood of all believers were actually rare among sixteenth-century Anabaptists and that evidence exists of both anticlericalism and high esteem for the ordained ministry. Koop's thesis is that although the laity played a heightened role in Anabaptist circles, most Anabaptists "affirmed the importance of genuine and qualified leadership."

Koop traces the commonalities between the anticlerical spirit of the Middle Ages and the anticlericalism of the Anabaptists, suggesting that the latter was not a theological innovation of the Anabaptists, but rather was a theological expression of a broader phenomenon known already in the late Middle Ages. Furthermore, this impulse was not fundamentally anticlericalism as such, but rather an impulse toward the reform of the clergy. The Kempen confession demonstrates that the language of anticlericalism actually exhibits a high view of congregational leadership. The theological burden of these Anabaptists was not some new proposal that congregations can or should operate without an ordained leadership; they desired that clergy be "true shepherds" rather than "worldly preachers."

Walter Sawatsky argues that the issues of leadership and authority must be addressed with a broader geographical, historical, and ecumenical awareness. Questions about leadership and authority tend to be reductionistic in their focus on the individual. They deserve a broader perspective. Shifting patterns in the role and practice of the ministry in the Mennonite traditions owe as much to the influence of business and societal changes as they do to whatever theological innovations the sixteenth-century Anabaptists made. Sawatsky's article is an argument for the value of sociology for understanding our theological debates. More specifically, he argues for appropriating Christian history in fullness—without the picking and choosing that sometimes characterize sectarian historiography—and for seeing our own history with its praxis and theology of ministry in interplay with other Christian traditions, Protestant and Catholic.

Mennonites have a congregationalist polity; but that says little. The quality of a congregationalist polity must be assessed in terms of how it maintains the links connecting leadership, a high view of church, and church as applied to all of life. Except for the Vietnam protest era in America, Mennonites have consistently held a high view of the charismata of ministry, and have observed rituals setting some apart for such ministry. However, Mennonites today need to grant more place to an apostolate or episcopate, practicing greater accountability to the whole church of Jesus Christ and its charismata by taking a long look at our history, especially in light of current episcopal and presbyterian church efforts to strengthen congregationalism in their churches.

Our theological discourse is poorer for the various ways in which it has been reductionistic. Many considerations have been ignored or largely unexplored, such as the ways in which migration—whether from the eastern United States to the Midwest, or from Russia to Canada—has influenced our patterns and structures of leadership. At the heart of the matter, concludes Sawatsky, is the task of incarnating Christ in a sinful world—a task never forgotten, yet never fully realized by the church. The role of the minister in that task is to exercise "authority and power consciously with clear accountability."

One would expect that a congregation would respect and take seriously the words of a pastor who speaks the Word of God to the congregation. But how does a congregation understand the authority of its pastor? What is—or should be—the role of "teaching authority" in the Mennonite church? Gayle Gerber Koontz picks up this question and addresses it in the context of the historical relationship between ecclesiology, authority, and ministry in the broader church since the Reformation.

Although the word of the prophet may be respected when it speaks to a community's need to address a contingent situation in response to the Spirit, the authority of the other kind of spoken word— the authority of tradition, received wisdom, and fidelity to a community's origins—has not fared as well in the Mennonite church. This suspicion of tradition may stem from the fact that Anabaptism originated in protest against the Roman Catholic Church and against Luther's consolidation of power and authority in response to the chaotic antiauthoritarian impulses of the Peasants' War. Our particular story is precious both because it is *our* story and because it represents a gift to the broader church. But with the ecclesiological strengths of the Anabaptist-Mennonite tradition come some weaknesses. The Mennonite church has been weakened by its lack of "appreciation and respect for the rightful authority of the spoken word that appeals to the memory and wisdom of the wider Christian church in interpreting the gospel." It is time to recover that appreciation and respect.

What is needed is not blind trust in the "right" people, but rather renewed appreciation for the gifts of knowledge and expertise in the Christian tradition. In particular, "congregations have special responsibility to call pastors with competence in two specific areas— ability to respectfully interpret the wisdom of the historical church in the process of looking toward the future, and commitment to and ability in relating to Christians of other denominations." In short, the Mennonite church needs pastors who are knowledgeable about and open to the Spirit of God moving in the people and the theological heritage of other traditions, who are able to see ways in which the history of theological discourse (whether that of Augustine or Menno Simons) may elicit wisdom for today's church.

In his essay, Perry Yoder argues that "that the church's failure to understand the pastoral role as a teaching role is a serious conceptual flaw, with deleterious consequences for congregations and for the larger church." The teaching ministry of the church is usually associated with "Christian education," which in turn is usually associated with Sunday school, and Sunday school with children and youth. In most of our congregations, Christian education (to say nothing about the children and youth themselves!) has a lower status than do pastoral care or ministerial leadership. Combine this perception with demands that compete for the pastor's time, especially on a Sunday morning, and it is easy to see why many pastors fail to take seriously their role as teachers.

Yoder traces the role of teaching in the Old Testament and in the ministry of Jesus. He concludes that leading the people of God requires connecting canon, community, and commentary—a three-cornered dialectic that can be maintained only when ministers take seriously their teaching role. Yoder does not argue that *only* an ordained pastor can fulfill the role of teacher and interpreter, but he does argue that the pastor has a special calling and responsibility to take that role seriously. Today's church will be both healthier and more faithful as pastors take up the challenge to provide pastoral care in the form of teaching. Yoder calls us to recover, embrace, honor, and exercise the ministry of teaching.

Jacob Elias reflects on his own call to the ministry—and how the debates of the 1960s and 1970s in the Dean's Seminar did and did not affect his understanding of the ministry and of his role as minister. He says, the "functional or charismatic understanding of ministry never seemed to sidetrack me from my sense of calling to the pastorate or undermine my authority to fulfill my pastoral responsibilities." Elias's experience would seem to confirm the potential for developing an understanding of ministry that holds the positive features of both functionalism and office without dichotomizing them or resorting to reductionism.

An area of broad consensus among German Protestant biblical scholars of the twentieth century was that one could trace a linear development in the early church from a charismatic, functionalist understanding of ministry and giftedness, seen in the life and teachings of Jesus and more clearly in the writings of Paul (the "early Paul"), to the structured institutionalism and legalism of the post-Pauline writings (the "late Paul"). This development within the first century C.E. was usually seen as a "fall" from the openness of grace and charisma to the dull legalism of institution and hierarchy. The phrase "early Catholicism" served as a shorthand expression for this way of describing these changes in the early church.

Elias describes the historical development of this understanding in the twentieth century, along with more recent critical assessments of it. Today's scholars are more likely to recognize that the first-century story was more complex—that signs of office and institutionalism existed in the earliest periods (cf. Phil. 1:1) *and* that egalitarian expressions of the giftedness of all are found in the supposedly post-Pauline writings (cf. Eph. 4). If a new consensus is emerging, it is that "official and charismatic understandings of ministry coexisted from the beginning." This emerging consensus has potential for informing the functionalism vs. office debate.

If one moves beyond the usual practice of focusing on the "titles" Paul used of leaders in the church to asking what metaphors or similes he employed in describing himself or others as ministers, one finds a remarkable variety of images, many of which reflect "tender family themes of vulnerability, nurture, and encouragement," including much maternal imagery. Elias concludes that whatever the forms of ministry or church structure, faithful ministers serve the gospel of Jesus Christ by being "servant-leaders affirmed and set apart by the community of faith for a ministry of proclamation and nurture and care." No debate about offices or structures need detract from such a ministry.

My essay examines the use of the word *ordain* in the King James Version to translate a wide variety of Hebrew and Greek verbs. I consider whether the political and theological context in the Church of England in the seventeenth century may have influenced the translators' use of the word *ordain*. I conclude that the sheer variety of Hebrew and Greek words behind the word *ordain* in the King James Version demonstrates the fluidity of what we call ordination. In fact, there was no concept of ordination in the New Testament—at least in the way that Catholic and Protestant churches use the word today.

Appeals to "office" in the free church tradition may depend unwittingly on the theological and political interests of King James I in his seventeenth-century English context. Finally, caution is warranted when one attempts to articulate a biblical theology of ordination based on any English version of the Bible without reference to the original languages.

In his essay, Ben Ollenburger explores the ways in which the offices and/or functions of pastor and prophet might be coterminous, overlapping, or opposing. He begins by contrasting the pastoral and prophetic offices as broadly understood in the church. For instance, pastors speak primarily to an *internal* audience; prophets speak primarily to an *external* audience. However, a closer look at the biblical record shows that prophets too spoke primarily to an internal audience—even when delivering oracles against the nations. Prophets were essentially poets, interpreters, and theologians who proclaimed and taught the Word of God to God's people. That is not so different from what pastors are called to do.

Some caveats remain, of course. The pastoral office is an office. Many prophets had no office, but spoke as God directed, through their own artistry and intellect. The congregation has a responsibility to do theology by testing and weighing the words of prophets—indeed, the people are to weigh any proclamation. Just as the prophets of both testaments did, pastors today address the community of faith on God's behalf as ambassadors of God's contested sovereignty. Our understanding of the ministry of the pastor will be greatly enriched if the biblical role and function of the prophet are sought and embraced.

Like Ollenburger, Ted Koontz sees this prophetic role as directed first of all internally. Much serious moral reflection needs to be done by the church on such issues as access to health care. The pastor has a vital role as preacher, teacher, and prophet in the congregation's discernment, proclamation, and embodiment of the implications of the gospel for key issues facing people in today's world. Neither discernment nor proclamation nor embodiment will suffice by itself; the clarity and strength of the church's witness depend on the integration of the three.

Mennonites have historically been viewed as prototypical of the "Christ against culture" type of H. Richard Niebuhr's famous typology—and not without reason. Mennonites have generally seen themselves as a separate people—a people defined by voluntary disciple-ship called to embody a different model, a different way of being from that of the world. Nonconformity was once seen as an essential expression of faithfulness among some Mennonites.

Two observations call into question the continued usefulness or adequacy of separation or nonconformity as the primary stance of the church in relation to society. First, times have changed. Mennonites have to a large degree made themselves at home in North American culture. Second, neither complete separation from nor identification with culture is really an option for any body of believers that claims the name of Christ. We all accept certain characteristics of modern culture, reject others, and debate yet others. Mennonites do not object on moral or ecclesiological grounds to driving on the right side of the road or attending an orchestra concert. Because of its inevitably ambiguous relationship with society and culture, the church must take up the challenge of ongoing moral discernment: it must sort out values, messages, technologies, and practices in order to "determine which are in harmony with God's reign and which oppose it." Here the prophetic role of the pastor becomes central. "Prophetic leadership is crucial if the church is to engage its surrounding culture critically (analytically, carefully, and thoughtfully, rather than reflexively)."

Picking up on Koontz's point that the church is inevitably implicated in the life of the world and never really separated from it, Mary Schertz proposes that the Mennonite church embrace more fully and intentionally the call to public leadership as an expression of Christian ministry. Whether as a result of our history of persecution, our fascination with our superior humility, or our insecurities, we have failed to make ourselves available to the world through public ministry. Schertz suggests that this failure is nothing less than a failure to love the world as God has loved it. She calls the church to embrace this more public role in our communities—not because we despair of or shrink from the task of signifying God's reign as the people of God, but precisely *as* signifying the reign of God in the world—and because God so loved the world. Ironically, perhaps the truest nonconformity to the world lies in loving it as God loves it.

Willard Swartley addresses another neglected aspect of pastoral ministry, that of healing. Despite the centrality of healing in the Gospels and the near equation of healing with salvation in the teachings and ministry of Jesus, neither today's church nor most ministerial candidates expect the gift or ministry of healing to be high on the list of qualifications for pastoral ministry. It is strange that the question "Are you a healer?" is seldom if ever asked in interviews with pastoral candidates. Swartley encourages pastors to take up this ministry and to embrace "healer" as an important part of their self-identity. He further calls on seminaries to include—if not organize their curriculum around—healing, in our preparation of people for congregational ministry.

In his essay, Arthur Paul Boers addresses both the identity and the task of the modern pastor. The task of thinking critically about God's action in and love for the world is best understood as the task of "spiritual theology." Spiritual theology is theoretical, personal, *and* formational. It is not just an intellectual discipline; it emphasizes pilgrimage, relationship with God, spiritual discipline, community, practical discipleship, justice, humility, and repentance. Many metaphors have been offered as the primary metaphor for understanding the role of the pastor. Some of these metaphors derive from the Bible and some have been identified as particularly important for our time in the essays of this book. Boers considers the adequacy of several of these metaphors to encompass the task of the pastor. Each is found wanting in some way. The alternative proposed by Boers is that we see pastoring as "spiritual orienting or orientation," with the pastor adopting the identity of a "spiritual orienteer." The pastor is one who, in all of the tasks of ministry, whether in preaching, in administration, or in crisis counseling, seeks always to orient the congregation—including himself or herself—to God.

June Alliman Yoder explores one of the often ignored tasks of the Christian minister: that of listening. Drawing on the insights of communication theory, Yoder maintains that communication is a complex task and that careful, thoughtful, intentional, attentive listening lies at the heart of it. Even when it comes to preaching— that stereotypical activity of the pastor—Yoder maintains that the only effective preacher is the good listener. For the pastor, "listening, or paying attention, is the single most important form of ministry and the activity that most defines the pastoral role."

The role of the pastor in ministry requires listening for God's call and listening for God's word. When it comes to preaching well, one must listen to the biblical text, to the congregation, to scholars who have studied the text, and to the broader historical and social context in which a congregation finds itself. Even during the delivery of the sermon, the preacher must attend to the Spirit of God, listen to his or her own sermon, and watch for the communication of the congregation. Finally, the pastor must listen to his or her own self, cultivating the self-awareness necessary for self-care. Few ministry tasks do not call for significant quantities of listening and sharp listening skills.

In her essay, Rebecca Slough explores pastoral ministry as an improvisational art. Anyone with experience in pastoral ministry knows that no manual exists that can say, "In such a situation, a pastor should always do this or say that." Effective ministry depends on one's knowledge and on one's abilities to read ministry situations and listen to the improvisational leading of the Spirit. Circumstances, situations, and people themselves are too complex for a formulaic approach to ministry. Thus, some improvisation is necessary in any effective pastoral interventions.

In true improvisation one does not begin with a blank slate. Improvisation requires, in fact, both knowledge and a number of advanced interrelated skills. Like good jazz musicians, pastoral ministers improvise on the basis of knowledge of their art. Pastors' improvisation rests on knowledge of the Bible and the story of our faith, as well as on the skill of thinking critically about theology and ethics. They need to have a whole range of ministry art skills from which to draw. They need to know their people, their community of faith. And like good jazz musicians, they need self-knowledge and self-awareness.

The development of pastoral counseling as a specialized activity and even separate profession has been a mixed blessing to the church, writes Daniel Schipani. On the positive side, pastoral counseling has empowered pastors to tend carefully to their skills of listening helpfully and constructively and to embrace this function as an important part of pastoral ministry. On the negative side, pastoral counseling has often been seen as an illegitimate stepchild of psychotherapy in which pastors pretend to act like "the professionals" but know that they are not. It has often measured itself against the standards of professional psychotherapy rather than by the measures of effective ministry.

When pastoral counseling is removed from the congregational context, pastors feel disempowered as counselors and neglect the rich resources of wisdom available in the Bible, the Christian tradition, and the community of faith. Pastoral counseling works best when it is understood and practiced as an expression of pastoral ministry, not when it is understood and practiced as a form of psychotherapy that can afford to ignore the wisdom traditions of the community of faith. Schipani seeks to reenvision pastoral counseling. It should be viewed, practiced, and taught pastorally; contextualized ecclesiologically; centered on Jesus Christ as the Wisdom of God; grounded in Scripture; viewed, practiced and taught as a unique form of the (re)creative process guided by the Spirit; and oriented toward the reign of God.

Much is at stake. Pastors who embrace the call to counsel are agents of change and growth toward the realization of the reign of God in their communities. But do pastors generally embrace the task of being change agents? Is being a "servant leader" compatible with being a change agent? By what authority can a pastor embrace such a role?

Nelson Kraybill explores issues of power and authority in his essay. Though some Christian leaders have tried to pretend that power and authority do not—or should not—exist in the church, these dynamics are a normal and necessary part of church life. Nevertheless, the New Testament church conceived of power and exercised authority in ways that departed from patterns of the surrounding Roman imperial culture. Systems theory has taught us that the effective leader is one who can effectively self-differentiate while maintaining relationships. Examination of the New Testament shows that it is full of leaders who did just that. The call to leadership in the New Testament is a call to a noncoercive change agency. Thus, both conflict management and vision setting are at the heart of empowering leadership.

In the final essay, Erick Sawatzky reflects on the changing patterns and conceptions of pastoral ministry in the last half of the twentieth century. He suggests that the rapid changes toward egalitarianism that characterized the third quarter of the century owed more to changes in the larger society than to more accurate readings of the New Testament. Many churches and pastors at the end of the twentieth century found themselves confused about and ambivalent toward leadership in general and toward the office of pastoral minister in particular. What is needed is a renewed authority in the office, an authority borne both by competence and by effective and empowering relationships.

Effective pastoral leadership is more than simply a matter of *doing*; it is also a matter of *being*. Competence in performing tasks is important, but so is the integrity of the person in the office. More than simply *doing* a prescribed set of tasks, *being* a pastor also entails filling a role that is larger than the sum of its parts: location, leadership, authority, and professionalism. It is not as though there is any one thing that only the pastor can do; rather, the uniqueness of pastoral ministry lies in the particular confluence of God's call, personal integrity, the position itself, and competence to do the work. Such a calling is one to be embraced by those called and honored by congregational members.

Is it possible to reform our understanding of ministry in a way that recognizes the particular calling and giftedness of pastors while empowering the laity to exercise their own gifts as well? Can the church believe in and practice the priesthood of all believers without the anticlericalism and disregard of the gifts of leadership and its authority that has often accompanied it? Is it possible to affirm and esteem the particular gifts and calling of the pastor in a way that honors both the individual and the office without dishonoring or disempowering the members of the body?

The debates between those who emphasize the priesthood of all believers and those who maintain the value of a trained, professional pastorate have been energized in part by fears about what might happen to the church if their side was neglected. The functionalists fear that the validity and value of the spiritual gifts of all God's people will be denied or ignored, while those who emphasize the "office" fear that "priesthood of all believers" language will disempower the pastor. History suggests that both fears have some basis in fact. History also shows that the most effective congregations have not been those that have sought a "balance" on this matter, but rather those that have honored and respected all of the gifts of the Spirit, including the gift or office of pastoral minister. May God grant us that grace!

This book is dedicated to the reappropriation and honoring of pastoral ministry, with all of the gifts and expressions of ministry that it entails—not because it is the one ministry that matters, but certainly because it is *a* ministry that matters. And while preaching, teaching, prophesying, healing, performing, listening, nurturing, discerning, embodying, improvising, interpreting, orienting, and counseling may all be part of that calling, it is ultimately God who gives the gifts and who will build God's church; we are but workers in God's vineyard.

1

"That some would be pastors"

Ross T. Bender

> The gifts he gave were that some would be apostles, some
> prophets, some evangelists, some pastors and teachers,
> to equip the saints for the work of ministry, for building
> up the body of Christ, until all of us come to the unity of
> the faith and of the knowledge of the Son of God, to
> maturity, to the measure of the full stature of Christ.
> (Eph. 4:11-13)

This text is a key New Testament passage on the subject of Christian
ministry. It is one of several (Rom. 12:3-8, 1 Cor. 12:4-31) that
employ the imagery of the body and its various organs (e.g., foot,
hand, eye, ear) as a metaphor for the church and its various ministries—
for the spiritual gifts given by the Holy Spirit. Of the various New
Testament texts on the meaning and practice of ministry, these three
were the primary ones chosen by participants in the Dean's Seminar
at Associated Mennonite Biblical Seminaries in the late 1960s as we
sought to develop a model for theological education in the free church.[1]

The Dean's Seminar study and its critics

To no one's surprise, the development of a model for free church
theological education sparked controversy both among those who
participated in the seminar and in the church as a whole. And the
controversy continues to this day. A quarter-century after publication
of the Dean's Seminar study, John A. Esau deplored the inadequacy of
what he labels its "functionalist theology of ministry," in which
pastoral leaders are merely those who fulfill certain tasks in the
church for which they are best qualified. "For all of its idealism and
apparent use of certain biblical images," Esau charges, we have been
left with "a theology that has failed," a theology that "has not served
us well."[2]

15

The Dean's Seminar took place at a time of ferment not only on the AMBS campus but also in the Mennonite churches. Nor was the question of the nature and practice of Christian ministry a uniquely Mennonite question. It was being debated among many denominations, along with the question of the nature of the church. However, some distinctively Mennonite issues and circumstances surrounded the conversations in Mennonite circles. The time for such a study was ripe for Mennonites. Goshen College Biblical Seminary and Mennonite Biblical Seminary were on the threshold of major changes in the structures of their cooperation, which led to the Goshen seminary's move to the Elkhart campus and to the complete integration of their academic programs.

In the late 1960s, seminary education was a relatively recent development among Mennonites. Mennonite Biblical Seminary was founded in Chicago in 1945, and Goshen College Biblical Seminary was founded on the campus of Goshen College in 1946. These followed several earlier efforts at training for ministry, both undergraduate and graduate, in both the General Conference Mennonite Church and the (Old) Mennonite Church.[3] Mennonites had a long tradition of a lay ministry, with ministers called from within their home congregations. With some exceptions, ministers were largely self-educated and self-supporting. A few were graduates of other-than-Mennonite seminaries. The lay ministry was a plural ministry with a threefold division of labor. The usual pattern included a bishop or *Ältester,* one or more preachers, and several deacons. Together these leaders were sometimes referred to as "the bench."[4]

In the movement toward professionalization of the ministry, older patterns gave way to new ones even as they existed side by side in some congregations for a period of time. The untrained, unsalaried, lay ministry was for the most part displaced by the seminary-trained, salaried, full-time professional ministry. The threefold lay ministry largely became a thing of the past. The single pastor took on the various roles and tasks carried earlier by the bench.

With the professionalization of the pastoral ministry, what congregations expected of their pastors expanded. Ministers in single pastorates began to feel the weight of the load they carried alone. As the older models of ministry dropped away, Mennonites tended to look to other denominations and seminaries for new models that fit the new situation. At AMBS, we saw the need to reflect on the adequacy and appropriateness of these borrowed patterns.

In this process of reflection, the seminar addressed these questions: "Do we have a distinctive vision of church life and a distinctive message in our time based on our heritage? At what points does a Free Church posture make a difference? At what points does it cut across and stand at variance with other contemporary options? How shall such a vision be translated into a program of theological education?"[5]

The seminar met for approximately seventy sessions over a period of two years. Participants were C. J. Dyck (Anabaptist and sixteenth-century studies), Leland Harder (practical theology and sociology of religion), William Klassen (New Testament), Millard C. Lind (Old Testament), J. C. Wenger (historical theology), John H. Yoder (theology and ethics), and myself (dean; Christian education). The group included a wide range of positions and perspectives, which made for stimulating discussion and debate. We tried to reach consensus on the issues. We hoped to be able to say "It seemed good to the Holy Spirit and to us" when we agreed, and at times we did.

One conviction presented persuasively and passionately was that the normative New Testament passages on the nature and practice of Christian ministry were the ones cited above, which refer to the church as the body of Christ. Just as a body has many members, each with distinctive functions, so the church as the body of Christ has many members with differing yet complementary ministering gifts.

On the face of it, this emphasis on the universal ministry of all the people of God would not appear to be a controversial assertion. It would, in fact, seem to be at the heart of biblical teaching on the nature and practice of Christian ministry: "For as in one body we have many members, and not all the members have the same function, so we, who are many, are one body in Christ, and individually we are members one of another. We have gifts that differ according to the grace given to us" (Rom. 12:4-5a). The complete text (12:3-8) elaborates this basic principle more fully, as do the texts in 1 Corinthians and Ephesians. The final report of the seminar drew heavily on these texts. It defined ministry as the exercise of the spiritual gifts given to the total people of God: "The Christian ministry is present in all its theological fullness wherever the people of God is gathered and its members are obedient in the exercise of their gifts."[6]

What were the contemporary issues that drew seminar participants to these texts? We were concerned that the Mennonite church was moving away from a shared plural ministry composed of leaders called out of the congregations they served, and that the seminary was moving uncritically in the direction of a Protestant pattern of ministry without adequate critical reflection about the appropriateness for Mennonites of these borrowed patterns.[7] Seminar participants feared that in the transition from a plural ministry to the single pastorate, the professionally trained, salaried pastor would take over responsibilities that belonged to all the members of the body. We had concerns about the potential for accumulation of power in one person, about a tendency to create distance between the pastor and the people in practices such as the use of the title "reverend," or in references to "clergy" and "laity." For these reasons, the biblical model of the church as the body of Christ with its many members engaged in ministry was appealing.

Some saw our reliance on these texts as creating an overemphasis, an imbalance, because we did not give equal attention to the texts in the pastoral epistles: 1 Timothy 3:1-13, for example, lays down the qualifications for the offices of bishop and deacon; Titus 1:5 enjoins appointment of elders in every town. Critics expressed concern about what appeared to them to be a denigration of pastoral ministry. They wondered whether the apparent neglect of the pastoral epistles in this study was influenced not so much by the Holy Spirit as by the spirit of the times, which called into question the relevance and viability of pastoral ministry. They worried about the lack of recognized leadership and the danger of competition and chaos inherent in a situation in which everyone is a minister and no one is in charge. They expressed concern about neglecting to recognize the symbolic role pastors play in representing the congregation in the community and in representing God to the congregation.

In the words of John Esau,

> This egalitarian theology of ministry made claims to being
> both biblical and Anabaptist, which in Mennonite circles
> is the near equivalent of claiming papal authority. . . .
> One could argue that these notions are more rooted in

the cultural revolution that was part of what was happening in North America at the time of Vietnam and Watergate. It has been a time in which all those who have been perceived as professionals (doctors, lawyers, politicians, and pastors) have been challenged as to their role and legitimacy. . . .

What this theology of ministry lacked was any understanding of the place of the pastoral "office." It explicitly rejected notions of representationalism, the concept that one person might symbolically speak and authentically act in behalf of the whole. Concepts about shared leadership tended to degenerate into meaning that the pastor lost the power and authority required to serve the church effectively.[8]

Toward resolution

At first blush, it may seem impossible to reconcile the different perspectives represented by the Dean's Seminar study and its critics. However, several points are germane to the potential resolution of some of these issues that divide these camps.

First is the recognition that pastoral ministry is not coterminous with Christian ministry. In the texts in Ephesians, Romans, and 1 Corinthians, pastoral ministry is distinct from Christian ministry; it is one of the ministries spoken of. Over the years pastoral ministry has come to be the main ministry in the congregation, and we have tended to lose sight of the fact that in this early stage of the development of ministry patterns, a number of leadership gifts were identified. According to Ephesians 4, the list of ministries includes apostles, prophets, evangelists, pastors, and teachers.

Second, these texts do not set the spiritual gifts apart from the offices of ministry. The offices too are spiritually endowed and are gifts from the Spirit to the church: "The gifts he gave were that some would be . . . pastors and teachers." All three texts emphasize repeatedly the multiplicity of spiritual gifts and at the same time emphasize the official ministries. The offices are not different in kind, for they too are gifts of grace given by the Spirit of God.

Third, the "official" ministries are plural in number just as the "charismatic" ministries are. A developing theology of ministry should also make room for such special ministries as pastors, teachers, evangelists, administrators, and others, as gifts and roles are discerned and ordered by the church.

Fourth, the official ministries should not be set over against the charismatic ones by the use of such slogans as "the one or the many," or even "the one and the many." Which of these diverse yet complementary ministries is to be understood as "the one"? Which one alone embodies within itself the defining characteristics that all the others lack?

Fifth, a developing theology of ministry must allow for changes to take place through the experience of the church over the years: old patterns will give way to new ones. In fact, the pastoral epistles reflect just such change, as patterns of ministry developed from an earlier period took on the more formal definition evident in 1 Timothy and Titus.

Finally, the pattern of ministry that is agreed on must provide for designated leadership. The offices of ministry in these texts are clearly leadership ministries. Without clear but flexible patterns of leadership, the body dissolves into chaos and descends into dysfunction.

The metaphor of the church as a body with many spiritual gifts does not immediately translate into a permanent pattern of ministry set in stone for all time. Nevertheless, as we have seen, it does provide some basic principles by which to evaluate emerging patterns. The report of the Dean's Seminar speaks to this process: "Although there is in the New Testament no one normative pattern of church life and ministry to be followed in each generation, and though there was considerable freedom for the Holy Spirit to guide the churches in developing such patterns, the Scriptures are instructive and authoritative in the matter of determining principles for modern structures of church life and ministry and for making judgments about the faithfulness and appropriateness of particular historical models."[9]

The pastor as navigator

My extended leave of absence from AMBS to serve as pastor of a congregation in the greater Denver area gave me opportunity to reflect from within a congregation on the nature and practice of ministry. I began my pastoral ministry in that place with another metaphor, the metaphor of a hand. Each finger represented one aspect of my ministry: preaching, teaching, leading worship, providing a pastoral presence, and being a theological resource. The hand itself represented an administrative role, providing cohesiveness and coordination to the various ministries of the five fingers as well as to the many-faceted ministries of the members of the congregation.

I did not, of course, do all the administration and coordination of congregational program, nor was I the only preacher, teacher, and worship leader. I came to see more fully how important was the role of providing a pastoral presence and being a theological resource. My pastoral office as it developed took shape in part because of my spiritual gifts and training and in part because of the needs and expectations of the congregation. It was gratifying to observe how deeply the members of the congregation were involved in their ministries both in the congregation and in the larger community.

As I neared the end of my five-year term, I hit upon another metaphor to describe my office as a minister, the metaphor of a ship and its navigator. The New Testament includes many references to ships. I drew from one of them, in Acts 20, for my farewell message to the congregation. This text refers to the ship on which Paul was traveling to Jerusalem, and to which the elders of the church at Ephesus came to bid him farewell.

In Gospel stories of Jesus in the boat with his fearful disciples, stilling the storm, Christian tradition has seen an image of the church. The church is in the world as a ship is in the stormy sea being buffeted by fierce winds and high waves. Some church architecture draws on this image of the church as a ship. The main body of the building, where the congregation meets for worship, is called the nave, from a medieval Latin word for ship.

The people are not passengers on a pleasure cruise, however; they are the working crew. Much work needs to be done. The sails must be kept in good repair. They must be unfurled when the ship leaves the harbor. They must be trimmed to catch the wind. The decks must be scrubbed. The cargo must be loaded and unloaded. Some crew members must climb the mast to the crow's nest and keep a sharp lookout along the horizon or toward the sky to give warning of any threats in the sea lanes or in the clouds. Someone must read the compass and someone must steer. Someone must see to it that an adequate supply of provisions is put on board and that food is prepared and served. Someone must take care of the sick and dying and arrange for burial at sea if necessary. Someone must rescue those who fall overboard. Someone is responsible to drop anchor and to weigh anchor again when it is time to leave each port of call and resume the voyage. There is plenty of work to be done, and it requires the full cooperation and best efforts of everyone on board.

In this analogy, the role of the pastor is not that of the captain. Jesus is the captain of the ship, the Lord of the church, the head of the body. He is in charge of planning the destination, the itinerary, and the schedule. The role of the pastor may more appropriately be compared to that of the navigator. The navigator is the one who maps out the course set by the captain. The navigator is responsible to check the chart and compass (the Scriptures and the heritage of faith) and to be sure that the ship is on course and on schedule. The navigator must be familiar with the sea lanes and the hazards that lie below the surface of the water. In short, the navigator is responsible to assist the captain in assuring a safe voyage and the ship's arrival at its appointed destination in good shape and on time.

Conclusion

Discussion about the nature and practice of ministry has continued over the past four decades, since we debated the issues in the Dean's Seminar. These continuing conversations have yielded fruit and eventuated in a 1992 statement adopted by the faculty and board in which AMBS committed itself to the conviction that "all Christians are called and gifted 'to participate in the ministries of the church.'"[10] At the same time, "to underline the distinctive character of pastoral and other church leadership ministries, seminary faculty have adopted the language of *office*. When one is called to hold an office in ministry—whether expressed in the role of pastoral minister, evangelist, pastoral counselor, or a teacher of the church—the church assigns not only particular responsibilities, but appropriate authority and standards of accountability in relation to other ministries in the church."[11] Of this statement of consensus I am pleased to join in the affirmation that "it seemed good to the Holy Spirit and to us."

Notes

[1] For an introduction to the Dean's Seminar, see Ross T. Bender, *The People of God: A Mennonite Interpretation of the Free Church Tradition* (Scottdale, Pa.: Herald Press, 1971), especially the foreword by the author and the introduction by Erland Waltner. Waltner identifies the three major issues debated by seminar participants in their attempt to develop a model for theological education in the free church: "(1) What is the nature of the Free Church, especially in the Anabaptist-Mennonite perspective stated in contemporary terms? (2) What is the essential nature of the church's ministry today? and (3) What is to be the character of theological education for ministry in the 1970's, reflecting faithfully the theology of the Free Church?" (13).

[2] John A. Esau, editor, *Understanding Ministerial Leadership: Essays Contributing to a Developing Theology of Ministry* (Elkhart, Ind.: Institute of Mennonite Studies, 1995), xi-xii.

[3] See *Growing in Ministry: 2000-2002 Catalog* (Elkhart, Ind.: Associated Mennonite Biblical Seminary), 178-79, for a brief history of AMBS.

[4] The transition from lay to professional ministry proceeded at different paces in different parts of the constituency, with the General Conference Mennonite Church in the United States moving earlier and further in the direction of a seminary-trained and salaried clergy than the GC churches in Canada and the (Old) Mennonites in North America.

[5] Bender, *The People of God*, 5.

[6] Ibid., 168.

[7] I must acknowledge, in all candor, that the plural ministry was lodged in the bench, which exercised most of the power positions in the congregation. The role other members played was largely passive. In that sense, the body theology of ministry represented a challenge to the older tradition, as well as to the emerging new pattern.

[8] Esau, *Understanding Ministerial Leadership*, xii.

[9] Bender, *The People of God*, 154.

[10] "Theological Education and Curricular Design at AMBS," *Growing in Ministry: 2000-2002*, 169. This statement is reprinted as Appendix 2 in the present volume (257-62; see esp. 258).

[11] Ibid.

2

Worldly preachers and true shepherds

Anabaptist anticlericalism in the Lower Rhine

Karl Koop

Although some scholars have given attention to issues of pastoral identity and leadership in Anabaptism,[1] most have concentrated on the heightened role of the laity and the egalitarian nature of Anabaptist communities. Almost a half a century ago, in his classic volume *The Anabaptist View of the Church*, Franklin Littell noted that in matters of polity, the congregation, not the clerics, were the center of authority. Littell did not deny the concept of leadership in Anabaptism, but he focused his attention on the way the Anabaptists made decisions on the basis of consensus and mutual agreement.[2]

Scholars writing in the last decades of the twentieth century have generally followed Littell's line of thought. In the work that emerged from the Dean's Seminar at Associated Mennonite Biblical Seminaries in the 1970s, theological educators observed that the Anabaptists reached their decisions by consensus, and that all people shared responsibility for the governance and work of the congregation.[3] In his research on Anabaptist hermeneutics John Howard Yoder noted that it was in the context of the congregation that Anabaptists came to understand the biblical text.[4] Similarly, sociologists J. Howard Kauffman and Leland Harder have asserted that the Anabaptists "emphatically rejected the established distinction between clergy and laity and considered every member to be a minister of one kind or another."[5] Studies by Adolf Ens and Stuart Murray have not ignored the fact that the Anabaptists had leaders, but the general thrust of their work has also sustained the notion that the Anabaptist community was egalitarian in its polity.[6]

Recently this emphasis on the role of the congregation in Anabaptism has come under scrutiny. Critics have not denied that Anabaptists rejected traditional leadership roles and church structures, but some have questioned whether the Anabaptists were as egalitarian as has sometimes been assumed. For instance, when Marlin Miller was asked to write an article for *The Mennonite Encyclopedia* focusing on the priesthood of all believers, he discovered that the concept, which originated with Martin Luther, hardly appeared in Anabaptist writings.[7] Historian John D. Roth has questioned whether the Swiss Brethren, the Hutterites, or Menno Simons consistently implemented the ideal of the hermeneutic community, and Roth has suggested that more research be carried out to ascertain the degree to which this ideal worked itself out in practice.[8] Gary Waite, in his study of the holiness of the laity among early Dutch Anabaptists, has argued that leaders in some Anabaptist communities were actually objects of veneration, as were the Anabaptist martyrs who had lived holy lives.[9] And Werner Packull, based on his studies of the Hutterites and Menno Simons, has noted that the concept of the hermeneutical community, as expressed in the writings of John Howard Yoder and others, may well be a modern interpretation of sixteenth-century Anabaptism.[10]

Even the critics do not call into question the heightened role of the laity in Anabaptist communities. Historians generally agree that the call for greater lay participation in the affairs of church and society was already widespread in the late Middle Ages.[11] During the Reformation period, even magisterial reformers such as Luther and Zwingli encouraged lay involvement, as did peasants, who revolted against political and ecclesial hierarchies in the uprising of 1525. Anabaptists were sympathetic to peasant aspirations, and some participated in the uprisings aimed at bringing about social and political reform. Anabaptists urged greater lay participation and understood biblical passages such as 1 Corinthians 14 to mean that each person within the congregation had something to contribute. The Swiss Brethren learned this lesson from Zwingli, who referred to this form of church involvement as the Rule of Paul.[12]

Clearly, the Anabaptist appeal to the working of the Holy Spirit in the lives of believers challenged accepted hierarchies of the day and allowed for the possibility of new social arrangements. Nevertheless, the questions posed by critics suggest that more attention needs to be given to the way the laity participated in their respective communities. Equally important is the need for scholars to examine the ways Anabaptist leaders carried out their roles in communities that expected a level of mutuality and accountability.

While not denying that the laity played a heightened role in Anabaptist circles, I maintain that Anabaptists, at least in the Lower Rhine regions of Germany, affirmed the importance of genuine and qualified leadership. I will focus attention on the anticlerical impulse among Anabaptists in the region as expressed in the Kempen confession of 1545. The use of the term *anticlericalism* may seem out of place here, because it could imply a negating of the clerical office. In some contexts, however, the term may point toward reforming, rather than eradicating, the clerical office. This impulse toward reform is apparent when one looks more closely at the anticlerical impulse in the early modern period.

Anticlericalism in the early modern period

The term *anticlericalism* first emerged in the context of controversies following the Enlightenment and the *Kulturkampf* in nineteenth-century Europe. The term referred to the way European society attempted to challenge clerical influence in politics and public life. It reflected antagonism toward the institutional church, and sometimes even a general turning away from Christianity.[13]

Anticlericalism was not unique to this period, however. John Van Engen has noted that anticlerical attitudes were frequent throughout Christian history and often grew "apace with the institutionalization of Christendom."[14] The more the church entered into the lives of people, the more intense anticlerical sentiments came to the surface. "By the high Middle Ages Europeans took for granted smoldering resentments directed against monks, friars, bishops, priests, and clerics who claimed this-worldly privileges by way of an other-worldly office."[15] As religious movements attained institutional status and infringed on the privileges of others, satire and critique inevitably followed. This reaction was evident at Cluny and among the Cistercians, whose bureaucracies and economic power dominated vast regions of Europe. Anticlerical feeling also emerged in the context of an increasingly imposing papacy. Disaffection with the clergy also emerged in village parishes, where various obligations, tithes, and fees intruded on the ordinary peasant, and where mendicant friars came begging for money.[16]

These anticlerical sentiments in the general populace led some would-be clerics to avoid the priestly office. In about 1374, Geert

Grote, who founded the *devotio moderna* and who had been an ambitious and successful cleric, experienced a major personal turnaround that led him to avoid ordination to the priesthood. The reasons for resisting ordination were well known during this time. "Common wisdom held that most of those who took vows were hypocrites, and Grote was determined not to join their number."[17] Grote's critique of the clergy was coupled with disdain for the educated, the assumption being that learning brought about confusion, perversion, and a loss of genuine piety. While literacy—even advanced latinity and university training—were not ruled out, the devotional emphasis was to remain central. Thomas à Kempis captured the tone set in the 1390s when he stated in his *Imitation of Christ*, "What good is it to dispute profoundly about the Trinity if you lack humility and so displease the Trinity? Truly, deep words do not make a person holy and righteous, but a virtuous life makes one dear to God. I would rather feel compunction than know its definition."[18]

The anticlerical spirit of the late Middle Ages permeated the Reformation period and became a primary engine of social, religious, and eventually, political change.[19] In his address to the German nobility, Martin Luther argued that the clerical estate was in shambles, the pope had failed, and it was up to the laity to rescue Christendom. Theologically, Luther pointed out that because of the justice imputed to humanity by God, the supposed mediation of salvation through the priestly office was not necessary.[20] Ulrich Zwingli, in his *Exposition and Principles of the Articles*, also spoke out energetically against the clerical institution, his break with Rome by this time being more or less complete.[21]

Among the radical reformers, anticlerical sentiments were even more pronounced. In 1519 Franz Günther and Thomas Müntzer were engaged in anticlerical struggle against Franciscan monks in the city of Jüterbog, and when Müntzer fled to Prague and penned his manifesto two years later, he left no doubt about his views on those "hell based parsons."[22] Similar sentiments ignited among Zwinglian radicals who marched to the monks' church in Zurich and heckled the priest for venerating the saints in his pious sermons. The authorities issued a warning, but at least one of the radicals, Conrad Grebel, remained impenitent and threatened violence: "If my lords do not allow the Gospel to advance they will be destroyed."[23]

Clearly some reformers were prepared to attack the clerical elite[24] verbally, and sometimes even physically. It may be more difficult to ascertain how to interpret this behavior. Referring to the medieval context, John Van Engen has asked whether anticlericalism was "generated by a resentful and destructive impulse or by an ameliorating and reforming impetus? Or indeed by some mixture of the two with all the range of ambiguity in between? Is it even right to label such outbursts, whether verbal or physical, 'anticlericalism'?"[25]

To put the question more sharply, was anticlericalism as it was understood in nineteenth-century Europe even thinkable in the Middle Ages or Reformation period? "If most people could not imagine a world without God, could they imagine a world without God's mediators or representatives? They could resent and criticize monks and priests; could they imagine simply doing without them or even doing away with them?"[26] It is striking that Geert Grote, who avoided the clerical office for himself, never rejected it in any formal or theological sense. "On the contrary, he set its standards so high as to be nearly unattainable."[27] To be sure, by the time of the Reformation the sacerdotal office, with its mediating qualities, was repudiated by many reformers. But at that time could they have conceived of church life in fully democratic or egalitarian terms, absent of real leadership, as has sometimes been contemplated in modern times?

The most influential proponents of anticlericalism during the Reformation period were themselves church leaders. While one can find examples of reformers who fled from or avoided the clerical office,[28] in general the removal of the clerics seems not to have been the primary goal of sixteenth-century anticlerical protest; it was more a critique of a lifestyle and misuse of power.[29] Moreover, this anticlerical stance was rooted in a heightened religiosity among the laity, coupled with a concern about salvation. The masses wanted access to God, but began to have doubts about that possibility when those mediating the Word and sacraments were corrupt or incompetent. The goal of anticlericalism during the Reformation period, in most instances, was not to get rid of the clerics but to bring about clerical reform.[30]

As will become evident in the next section, that goal was also inherent in the anticlerical impulse among Anabaptists who began settling along the Rhine near Cologne, who lashed out against "worldly preachers" and set out to define the identity of the "true shepherds."

Anticlericalism among Anabaptists in the Lower Rhine region

The story of North German Anabaptists along the Rhine is not well known. It has sometimes been assumed that Anabaptists in the region were Swiss Brethren.[31] By the middle of the sixteenth century, Swiss Brethren or Upper Germans were indeed moving northward into the Lower Rhine territories.[32] Dutch and German historians in recent decades, however, have pointed out that the first Anabaptists in the area were from the German province of Westphalia, and the Münsterite Anabaptist Heinrich Rol in all likelihood played a pivotal role in the emergence of Anabaptism in the region.[33] According to J. F. G. Goeters, Heinrich Rol in early 1534 baptized Gerhard Westerburg, who then returned to his native Cologne to introduce Anabaptism there. On February 21, 1534, Rol himself left Münster to visit the cities of Wesel and Maastricht, where more adult baptisms took place. These new converts, in turn, brought Anabaptist ideas to Kleve and Duisburg. In the ensuing years Anabaptist ideas were well received in the Lower Rhine regions, especially among those who had already been introduced to sacramentarian ideas.[34]

The Anabaptists along the Lower Rhine eventually came under the influence of the Dutch Anabaptist Menno Simons, who visited the area from 1544 to 1546. Menno possibly resided in the diocese of Cologne, in the Niederstift, close to Odenkirchen, and in Kempen. Menno may have come to the region for several reasons. Herman von Wied was archbishop of Cologne during this time, and along with Albert Hardenberg was introducing a moderate reformation that was relatively sympathetic to Anabaptist ideas.[35] There were already Anabaptists in the area, including Menno's colleague Dirk Philips.[36] Jacobus ten Doornkaat Koolman states that Menno had contact with local leaders Theunis van Jüchen of Sasserath and Michiel Oistwart.[37] About a thousand Anabaptists probably lived in the Gladbach area during this time, inhabiting "towns like Kempen, Krefeld and Rheydt west of the Rhine River between Duisburg and Düsseldorf."[38] Theunis (also Thönis) was an energetic leader, accepting the office of teacher and elder after the death of the elder Leitgen in 1545. Theunis's missionary travels took him to Visschersweert in 1545; he was also involved in Anabaptist conversations at Goch in 1547 and later participated in Anabaptist activities in the Eifelgebergte hinterlands. On June 30, 1551, he was burned at the stake in Linnich on the Roer.[39]

It was Theunis who authored the Kempen confession, which was then used by the Anabaptists around Kempen and presented to the officials of Electoral Cologne on March 28 and June 17, 1545.[40] The congregation in Kempen was relatively small, consisting of about twelve families who had initially joined the Protestant cause and had only recently become Anabaptist. According to the court records, none of the people belonging to the congregation at Kempen had been baptized for much more than a year.[41] Goeters indicates that the congregation consisted mainly of young couples with children; they met occasionally in the home of locksmith Reynar Piper for communion services.[42] When the group was called on for cross-examination by the local officials, representatives of the congregation—a goldsmith Georg, and mason Tewes Rubsam, both from Kempen—submitted the confession as an account of their faith.[43]

The confession was a statement of faith in six articles, dealing with (1) the incarnation, (2) baptism, (3) the Lord's Supper, (4) ministry, (5) civil authorities, and (6) the weapons of the faithful.[44] It reflects theological concerns of North German/Dutch Anabaptism in its emphasis on Christ's heavenly origins, the new birth, and the view that only true believers can receive holy baptism and participate in the Holy Supper. Written ten years after the collapse of the kingdom of Münster, the confession rejects revolutionary Anabaptism, recognizes the legitimacy of government, and identifies the weapons of the true Christian solely in spiritual terms.[45]

By far the longest section in the confession is the fourth article, on ministry, which focuses on the reasons why true Christians should not listen to the preachers of the world nor associate with their followers.[46] The article points out why the Anabaptists of Kempen cannot bring themselves to cooperate with the direction of the reform movement in the Rhine region.[47] The article is anticlerical in sentiment but in no way diminishes the importance of the clerical office. The Anabaptists are concerned to redefine the identity of the true shepherd, the authentic pastor who leads his flock according to the teachings of Christ.

Goeters maintains that a number of themes in the confession, including the article on ministry, reflect the influence of Menno Simons.[48] In January 1544 Menno had debated with Johannes à Lasco of Emden on the incarnation and on the office of the preacher.[49] Menno had argued passionately that true preachers had been sent by Christ

Jesus, were blameless in doctrine and life, and were of "one body, spirit, and mind" with Christ, even as Christ was "one with the Father."[50] True preachers were not to seek dominion over others, nor should they serve for the sake of certain benefices, pensions, or salaries, "but solely for the gain of the souls which Christ Jesus [had] so dearly bought with His precious blood."[51]

Menno also noted that genuine preachers did not waver in their responsibility to "reprove the great as well as the small, the rich as well as the poor, the learned as well as those that were unlearned."[52] The problem with the preachers in the evangelical churches was that their doctrine was corrupt; they possessed "no power, no fruit of the Spirit, no true fear of God, and no brotherly love."[53] They took on their clerical functions, motivated by their bellies and other benefits, and were therefore mere hirelings who did not genuinely care for the sheep.[54] Menno referred more than once to John 20:21, which formed the basis of his understanding of leadership as well as of the church "without spot or blemish": "As the Father has sent me, so send I you." In the same way that Christ Jesus was one with the Father, so also should the leadership in the church be one with Christ, because that oneness was the very nature of the church itself.[55]

The Kempen confession follows the spirit of Menno Simons at several points. According to the confession, true Christians are those who have been born of Christ, are guided by his Spirit, and follow the way of Christ. They avoid the things of the world that are visible, customary, and transitory, and they are literally willing to follow Christ and his way of the cross, which leads to oppression, scorn, and suffering. True Christians have become new creatures; they have been born anew. For them the old has passed away, and a new righteousness has come, recognized by its fruits in the believer's life.[56]

The confession does not support a Lutheran concept of imputed righteousness, a belief that God "declares" the believer righteous on the basis of faith alone. Rather, following the spirit of the Radical Reformation, the confession teaches that believers actually "become righteous." Here emerges the medieval and patristic soteriological presupposition, which holds that a new ontological righteousness is possible. Following the teachings of the ancient church, the confession implicitly assumes that God became human so that humanity, in union with Christ, could become divine.[57]

The article about the preaching office is polemically anticlerical, drawing from many Scripture texts for theological ammunition. The worldly preachers cannot be trusted because they do not recognize Christ's divine power, nor his divine nature, and are essentially hirelings (John 10).[58] Christ has not sent them; rather than serve others, they prefer to be served. "They misguide and do not teach; they kill and do not bring life (Mt. 13); scatter rather than gather; they concern themselves at all times with themselves, not the concerns of Jesus Christ and those next to them, etc."[59] Their doctrine and life are not in keeping with the word of the Lord; for this reason such preachers and their followers are to be avoided.[60]

Despite its harsh critique of clerical abuses, the confession at no point suggests that the church should put leadership aside, or even de-emphasize it. In fact, the confession affirms authentic leadership in the church. Its anticlerical sentiment is therefore not a condemnation of the clerical office as such, but a call for clerical reform. The thrust of the article is that believers must distinguish between worldly preachers and true shepherds. Unlike the worldly preachers, true shepherds are cleansed of false practices and understand the meaning and teachings of Christ. They speak words of penance and grace to all.

In agreement with Menno, the confession affirms that true shepherds do not discriminate among their parishioners, and they hold even the magistrates accountable for their actions. "Regardless of person they punish lords and princes, the high and the low, the educated and the uneducated, male and female; for they also know that the powerful, penetrating word of God has been given to all flesh."[61] They carry out the sacraments of baptism and the evening meal according to the Word of God.[62] Their authenticity is rooted in the fact that Christ and the Father have sent them. The consequences of such sending are significant: as they work in Christ's vineyard they are like sheep among wolves (Matt. 10:16; John 17:14).[63]

Given what we know about the heightened role of the laity in Anabaptism, we may find it odd that the Anabaptists of Kempen did not give attention in their confession to the congregation. Did they not see the possibility of lay participation and congregational engagement? That conclusion seems unlikely, because both the earlier and later writings of the Anabaptists and Mennonites in the Low Countries point to the fact that congregational involvement was assumed, and we have no reason to doubt that things were different in Kempen.

That the Anabaptists of Kempen did not address the issue of lay participation likely had to do with the purpose of their discussions with the authorities—to indicate why the Anabaptists could not participate in the reform currently underway in the region. Their reasons were theological: a central issue was their conviction that if worldly preachers lead the effort, genuine reform will not be the result. In this context, these Anabaptists' anticlerical sentiments were meant to convey to the authorities their belief that true reform is possible only when faithful and authentic leadership is in place.

Conclusion

Although Rhenish Anabaptists expressed anticlerical sentiments, their rhetoric in the Kempen confession focuses on making the distinction between worldly preachers, who had attained their position for all the wrong reasons, and true shepherds, who were genuinely called of God. Essentially these Anabaptists supported the clerical office; it is unlikely that they would ever have considered a congregational polity that excluded all forms of pastoral leadership. The goal of the Anabaptists of the Lower Rhine region, evident in this article of their confession, was not to condemn leadership in the Christian community but to reform it.

The Kempen confession offers an outstanding discourse on anticlericalism, yet it leaves many questions unanswered. Although it affirms pastoral leadership, it does not give us an account of all the responsibilities that pastors should have. Further, we cannot assume that all Anabaptist communities had as positive a view of pastoral leadership. Did other Anabaptists in other regions esteem as highly the role of true shepherds in the life of the church?[64] What role did these sixteenth-century leaders play in worship, catechetical instruction, preaching, and pastoral care? How was their status similar to, or different from, the status of leaders in Catholic or Protestant churches? Clearly, these questions, and others related to sixteenth-century pastoral identity, merit further scholarly exploration.

Notes

[1] See, for instance, Christoph Bornhäuser, *Leben und Lehre Menno Simons':
Ein Kampf um das Fundament des Glaubens* (Neukirchen-Vluyn: Neukirchener
Verlag, 1973); William Echard Keeney, *The Development of Dutch Anabaptist Thought
and Practice from 1539-1564* (Nieuwkoop: B. De Graaf, 1968).

[2] Franklin Littell, *The Anabaptist View of the Church: A Study in the Origins of
Sectarian Protestantism*, 2nd ed. (Boston: Starr King Press, 1958), 92-93.

[3] Ross T. Bender, *The People of God: A Mennonite Interpretation of the Free
Church Tradition* (Scottdale, Pa.: Herald Press, 1971), 86, 88, 154.

[4] John Howard Yoder, "Hermeneutics of the Anabaptists," in *Essays on Biblical
Interpretation*, ed. Willard Swartley, Text Reader Series, no. 1 (Elkhart, Ind.: Institute
of Mennonite Studies, 1984), 20-21. See also John Howard Yoder, *The Fullness of
Christ: Paul's Vision of Universal Ministry* (Elgin, Ill.: Brethren Press, 1987), 41-42.

[5] J. Howard Kauffman and Leland Harder, *Anabaptists Four Centuries Later: A
Profile of Five Mennonite and Brethren in Christ Denominations* (Scottdale, Pa.:
Herald Press, 1975), 183-84.

[6] Adolf Ens, "Theology of the Hermeneutical Community in Anabaptist-
Mennonite Thought," in *The Church As Theological Community: Essays in Honour of
David Schroeder*, ed. Harry Huebner (Winnipeg, Man.: CMBC Publications, 1990),
69-89; Stuart Murray, *Biblical Interpretation in the Anabaptist Tradition* (Kitchener,
Ont.: Pandora Press, 2000), 157, 164-65.

[7] Miller found only a few references to the priesthood of all believers in the
writings of Menno Simons. Menno seems to have used the term to stress the
importance of holy living rather than to make a point about congregational polity.
See Richard A. Kauffman and Gayle Gerber Koontz, eds., *Theology for the Church:
Writings by Marlin E. Miller*, Text Reader Series, no. 7 (Elkhart, Ind.: Institute of
Mennonite Studies, 1997), 121-23. Miller's article, "Priesthood of All Believers," is
found in *The Mennonite Encyclopedia,* ed. Cornelius J. Dyck and Dennis D. Martin
(Scottdale, Pa., and Waterloo, Ont.: Herald Press, 1990), 5:721.

[8] John D. Roth, "Community As Conversation: A New Model of Anabaptist
Hermeneutics," in *Essays in Anabaptist Theology*, ed. H. Wayne Pipkin, Text Reader
Series, no. 5 (Elkhart, Ind.: Institute of Mennonite Studies, 1994), 40.

[9] Gary K. Waite, "Dopers anticlericalisme en lekenheiligheid: Doperse heiligen
en de status van heiligheit in de Nederlanden," *Doopsgezinde Bijdragen*, new series
25 (1999): 65-84.

[10] Werner O. Packull, "Menno Simons und die Auslegung der Heiligen Schrift,"
Mennonitische Geschichtsblätter 53 (1996): 54.

[11] See, for instance, several essays on the late medieval setting, in *Anticlericalism
in Late Medieval and Early Modern Europe,* eds. Peter Dykema and Heiko Oberman
(Leiden: E. J. Brill, 1994).

[12] Ens, "The Hermeneutical Community," 76.

[13] See Hans-Jürgen Goertz, "'What a Tangled and Tenuous Mess the Clergy
Is!' Clerical Anticlericalism in the Reformation Period," in Dykema and Oberman,

Anticlericalism, 501-2; and Hans-Jürgen Goertz, *Antiklerikalismus und Reformation: Sozialgeschichtliche Untersuchungen* (Göttingen: Vandenhoeck & Ruprecht, 1995), 10-12.

[14] John Van Engen, "Late Medieval Anticlericalism: The Case of the New Devout," in Dykema and Oberman, *Anticlericalism*, 19.

[15] Ibid. "For its part this clerical caste frequently displayed attitudes we might call 'anti-laicism,' religious contempt for lay people said to think mostly about their bellies and their genitals and their honor with no receptivity to a higher eternal good" (ibid.).

[16] Ibid., 20.

[17] Ibid., 23.

[18] Van Engen, "Late Medieval Anticlericalism," 47.

[19] Low German–speaking Mennonites may be familiar with the proverb *Je jeliehrda je vertjierda* (The more learned, the more perverted). This phrase—in modern German, *Die Gelehrten die Verkehrten*—was one of the best-known Reformation slogans in sixteenth-century pamphlet literature. Memorable sayings, including this one and *Affen–Pfaffen* (The cleric is an ape), proved important in the service of the Reformation from 1515 to 1525. But obviously these sentiments were already present in the late Middle Ages. See Heiko A. Oberman, *"Die Gelehrten die Verkehrten:* Popular Response to Learned Culture in the Renaissance and Reformation," in *Religion and Culture in the Renaissance and Reformation*, ed. Steven Ozment (Kirksville, Mo.: Sixteenth Century Journal Publishers, Inc., 1989), 43-63. The proverb *Je jeliehrda je vertjierda* can also be found in Anabaptist writings. See, for instance, Dirk Phillips, "The Sending of Preachers or Teachers," in *The Writings of Dirk Philips 1504-1568*, trans. and ed. Cornelius J. Dyck, William Keeney, and Alvin J. Beachy (Scottdale, Pa.: Herald Press, 1992), 199.

[20] Goertz, "'What a Tangled and Tenuous Mess the Clergy Is!'" 505, 513. See Martin Luther, "An Appeal to the Ruling Class of German Nationality As to the Amelioration of the State of Christendom, 1520," *Martin Luther: Selections from his Writings*, ed. John Dillenger (New York: Doubleday, 1961), 403-85.

[21] Goertz, "'What a Tangled and Tenuous Mess the Clergy Is!'" 507. See Ulrich Zwingli, "Sixty-Seven Theses," in *A Reformation Reader: Primary Texts with Introductions*, ed. Denis R. Janz (Minneapolis: Fortress Press, 1999), 155-58.

[22] Goertz, "'What a Tangled and Tenuous Mess the Clergy Is!'" 506; Thomas Müntzer, "The Prague Protest: A Protest about the Condition of the Bohemians," in *The Radical Reformation*, ed. and trans. Michael G. Baylor (Cambridge: Cambridge University Press, 1991), 2. Müntzer did not mince words in his critique of the clergy and the educated: "Freely and boldly I declare that I have never heard a single donkey-fart doctor of theology, in the smallest of his divisions and points, even whisper, to say nothing of speaking loudly, about the order [established in God and all his creatures]" (ibid., 2).

[23] Hans-Jürgen Goertz, *The Anabaptists*, trans. Trevor Johnson (London: Routledge, 1996), 8.

[24] See, for instance, Heinhold Fast, "Reformation durch Provokation: Predigtstörungen in den ersten Jahren der Reformation in der Schweiz," in *Umstrittenes Täufertum 1525-1975: Neue Forschungen*, ed. Hans-Jürgen Goertz (Göttingen: Vandenhoeck & Ruprecht, 1975), 79-110.

[25] Engen, "Late Medieval Anticlericalism," 20.

[26] Ibid.

[27] Ibid., 28.

[28] Heinhold Fast argues that Jörg Maler, an Anabaptist, avoided ordination on principle, preferring to maintain his office as "reader" (Heinhold Fast, "Vom Amt des 'Lesers.' Zum Kompilator des Sogenannten Kunstbuches: Auf den Spuren Jörg Malers," in *Außenseiter Zwischen Mittelalter und Neuzeit: Festschrift für Hans-Jürgen Goertz zum 60. Geburtstag*, ed. Norbert Fischer and Marion Kobelt-Groch [Leiden: Brill, 1997], 187-203). See also Heinold Fast, "Zur Überlieferung des Leser-Amtes bei den oberdeutschen Täufern," in *Mennonitische Geschichtsblätter* 54 (1997): 61-68.

[29] Hans-Jürgen Goertz, "Kleruskritik, Kirchenzucht und Sozialdisziplinierung in den Täuferischen Bewegungen der Frühen Neuzeit," in *Kirchenzucht und Sozialdisziplinierung im frühneuzeitlichen Europa*, ed. Heinz Schilling (Berlin: Duncker & Humblot, 1994), 185. That Anabaptists did not reject the office, but were concerned primarily with the way in which it was abused, has also been observed by John A. Esau. See "Recovering, Rethinking, and Re-imagining: Issues in a Mennonite Theology for Ministry," in *Understanding Ministerial Leadership: Essays Contributing to a Developing Theology of Ministry*, Text Reader Series, no. 6 (Elkhart, Ind.: Institute of Mennonite Studies, 1995), 12-13.

[30] Hans-Jürgen Goertz also makes this point in his book *Antiklericalismus und Reformation: Sozialgeschichtliche Untersuchungen* (Göttingen: Vandenhoeck & Ruprecht, 1995), 15.

[31] See Leonard Gross, *Golden Apples in Silver Bowls: The Rediscovery of Redeeming Love* (Lancaster, Pa.: Lancaster Mennonite Historical Society, 1999), 1-2.

[32] For background to this development see John S. Oyer, "The Strasbourg Conferences of the Anabaptists, 1554-1607," *Mennonite Quarterly Review* 58 (July 1984): 218-29.

[33] See Werner Packull, "Peter Tasch: From Melchiorite to Bankrupt Wine Merchant," *Mennonite Quarterly Review* 62 (July 1988): 278.

[34] Goeters, "Die Rolle des Täufertums in der Reformationsgeschichte des Niederrheins," *Rheinische Vierteljahrs Blätter* 24, no. 3/4 (1959): 228-29. Goeters is partially dependent on A. F. Mellink, *De wederdopers in de noordelijke Nederlanden 1531-1544* (Groningen: Wolters, 1954). Cornelius Krahn believes that the connection to Münster is too strong and that the question of Anabaptist origins needs to take the sacramentarian movement more seriously (Cornelius Krahn, *Dutch Anabaptism: Origin, Spread, Life, and Thought* [Scottdale, Pa.: Herald Press, 1981], 185).

[35] According to Krahn, Herman von Wied, who occupied the see of the

archbishopric from 1517 to 1546, "issued a severe edict against the Anabaptists dated August 23, 1534, which initiated the persecution and martyrdom of the Anabaptists in this territory" (Krahn, *Dutch Anabaptism*, 187). After 1538, however, he became interested in a gradual and humanistically oriented reformation. Eventually "he came to the point of lining up more fully with the Reformation. As a result he was forced to give up his position in 1546" (ibid., 35). See also J. F. G. Goeters, "Das älteste rheinische Täuferbekenntnis," in *A Legacy of Faith: A Sixtieth Anniversary Tribute to Cornelius Krahn*, ed. Cornelius J. Dyck (Newton, Kans.: Faith & Life Press, 1962), 197.

[36] Krahn, *Dutch Anabaptism*, 182-83.

[37] Jackobus ten Doornkaat Koolman, *Dirk Philips: Friend and Colleague of Menno Simons, 1504-1568*, trans. William E. Keeney, ed. C. Arnold Snyder (Kitchener, Ont.: Pandora Press, 1998), 25.

[38] Krahn, *Dutch Anabaptism*, 189.

[39] Koolman, *Dirk Philips*, 26.

[40] Participants on the Reformed side included Wilhelm von Rennenberg and Dietrich Vollebier of Kempen, Heinrich Zell of Bonn, Johannes Praetorius of Andernach, among others. See Goeters, "Täuferbekenntnis," 197-98.

[41] Ibid.

[42] Ibid., 198.

[43] Ibid. Krahn, *Dutch Anabaptism*, 188.

[44] The complete text of the confession is found in Goeters, "Täuferbekenntnis," 199-210.

[45] Krahn, *Dutch Anabaptism*, 189.

[46] The title of article four is as follows: "Wairum wir dieser Werlt Predycanten neyt en sullen noch moyssen horen off ouch ire Junger nety geseyn konnen." See Goeters, "Täuferbekenntnis," 203.

[47] Ibid., 211.

[48] Ibid., 210.

[49] See Menno Simons, "Brief and Clear Confession, 1544," in *The Complete Writings of Menno Simons c. 1496-1561*, trans. Leonard Verduin, ed. John C. Wenger (Scottdale, Pa.: Herald Press, 1986), 422-54. The treatise is divided into two sections, the second part dealing with the calling of ministers (ibid., 440-54).

[50] Ibid., 441.

[51] Ibid., 442.

[52] Ibid., 443.

[53] Ibid., 446.

[54] Ibid., 444. Here Menno was drawing from John 10:12, a favorite anticlerical text in Reformation Zurich that had been used by Zwingli in his Sixty-Seven Theses, and by his followers such as Conrad Grebel. See Arnold Snyder, "Biblical Text and Social Context: Anabaptist Anticlericalism in Reformation Zurich," *Mennonite Quarterly Review* 65 (April 1991), 169-91; esp. 173.

[55] Ibid., 448-49.

[56] Goeters, "Täuferbekenntnis," 203.

[57] Scholars have pointed to the Eastern theologians as early proponents of this soteriological emphasis on divinization. See, for instance, Irenaeus, "Against Heresies," in *Invitation to Christian Spirituality: An Ecumenical Anthology*, ed. John R. Tyson (New York: Oxford University Press, 1999), 66-67.

[58] Goeters, "Täuferbekenntnis," 203.

[59] Ibid., 206.

[60] Ibid., 203-6. Here the confession draws from many biblical texts.

[61] Ibid., 204.

[62] Ibid.

[63] Ibid., 205.

[64] A cursory reading of the Schleitheim articles suggests that the Swiss Brethren believed pastoral presence to be crucial. Article 5 states: "But if the shepherd should be driven away or led to the Lord by the cross, at the same hour another shall be ordained to his place, so that the little folk and the little flock of God may not be destroyed, but be preserved by warning and be consoled" (*The Legacy of Michael Sattler,* trans. and ed. John Howard Yoder [Scottdale, Pa.: Herald Press, 1973], 39).

3

Mennonite ministry and Christian history

Walter Sawatsky

We have learned from social historians, sociologists, and even socialists, to think in terms of social processes that develop over an extended period of time. Marxists historians, for example, presented all of European history within a threefold scheme: the feudal era of rule by aristocrats, the era of the middle class or bourgeoisie whose power base was mercantile, and finally the democratic era when the masses—laborers and peasants, the powerless—came into their own.

Within this conceptual scheme religious movements had a place. The Protestant Reformers, especially Luther, provided intellectual leadership for the revolution of the bourgeoisie, but these leaders' ideas were necessarily couched in the language of theology, given the times. Princes of emerging nation states were able to consolidate their power by aligning themselves with business leaders and supporting the theologians who were pushing for change. Yet already in the early sixteenth century, according to Friedrich Engels, Anabaptist leaders served as proponents of the position of the common people. The Anabaptists were ahead of their time; the bourgeois era needed time to replace the aristocrats, and then to demonstrate its own limitations as a class. When the socialist revolutions came to power, even the consciousness of the masses had moved beyond the religiosity of Anabaptists, beyond earlier Christian humanisms, to a full humanism that needed no transcendent gods.

During the decades when that Marxist project was faltering seriously, we learned from humanistic and revisionist Marxist thinkers to pay more attention to the role of intellectuals in the enterprise. Whether we read Djilas speaking in political terms,[1] or American Marxist sociologist Alvin Gouldner writing on the role of the intellectuals,[2] we were reading about what had gone wrong with the democratic enterprise: the shepherds of the people—the intellectuals—

had misused their power, had looked after their own interests and gratifications. They had not been true intellectuals, who would have been servants of the people. Whether this secular variant reminds one of the critique of shepherds of the people of Israel in Ezekiel 34, or of Jesus' frequent contrasting of bad shepherds with the good shepherd, the framework of thinking has remained constant. As was true of the Anabaptist critics of the clergy, these theorists did not seek to eradicate the shepherds but instead called them to become good shepherds.

My purpose for starting with secular sociologists from the left is to locate Mennonite thinking about leadership and ministry in a broader context. We tend to notice Mennonite distinctive patterns because our usual comparison is of the Anabaptist-Mennonite vision with that of other reform movements that did not go far enough. By going back "far enough" we have often meant returning to primitive Christian roots in order to replicate the church as it was before it became apostate. Christians commonly assume that Marxist radicalism went "too far," because it sought to build the good society without God. But the way the Marxists wrestled with the role of the leader reminds us that contemporary Mennonite questions about the position, power, and authority of the minister have much in common with questions raised by human history in general, and even more by Christian history as a whole.

Is there an essential heart of the matter?

The heart of the matter for current reflections on pastoral ministry, according to Erick Sawatzky, is a relationship. The leader of the church, often the pastor in modern America, is leading from the heart, from a center of integration of spirit, mind, and body. The relationship between pastor and people is one of integrity between the head and the body, that image of Christ and Christ's church that has been most prominent throughout Christian history. To mix metaphors, the shepherd of the sheep is to serve as head of the body, in the way that Christ is the good shepherd and loves the church. The negative images that Jesus used had to do with bad shepherding, with bad headship.

When Hans Küng constructed his theological review of Christian history, he, like many historians, started by attempting to identify what was at the heart of the matter. What was the essence of Christianity?[3] The phrase "the essence of Christianity" calls to mind

Feuerbach's book by that title of 150 years ago, which served as Bible for the Marxists. The essence, according to Küng's critique of Feuerbach and many others, is relationship to the person Jesus Christ, the one central to the first confession of faith, "Jesus is Lord."[4]

Küng's historical review helps us see more clearly the paradigm shifts through which Christianity has moved during two millennia. His approach is certainly superior to one that simplistically describes Christianity's apostasy, when it became an imperial church in the wake of Constantine's conversion, followed a thousand years later by various reformations seeking to recover from that apostasy. Küng kept asking how the criterion of the essential relationship to Jesus the Christ must be formulated with each successive shift. In so doing, he concentrated on how the leaders functioned, but measured their functioning against how well the people were enabled to discover and sustain relationship to Christ. Küng's analysis also involved paying attention to ways leadership and church life were institutionalized, to how the church came to understand and pass on apostolic faithfulness. A holy, living, constantly changing tradition (*paradosis*) was at the heart of the matter.

Much of the debate about the appropriate role of leaders, whether intellectual, political, corporate, or in the church, has revolved around issues of power and authority or legitimacy. Framing reflections on Mennonite thought and practice within the context of Christian history as a whole encourages us to notice developments that have been pushed aside when we look only at biblical models of ministry. To ask what the ministering person did, or what qualities of character that person was to have, and to mine the New Testament (and then, more reluctantly, the Old Testament) for answers has tended toward individualization or personalization, at the expense of thinking in terms of the whole body of Christ.

During the subapostolic period a system of organization emerged, through exercise of power and authority by bishops.[5] Several centuries of various patterns of such leadership in ministry passed before it became possible to argue for the supremacy of Roman papal leadership. In the current climate of more inclusive approaches to historical examination of the role of the episcopacy, Catholic and even Orthodox voices are showing openness to acknowledging the legitimacy of nonepiscopal churches and the charismata of their ministers.[6] In reciprocity, free churches need to reassess to what degree their own understandings of polity are driven by opposition to papal power claims, claims that some in Catholic circles are now calling into question. Bodies of both kinds should now attempt to think toward a reconciliation of churches through full communion, in which the power and authority of the church's leaders at all levels are recognized and legitimated.

The changing traditions of North American Mennonites

In Küng's terms, the American Mennonite story involves transitions from Reformation through Enlightenment to postmodern or ecumenical paradigms for mission and ministry. The American Mennonite experience is better understood, however, if we also draw attention to several particular features.

For Amish and Mennonite immigrants from Switzerland, Alsace, and south Germany, the challenge was to construct a church structure across the slowly expanding American frontier. In a context of religious freedom, they needed to learn to be a growing church instead of a surviving church. In facing this challenge their sixteenth-century for–mulations were of limited help. The anticlerical rhetoric of the early Anabaptists served to deconstruct both church as institution and church as clergy, but the American context had no dominant church and no dominant hierarchy, merely a dominant Protestant ethos.[7] In the new context, leadership categories of bishop, minister, and deacon had remarkable persistence, even as terms and titles got translated freely in the English milieu. Also noteworthy was a deep-seated resistance to forming structures for a national Mennonite church.[8]

The Russian/Prussian Mennonites arrived more recently in America. By 1874 when they began to settle in the Midwest, they had well-established leadership and institutional structures honed in settings of toleration, and they had even developed a self-understanding that included engagement in mission. This Mennonite tradition failed in its attempt to replicate the Russian and German structures in the new American context with its more intense and broad societal commitment to building a democratic republic (U.S.) or a democratic dominion (Canada). Nevertheless, these Mennonites found themselves adapting to conference structures that were national and international in scope.

Throughout the twentieth century, institution building in the American Mennonite church followed the model of other denominations, which increasingly adopted notions of management and self-regulation that were emerging in the business world. Particularly between 1970 and 2000, Mennonite church structures mirrored the professionalization taking place in the business community, as church agencies adapted regulations drawn from that arena for their own accounting and staff relations. Both the Mennonite Church and the General Conference Mennonite Church adopted credentialing guidelines that parallel guidelines for the teaching and other social service professions. Similarly, the drift to deregulation in the business world might well account for the looser structures in the recently united Mennonite Church USA.

A second development was the shifting role of spiritual leaders as a result of the immigration process. We still lack the detail we need to tell the story of the role played by spiritual leaders as eastern Mennonites moved westward. Much more so than was true in the formation of local congregations along the eastern seaboard as Franconia, Lancaster, and Virginia conferences formed, local congregations in the Midwest and West appear to have been shaped by individual leaders.[9] Russian Mennonite immigrations usually involved recognized elders or bishops traveling with their flock, and new settlement building included attention to forming congregations where clusters of Mennonites found land, or in cities where they found work. Those who have observed Russian Mennonite immigrants who moved to Germany between 1971 and 1993 have commented on a pronounced sense of a community moving, where initial purchase or construction of a church building entailed sacrifice. The image of ordained ministers leading the move, and authorizing someone to lead the remnant left behind, points to the spiritual leader as leading a pilgrimage.

The published biographies of Russian Mennonite leaders of the immigrations show those leaders spending almost more time negotiating with central authorities, overseeing major loans, raising committees and funds to found schools and other institutions, than in preaching and pastoral care.[10] In many cases, spiritual leaders were not salaried by the congregation and at best drew a salary related to those organizational roles undertaken in behalf of their people. If we include in our purview the Russian Mennonite immigrants re-establishing themselves in Paraguay, Uruguay, and Brazil, their spiritual leaders' activism in the economic and structural life of the colonies is still prominent. The image is of the spiritual leader of a people, most often of a group of such leaders who kept in close communication.

Finally, in light of the long tradition of high levels of lay involvement in spiritual life, the story of the establishment among Mennonites of a professional clergy, meeting the standards of an M.Div. degree, is distinctive. Societal standards for recognizing clergy, and visa requirements for sending missionaries since the era of independence were factors easily overlooked but important in the emergence of a professional, salaried clergy, with steadily increasing rationalization of fringe benefits. Churches that had avoided participation in health and life insurance plans and retirement policies now attempted to develop theologically appropriate mutual aid programs. At present the policies of such mutual aid societies are fully part of the American and Canadian economies, and standard actuarial principles and policies prevail, although special sharing projects seek to sustain that Mennonite legacy of mutual aid for some. Those who attend seminaries of more presbyterian or episcopal groups in North America are often ordained upon graduation; in contrast Mennonite seminarians completing an M.Div. degree obtain less formal recognitions for ministry, which allow them to list themselves for potential openings. Ordination typically follows a period of service in a congregation or other ministry setting.

This tracing of the broad outlines of the process of becoming denominations in the American sense and developing a corps of clergy that circulate within such denominations suggests a more steady development in a given direction than was true in specific regions.[11] Adding to the unevenness was confusion engendered by use of a specific Reformation legacy, the "recovery of the Anabaptist Vision," as a way of fostering the denomination's development.

H. S. Bender and his generation used this concept to foster the respectability of Anabaptist scholarship and thus to aid recognition of Mennonite groups as free churches and Protestant denominations. But the next generation used the idea of recovery of the Anabaptist Vision for more radical purposes. In the 1960s and 1970s this generation fostered a seminary program and Christian education curriculum that renewed the anti-institutional and anticlerical elements of the legacy, expressing it in the idiom of the Vietnam protest movement. That is, at a potential takeoff point in the professionalization of the clergy, American Mennonites began fostering the image of the pastor as salaried and trained, but not as congregational leader. They saw pastors as ones whose gifts were to be matched with the gifts of other ordained and lay people in congregations in order to achieve greater fullness.[12]

Toward the end of the twentieth century, appeals to radical Anabaptism took yet another form, now appearing as a marketing strategy. Mission statements of new church planting projects, or programs for North American or overseas ministry were described as bringing to a setting an "Anabaptist" orientation, that special something that justified competing for converts and keeping Mennonite ministries separate from those of other Christian churches, although in most other respects, contractual arrangements like those of other denominations prevailed.

At this point it may be instructive to note discussions within the Faith and Order committee/forum of the National Council of the Churches of Christ in the USA. Both member churches and non-member bodies, such as most Mennonites, have begun conversing on their understandings of the authority of the church. The conversation has sought to identify the appeals to authority within each denominational tradition, and to ask what authority the churches have, or should have, in society. Representatives of the traditions pointed to the central Christian traditions—the authority of God, of the Trinity, of Scripture, and for some, the authority of the Nicene or Apostles' Creed. Then they pointed to ways in which the authority of specific Reformation traditions has been sustained. For example, the 1530 Augsburg Confession continues to serve as a central point of unity for Lutherans, whereas within the Reformed tradition one can detect alignments more associated with the Synod of Dort (Dutch), the Westminster Confession (British), or Confessio Helvetica (Swiss).

But when the spokespeople described how appeals to authority function today, and how denominationally binding decisions and acts of discipline come about, most began acknowledging extensive diversity. The democratization of society and the impact of pluralism on virtually all spheres of church life account for the fact that appeals to authority are becoming awkward.[13]

Differentiations that matter
for the American Mennonite story

Early in 2002 the director of a conference-based leadership development program in Pennsylvania circulated a set of questions that had been posed by a conference minister for churches among new immigrant communities wanting to become Mennonite. The key question was: How do we define "apostolic leadership"? A series of interrelated questions followed, which emerged from the desire of more charismatic Mennonites for leadership that manifested the charism of authority, and from the hesitancy of other Mennonites about aggressive entrepreneurial leaders of growing churches, attracted by megachurch models. Instead of drawing attention to the classic marks of the church as one, holy, catholic, and apostolic, and asking how we might get back on course, one question pointed out that according to Ephesians 2:20 the church is built on the apostles and prophets; the questioner wanted to know whether the role of apostle is ongoing.

As if in answer, several weeks later Martin Marty weighed in, in his M.E.M.O in *Christian Century,* on "bishoping."[14] Marty was commenting on a newspaper article about "grade inflation" among pastors: leaders in historically nonepiscopal churches, such as the Baptists, were no longer content to be called "reverend," "pastor," or "elder" but had become self-styled bishops. Marty also noted the increasingly widespread use of the Doctor of Divinity degree, an honorary degree that someone has called the "donated dignity doctorate."

Waxing more serious, Marty pointed out that his own ELCA denomination is now in full communion with churches "that are episcopal, presbyterian, synodical, congregational, conferential and, if full communion with the United Methodists comes off, connectional." What matters, according to Marty, is that "all polities are to be measured in respect to the servant-hood of the whole people of God." To be measured by servanthood would elicit broad assent among Mennonites as right, as biblical. But Marty, a leading authority on American church history, also made this disturbing comment: "There can be tyrants in all polities—my observation is that congregational versions produce most, and most easily."

From the beginning Mennonites have practiced the laying on of hands, a ritual setting some apart for specific ministry. In American English that ritual is now called ordination, although the terms *Einsegnen, Hände auflegen, Bestätigen,* or *Ordinieren* earlier used by Mennonites have been too easily equated with *ordination* as an American legal term for recognizing clergy.[15] People used to be "ordained" as deacons, as ministers of the Word, and as bishops.[16] Given the heightened focus on the Word in both Lutheran and Reformed traditions, *ordination* soon had a more Protestantized meaning for the dominant Protestant traditions. They sought to render the Protestant clergy less sacrosanct than Catholic priests, who administered the sacraments as means of grace and exercised controlling authority in the confessional.

Along that sliding scale of desacralization, Mennonites tended to stress the accountability before the church of the one who was ordained: to challenge the word of the ordained minister, by appeals to Scripture, had a heightened value among Mennonites. As was true of the major reform traditions, the root of sin was no longer centered in the sex act; ordained leaders were to be married and lead exemplary families. Although women were vocal in leadership, there is no clear evidence of ordination of women until the twentieth century. Apparently application of the Scriptural evidence for the equal role of women and men, slaves and freemen, Jews and non-Jews had to wait until the logic of the democratization process had developed sufficiently. Given the stronger lay ministry tradition among Mennonites, one would expect ordination of women to have occurred sooner than among Lutherans and Reformed.

To understand the uneven significance of ministerial authority and identity within the uniting Mennonite church bodies in the U.S. and in Canada, we must differentiate some congregationalist types. The picture is not sufficiently clarified by asserting that Anglicans and some Lutherans retained an episcopal polity akin to that of Catholics and perhaps Orthodox, whereas the Reformed developed a presbyterian polity, and Anabaptist-Mennonites developed a congregational polity. After all, as the Reformation project struggled along in Britain, congregationalist and "independent" polities emerged among the Reformed. Then came the Baptists with a particular variant of congregational polity, and Quakers with an individualist polity without the institution of ordained clergy.

The boundaries of *Gemeinde* within Anabaptism in its first generation are unclear. It is helpful to think of communities, whether local gatherings or a network of meetingplaces in close proximity, developing an increasing sense of common purpose. This agreement they sometimes confirmed in a statement of confession, as at Kempen in 1545, while subsequently more communities began to refer to commonly valued writings (e.g., *Dat Fundamentboeck*). Eventually most Mennonites affirmed the Dordrecht confession of 1632.

Within the first two centuries of Mennonite development, the "congregational" polity in effect was a loose linkage of local communities in a specific linguistic/national region where one or several elders/bishops attempted to visit regularly. Generally speaking, during the eighteenth century when Mennonites were beginning to be tolerated more, stronger churchly organizations emerged. These regularized gatherings of ministers took counsel together on specific spiritual issues, or dealt with matters to be negotiated with state officials.

In 1811 the complicated story of schismatic Dutch Mennonites under numerous designations reached a turning point, with the formation of the Allgemeene Doopsgezinde Societeit (ADS).[17] Earlier a relief committee of several large urban churches in the south of Holland had given financial assistance to the other Dutch Mennonites as well as to Swiss Mennonite refugees. In 1811 the ADS organized a seminary for the training of clergy. By mid-century the society had also organized its own mission committee and program, and at the end of the nineteenth century it launched brotherhood homes, a newspaper, peace society, and other means of fostering service in the world and renewal within the church.

Among the widely scattered communities of Mennonites in south Germany, a different pattern developed. Widespread across the region was a pattern of worship among a few families, and a gathering at monthly intervals of a larger church headed by an elder. By 1850 the Ältesten, Prediger und Diakonen Versammlung (APDV) had begun meeting quarterly. All decisions about election, ordination, baptism, etc., were taken as if the *Gemeinde* (congregation or church) was fully constituted when this representative body met. The congregational polities in north Germany were centered much more around independent urban congregations. In the congregational life that developed in Poland/Prussia, leading elders served the equivalent of diocesan regions, and local congregations relied on ordained ministers and deacons, usually self-employed farmers. Urban centers such as Danzig began paying for a salaried clergy in the middle of the nineteenth century.

In the Russian colonies, it became common to ordain enough ministers and deacons to cover each village, whereas the elder/bishop provided oversight for an entire colony. Later, as colonies grew, several bishops shared responsibility for a colony. Much more even than in Poland, spiritual leaders met regularly for consultation. Decisions were made and elections conducted, however, at gatherings of the entire brotherhood, which included all baptized males. The brotherhood provided for lay accountability; it heard reports from the Schultze (civil administrators) and took decisions for the whole.

Mennonites transported many of these patterns to America, including the South German Ältesten, Prediger und Diakonen Versammlung, with the definition of *Gemeinde* it assumed. Also imported was the Predigersitz of the elders and ministers in the Russian tradition, whereas the tradition of individual congregational autonomy was represented at specific localities in immigrant America.

As is evident, the boundaries for decision making and accountability of these various "congregationalist" Mennonites were not the same. The expansion along the American frontier, and more recently the transitions to urban centers have hastened the narrowing of the boundary of church or congregation to mean the members of a legally organized church meeting in one place. Perhaps this description sounds too much like the story of a continuous social process that fails to give enough weight to the cases of abuse of episcopal power on one hand, or of excessive congregationalism on the other. The point is that those conflicts over power were symptomatic of systemic changes where the change initiators and change inhibitors used particular issues and arguments that mattered less than the systemic shift. Yet we do have a legacy of struggle over ministry and over definitions of the locus of authority for decision making.

It could be instructive to note that where sixteenth- and seventeenth-century Mennonites developed a polity and an ordained leadership, the primary tradition against which they measured themselves was the Reformed. In both the Swiss German cantons and the Dutch principalities, Catholics had lost dominance. The Reformed became the state church within whose ranks the theological struggles, such as those over a strict or Arminian Calvinism, took place.[18] Their influence on the Mennonites is too easily underrated.

Lutheran, Reformed, and Catholic majority cultures were the cultural contexts that shaped North German, Polish/Prussian, and eventually Russian Mennonites. In a general sense, until American Mennonites developed their own colleges and seminaries, Mennonite clergy tended to attend schools and read literature from publications, Baptist or Presbyterian, that were within the Reformed theological tradition. If much of the north European and Russian Mennonite world in the nineteenth century was part of the Pietist renewal movement that had a strong social and mission ministry dimension, the Mennonites of North America found themselves influenced increasingly by the holiness tradition, Methodist and later Pentecostal.

There is some truth to the generalization that contrasts Swiss-origin Mennonites' tendency to rely on the charisma of a few major leaders with Russian Mennonites' tendency to rely on institutions. However, we would build on a stronger legacy of spiritual leadership if we were to take more notice of the impact of many more leaders. After all, when the Anabaptist leaders trained in monasteries and universities had disappeared, the subsequent centuries of discrimination and persecution required that much of the *paradosis* was indeed an apostolic succession in which experienced ministers and elders mentored younger ones, modeling ministry.

In his valuable history of the development of doctrine, Jaroslav Pelikan observed that during the first five or six centuries the primary leaders in articulating doctrine in response to shifting contexts were the apostles and teachers of the Word, the fathers of the church whose recorded idiom was mostly exegetical sermons. They were generally bishops. When the bishops as a decision-making body gathered in council as representative of the entire *oikoumene,* they became a body with the highest charisma of authority.

Between 600 and 1500 most theologians were monks, according to Pelikan. It was in the century preceding the Reformation that the professional doctors of the church began to replace the bishops or monks as theological and perhaps also spiritual leaders.[19] Pelikan uses this observation to draw attention to the waning of the authority of the theologians during the course of the twentieth century. He notes that we now lack a clear body with the charisma of spiritual and theological leadership to replace the authority of the theologians. This situation is a reaping of the whirlwind in Protestantism, and in part accounts for the excessive claims to papal authority in Catholicism in spite of equally diverse theological trends within that communion.

So it is when we attempt to assess more contemporary efforts to articulate the charisma of authority that Mennonites are challenged to grant more place to an apostolate or an episcopate. It may help to delineate briefly some of the leadership legacies upon which to build. The American legacy of the South German Ältesten, Prediger und Diakonen Versammlung (decision making by an ordained leadership body of men) continued within the Old Mennonite denomination, generally through the generation of the 1960s. To the present in Lancaster Conference a bishops council, meeting together with all ordained men, is the body that makes all major decisions.

Franconia Mennonite Conference experienced an era of transition between 1950 and 1975 that was not marked merely by the abandoning of the plain coat and head covering but by the rise of a spiritual leadership elite who were not necessarily ordained. If Bishop John E. Lapp was looked to for direction during the 1950s, a generation later two of his sons were administrators of Mennonite colleges, and one headed Mennonite Central Committee. By virtue of these offices these men were recognized as spiritual and theological leaders, though without ordination. Indeed, Orie Miller as primary leader of MCC staff for the first forty years, and as chief executive of Lancaster conference's own missions committee, exuded a charisma of leadership second to none, without being ordained.

If we turn to the colony/conference tradition of the Russian Mennonites, there also many individual leaders stand out. Thanks to the mythology of tsarist favoritism, Johann Cornies the entrepreneur is remembered as primary shaper of Molotschna colony. Yet there were a series of elders of the Gnadenfeld congregation whose spiritual leadership extended beyond that community. Heinrich Dirks during the final third of the nineteenth century left an impact as motivator for mission. As I have noted elsewhere recently, leadership throughout the twentieth century in Russia was remembered in terms of loved and respected elders and teachers.[20] In the world of Kansas, where theological education was fostered early, we recall the legacy of H. P. Krehbiel, C. H. Wedel, and E. G. Kaufman as leaders through Bethel College, followed in the second half of the twentieth century by the leadership of Erland Waltner at Mennonite Biblical Seminary.[21]

As we trace the emergence of a renewed church through efforts at evangelism or revivalism, as well as through education, it is hard to tell that story without particular attention to John F. Funk, Daniel Kauffman, Ernest and Orie Miller, H. S. Bender, J. C. Wenger, John Howard Yoder, and eventually Marlin Miller. We recognize in Virginia the role of three generations of Brunks, and numerous Augsburger brothers. For western Canada a short list of leaders necessary to any telling of the story includes H. H. Ewert as founder of Mennonite Collegiate Institute, David Toews as bishop and leader of the Immigration and Colonization Council, J. J. Thiessen picking up many of these roles thereafter, and being instrumental in the formation of Canadian Mennonite Bible College. In addition a long list of Mennonite Brethren leaders shaped that tradition and left an impact through cooperation with other Mennonites. They include B. B. Janz as leader in the immigration, several generations of Toewses associated with the shaping of Mennonite Brethren Bible College, the Mennonite Brethren mission board, Mennonite Brethren Biblical Seminary, and eventually Conrad Grebel College.

Ministry that matters for the twenty-first century

Ministry that matters for the twenty-first century must be a ministry of leadership that exercises authority and power consciously with clear accountability. To assert leadership, authority, and power so unequivocally represents a response to a debate of more than thirty years within the Associated Mennonite Biblical Seminary community.

At a conference on church-related institutions sponsored by the Young Center (Elizabethtown, Pa.) in 1996, Rodney Sawatsky addressed the group under the simple theme "Leadership, Power and Authority."[22] This statement of a positive theology of power and authority in church leadership furthered a position that Sawatsky and others had been advocating for more than a decade.

Sawatsky's article became the focus of two forums at AMBS in 1998. He had spoken of an "implicit anti-leadership, anti-authority, anti-power mythology shaped in the 1960s" which had found "a systematic voice" in Ross Bender's *People of God* (1971). Sawatsky went on to emphasize that he viewed John Howard Yoder as primary formulator of the mythology. The anti-institutionalism or anti-clericalism was not so much a sixteenth-century Anabaptist position, but was part of the "unfinished reformation." As Yoder had put it in 1987, "The universalism of ministry is the radical reformation that is still waiting to happen."[23]

At the forum held at AMBS in 1998, participants in the Dean's Seminar—William Klassen and C. J. Dyck in particular—responded to Sawatsky's critique by helping us see the context better. For example, women in ministry had not been a serious option in 1970, yet as a result of the emphasis on mobilizing the laity, women began to enter numerous ministries. In a published response to Sawatsky, William Klassen challenged the implication that "we were mesmerized" by John Howard Yoder and that the published record of other faculty of the time did not fit the "anti-institutionalism" charge.[24]

Dyck also reminded us of the impact of Vatican II, which he had attended. Its Dogmatic Constitution on the Church defined the church not as the clergy but as the people of God. The pope had called on the clergy to see themselves as servants to the servants of God. Klassen's key point, worth restating, was that the Dean's Seminar had come after the death of Bender, and at a time when "two models of pastoral leadership—Old Mennonite and General Conference—had to begin communicating with each other." The task was "to begin negotiating a common front for theological education."[25] The 1998 forum was an opportunity, particularly for Klassen, to warn current AMBS faculty against too easy a drift into clericalism, into becoming a training place for clergy professionals.

It is easy to see that such debates about the role of charisma—for individuals or for institutions—is at the heart of the matter; any "corrective" quickly elicits a "countercorrective." The sociological concept Sawatsky and his interlocutors used was the contrast between first and second generation believers. There is a long lineage to the notion that the first generation relies on charisma—meaning dynamism, inventiveness, novelty—whereas the second generation relies on routinization—meaning power, control, loss of the real thing. Although I have approached the topic through heavy reliance on social history, I find use of typologies of generations of limited value, and the meaning assigned to charisma too narrow and popular.

The leadership of the good shepherd that Jesus called for was in keeping with the concept of leaders of the people as good shepherds that the prophet Ezekiel had spoken of. These were not instances of momentary care; the operative point of view was of a people living faithfully over time, who tended to stray and needed to be brought back often. As seminary professors now teach, the life of faith of individual people and of a people is a developing story, perhaps with stages of development. The charisms for the leader, indeed the charism for each in his or her specific ministry, is the gift of God. Sometimes that charism causes us to notice, and we say that a leader has charisma. At other times, to notice the charism too obviously itself constitutes a problem.

That the remembered Yoderian legacy is strongly anti-institutional and suspicious of professional clergy is true. It is also true that to criticize Yoder on those points ensures reactions of protest or of concern from fellow Mennonites, especially at a time when Yoder's reputation as theologian looms large. At the same time affirming the charism of institutions should never lead us to an uncritical affirmation of churchly institutions. For this reason, advocating one particular model for ministry, one model for being church even, is fraught with danger as tending toward unidimensional thinking.

Within the Mennonite historical trajectory we have surveyed, the definition or boundary for *congregation* has differed among traditions, and has changed over time. It behooves us to listen carefully and critically whenever a call to congregationalism emerges; in most cases the congregation we mean cannot claim to be the church in its fullness. Similarly the leadership in ministry toward which we seek to teach has been one of considerable diversity. To discover consensus would simplify the teaching endeavor, but the task is much more one of recognizing the gifts, the charisms, as truly fitting within the common story centered on Jesus Christ.

If during the Bender era the theology of the Anabaptists—their concept of the church, the principle of voluntarism, and their practice of ministry—was recognized as a legitimate Reformation tradition, by the year 2000 the congregationalist church model had become much more widespread. In explaining why he intended to develop an ecclesiology of a "polycentric participative church" for the postmodern world, Miroslav Volf pointed out that free churches represent the largest Protestant grouping worldwide, yet are too often ignored in ecumenical circles.[26] Volf's delineation of the meaning of the ordained office in a participative church is worthy of consideration. The priesthood or ministry of all believers is grounded in baptism. All have become priests on the basis of baptism, but the priesthood for which some are specially ordained is a recognition of a different dimension of service. Those so ordained have the charismata of office for expressing the unity of the whole local church.[27] The present widespread recognition of the mutuality between officeholders and the ministry of the laity should cause Mennonites to face the ecumenical implications of their practice.

On one hand, we witness in Catholic circles the renewed validation of all the baptized as gifted for ministry. Several factors portend a shift toward both married and female clergy, as well as a heightened role of laity in the ministries of the church. These include the fact of clergy shortages, the theological background for the failure to find enough candidates responding to a vocation of celibacy, and the exercise of the charismata by women and other lay people.

What Mennonites and other free churches have often failed to notice are the fact and fiction of the election of bishops and popes by "the people." Built into the concept of legitimizing the charism of leadership, whether of priest, bishop, or pope, is the understanding of a leadership arising from the people and accepted or received by the people. So Volf can write of officeholders who must have a call from God, who are elected, partly because they "imposed themselves in response to the call and gifting of God's Spirit." Volf's readers may not know whether he refers to Catholics, Anglicans, Baptists, or Mennonites. This interplay of election and imposing "is the power factor in every charismata of office, one that becomes repressive only if that power does not halt before the critical reception on the part of the congregation."[28]

Mennonites have often been forced to face the ecumenical issue in mission and evangelistic settings, over the question of shared ministry. Alle Hoekema reflects instructively on Dutch Mennonite experience in Indonesia nearly a century ago, when missionaries participated in a shared ministry but drew the line at performing infant baptism.[29] Mennonite pastoral practice in North America can hardly avoid the issue of recognizing the ordinations of ministers from other traditions, and Mennonite pastors can expect to have their own charism recognized. Indeed taking note of such mutual reception of charismata and possibly the reciprocity of accountability happens even more in the leadership ministries of interchurch projects in social service, peacemaking, or in general seeking the peace of the city. The ecumenical project in America since the 1960s, known as the Consultation on Church Union (COCU), seemed too concerned for structural union for separatist Mennonites to notice. But in recent years with a shifting focus toward mutual recognition and support, as well as shared projects such as a lectionary series or week of prayer events, the challenge for Mennonite participation in many places locally, and perhaps also centrally, grows more compelling. Jesus, in John 17:20-21, prays that his followers will be united so that the world may believe; is this prayer relevant when Mennonites speak of missional church?

Common to all Christian traditions is the authority of baptism as basis for the exercise of the charismata of ministry. This commonality exists despite the fact that recognition of each other's baptisms remains distant. Common to all Christian traditions has also been a recognition of the authority of ordination to designated offices, an authority to be exercised under accountability before the whole church. Although the vagaries of history have tended to obscure the commonality, ministers—whether through the laying on of hands in baptism, or through the laying on of hands for set-apart ministries—do gain in authority through knowledge and training. Even the nonsacramental churches are coming to recognize the power and authority of ritual for major moments in ministry, and hence the need to conduct such rituals responsibly.

Finally, at the heart of all the baptized ones, of all called to ministry, must be relationship to Jesus Christ. At the heart of the matter is incarnating Christ in a sinful world, a commitment never quite forgotten in the history of the church, and never fully attained.

Notes

[1] Milovan Djilas, *The New Class: An Analysis of the Communist System* (New York: Frederick A. Praeger Press, 1957).

[2] Alvin W. Gouldner, *The Future of the Intellectuals and the Rise of the New Class* (New York: Seabury Press, 1979). Cf. György Konrád & Iván Szelényi, *The Intellectuals on the Road to Class Power* (New York: Harcourt Brace Jovanovich, 1979).

[3] Hans Küng, *Christianity: Essence, History and Future* (New York: Continuum Press, 1995), esp. 1-46.

[4] Ibid., 47. In a key summarizing statement, Küng writes: "The name of Jesus Christ is rather like a golden thread in the ever-renewed fabric of Christian history, which is so often torn and dirty: the binding primal motif in Christian tradition, liturgy, theology and piety which is never simply lost, for all the decadence" (25).

[5] Everywhere that Christianity spread during the first three centuries, the offices of deacon, minister (preacher, presbyter), and bishop emerged, and a system for consulting within and between regions through representatives emerged. Its variety ranged from the picture of the Jerusalem Council of Acts 15 to later "local" and ecumenical councils.

[6] See, for example, statements in the review by Jeffrey Gros of *From Apostles to Bishops: The Development of the Episcopacy in the Early Church,* by Francis A. Sullivan (New York: Paulist Press, 2001): "One implication, which certainly needs deeper exploration, concerns the ecclesial character of communities that have not retained the episcopate . . . [that] have led numberless Christians to grace and salvation through the effective preaching of the Word of God and the fruitful pastoral ministry. I do not believe we [Catholics] have done full justice to such communities when we simply declare that they are not churches in the proper sense." Gros's review appeared in *Midstream* (January 2002): 88.

[7] For a recent analysis of the way Anabaptist anticlericalism prompted the magisterial reformers to articulate a model between Catholic and Anabaptist, see D. Jonathan Grieser, "Anabaptism, Anticlericalism and the Creation of a Protestant Clergy," *Mennonite Quarterly Review* 71 (October 1997): 515-43.

[8] The Mennonite Church General Conference was formed in 1908, nearly forty years later than the General Conference Mennonite Church (1860), but even in its more functional reorganization after 1970 it lacked the authority and power of counterparts such as the General Conference Mennonites or the Mennonite Brethren. The professionalization of staff in the second half of the twentieth century was centered in the mission and publishing boards, which were largely autonomous, and in several of the long established regional conferences.

[9] To illustrate, J. Denny Weaver, *Keeping Salvation Ethical: Mennonite and Amish Atonement Theology in the Late Nineteenth Century* (Scottdale, Pa.: Herald Press, 1997), treated a half dozen preachers as theological leaders and shapers of their communities.

[10] For a recent illustration see Esther Epp-Tiessen, *J. J. Thiessen: A Leader for His Time* (Winnipeg, Man.: CMBC Publications, 2001).

[11] James C. Juhnke, *Vision, Doctrine, War: Mennonite Identity and Organization in America, 1890-1930,* The Mennonite Experience in America, vol. 3. (Scottdale, Pa.: Herald Press, 1989); and Frank H. Epp, *Mennonites in Canada, 1920-1940* (Toronto: Macmillan of Canada, 1982), present the broad outlines, whereas regional conference and separate denominational histories enable one to notice the uneven patterns and timing.

[12] For a fuller treatment of the discussions that were to be called the Dean's Seminar, with a resultant statement on philosophy of seminary education that was published in the AMBS catalog, see Ross T. Bender, *The People of God: A Mennonite Interpretation of the Free Church Tradition* (Scottdale, Pa.: Herald Press, 1971). Henry Poettcker, "Policy Changes and Development in Leadership Patterns in the Conference of Mennonites in Canada 1950 to the Present" (paper presented at a CMC-sponsored History Symposium, Winnipeg, Man., July 1997), takes a different approach to constructing the story, at least within Canada, which has influenced my presentation here.

[13] I am relying on papers from the Faith and Order meeting in Chicago, September 2000, circulated for participants, and my own summary of the discussion.

[14] Martin Marty, "Bishoping," *Christian Century* (February 13-20, 2002), 79.

[15] The North American significance of ordination in law had to do with state recognition of marriages performed by clergy. In western Europe, in contrast, civil weddings became the norm as states such as the German Reich under Bismarck, or the French in earlier secularization actions moved away from state churches. Hence the church wedding of a German Mennonite did not need a recognized member of the clergy. In contrast, priests and Protestant clergy, when fully recognized by the modern German state, swore an oath as civil servant—an option not open to leaders in the free churches.

[16] In most of the European Anabaptist-Mennonite traditions, the preferred term was "senior leader" *(Ältester, Ancien, Starshchii)* that came to be translated as *bishop* in America, since the American English meanings of *episcope*—elder and overseer—carried a lesser administrative significance, no doubt shaped by New England Presbyterian and Methodist terminology during the era of the Protestant Empire.

[17] Though a detailed survey of Dutch Mennonite historical developments in English is not yet available, one gains fruitful insights from Sjouke Voolstra, "Mennonite Faith in the Netherlands: A Mirror of Assimilation," *Conrad Grebel Review* (fall 1991): 277-92; and from essays in Alistair Hamilton, Sjouke Voolstra, and Piet Visser, eds., *From Martyr to Muppy: A Historical Introduction to Cultural Assimilation Processes of a Religious Minority in the Netherlands: The Mennonites* (Amsterdam: Amsterdam University Press, 1994).

[18] For example, Sjouke Voolstra, "The Path to Conversion: The Controversy between Hans de Ries and Nittert Obbes," in *Anabaptism Revisited,* ed. Walter Klaassen (Scottdale, Pa.: Herald Press, 1992), 98-114.

[19] Jaroslav Pelikan, *The Emergence of the Catholic Tradition, 100-600,* vol. 1 of

The Christian Tradition: A History of the Development of Doctrine (Chicago: University of Chicago Press, 1971), 5.

[20] Walter Sawatsky, "Historical Roots of a Post-Gulag Theology for Russian Mennonites," *Mennonite Quarterly Review* (April 2002): 149-80.

[21] See James C. Juhnke, *Creative Crusader: Edmund G. Kaufman and Mennonite Community,* Cornelius H. Wedel historical series, no. 8 (North Newton, Kans.: Bethel College, 1994); and James C. Juhnke, *Dialogue with a Heritage: Cornelius H. Wedel and the Beginnings of Bethel College,* Cornelius H. Wedel historical series, no. 2 (North Newton, Kans.: Bethel College, 1987).

[22] Rodney J. Sawatsky, "Leadership, Authority and Power," *Mennonite Quarterly Review* (July 1997): 439-51.

[23] Ibid., 440.

[24] William Klassen, "Another Perspective on 'Leadership, Authority and Power,'" *Mennonite Quarterly Review* (January 1998): 96-102.

[25] Ibid., 98.

[26] Miroslav Volf, *After Our Likeness: The Church As the Image of the Trinity* (Grand Rapids: Eerdmans, 1998), 19-21.

[27] Ibid., 246-47.

[28] Ibid., 256.

[29] Alle Hoekema, *Dutch Mennonite Mission in Indonesia: Historical Essays,* Occasional Papers, no. 22 (Elkhart, Ind.: Institute of Mennonite Studies, 2001), 117-44.

4

Ecclesiology, authority, and ministry

An Anabaptist-Mennonite perspective

Gayle Gerber Koontz

Sometimes it takes the mirror of a neighbor to see oneself clearly again. Several weeks ago, while tracing part of a conversation about authority in the church among Roman Catholic theologians in the early 1980s, I was struck by their strong calls for "democratization" in the church. George De Schrijver argued that many find "it is hard to accept the magisterium's continued use and implementation of a rather aristocratic model of government in which decisions are made from the top" because this "pyramid-model of government violates the sensibilities of people trained in democratic procedures of co-responsibility."[1] Joseph Moingt agreed that believers who are mature people in all other areas of society are impatient when they are not recognized in their own church. Tired of "being treated as minors," some eventually leave it.[2] And Leonard Swidler's words veritably shouted from the page: "It is clear not only from reason that the Church can be a democracy but also from the fact that the Church *has* for centuries been democratic that it *can* be democratic. In fact, it is also clear from reason, Scripture, and early tradition that the Church *ought* to be democratic and was so understood and lived by the early Christians."[3]

As a North American Mennonite observer, I was struck by how foreign such passionate concern about democracy and authority is to our experience of church. If by definition democracy means that fundamental issues of "public life" in the church are decided on by the people,[4] Mennonites currently live in a strongly democratic church. Decisions that affect congregational belief and practice are decided largely at the local level in committee or at congregational members meetings. Denominational directions and conference agreements are determined by representatives appointed by congregations or districts, representatives who may or may not be ordained ministers.

As a result, the North American Mennonite challenge in relation to authority and ministry appears to be just the opposite of the North American Roman Catholic challenge. While Catholics struggle to recognize and affirm the authority of the spoken word in local congregations, Mennonites struggle to recognize and affirm the representational and teaching authority of ministers who seek to preserve the traditional witness of the Christian church and to relate to the larger church beyond the congregation and denomination.

Apostolic faith and practice, meaning the apostolic witness and practice of the early followers of Christ as depicted in the New Testament, is important to Mennonites. But "apostolic succession" (succession of the apostolic ministry) tends to be a negative term associated with its use by orthodox Christians to claim truly authoritative teaching and practice, in distinction from Protestants. What Mennonites do hold to constitute primary authority for faith and action is Scripture, or the written Word, interpreted by individual believers or congregations of believers through the power of the Holy Spirit.

Interpretation of Scripture as well as related theological reflection on Christian practice draw on Mennonite "tradition," reason, and life experience, to various extents. But one does not often hear Mennonites appeal explicitly to the post-biblical "received teaching" of the wider church, and Mennonites never appeal to "the teaching authority of the church" understood as embodied in the office of ministry, as in the Catholic magisterium, for example.[5]

Teaching authority was an important development in the early church, as Joseph Moingt explains in the essay on authority and ministry cited above. Appeal to the apostolic tradition was critical for the sake of continuity in witness about Jesus and for the sake of unity in a rapidly growing group of Christians. But attention *only* to this dimension neglects another important one in the life of the developing church. Moingt suggested that in the New Testament period there was a "double ministry of the word," or two forms of the "spoken word" testifying to the work of God through Christ. One was the spoken word which "appeals to the authority of a tradition, a tradition concerned about fidelity and conformity to the period of origins." But another form of spoken word "is freer, more innovative, more attuned to the inspirations of the present moment, and more sensitive to differences of culture and settings." The first is related more to developments in doctrine over time and the authority of teachers responsible for continuity of memory and witness, while the second has "a more prophetic and sapiential character" and is focused on "helping the community respond to new calls of the Spirit."[6] Both forms of the spoken word, he argues, were critical in the life of the New Testament church.

I believe that Moingt is right in insisting that honoring both forms of the spoken word is important for the faithful church. The biblical narrative itself testifies to the work of God as having continuity over time and also as creating what is new. As narrated in Acts 15, the discernment of the church gathered in Jerusalem demonstrates appeal to God's purposes in history as understood in Jewish Scripture and tradition, newly interpreted in light of developments in the mission of the church. Both the memory and wisdom of the righteous *and* new outpourings of the Spirit consistent with Christ are seen to be gifts of God and authoritative for belief and practice of the church.

Further, it appears to me that Mennonites, in the larger scheme of things, have given priority to the second form of the spoken word with its "prophetic and sapiential character" in interpreting Scripture for life. Such an emphasis provides for ongoing renewal in the church and permits Scripture to speak with flexibility and power to life in different local settings. What tends to be lost is appreciation and respect for the rightful authority of the spoken word that appeals to the memory and wisdom of the wider Christian church in interpreting the gospel.[7] As the irenic Catholic theologian David Burrell reminded his listeners, most of them heirs of Anabaptism, at a conference in March 2002, rightly understood it is not some fixed and unchanging "deposit of the faith" that is sacrosanct for the Catholic Church. But "reading of Scripture *through the eyes of the historic church*" is critical and "leads the church to wisdom."[8]

State-supported and congregationally-supported Christian authority

While all Christian traditions affirm that the authority for pastoral and teaching ministry is rooted in Jesus Christ, this authority was institutionalized over time in different ways in the Roman Catholic, Reformed, and Anabaptist-Mennonite traditions. One of the differences between initial Lutheran and Anabaptist-Mennonite perceptions of authority and ministry, for example, was their different relationship to the political states in which they found themselves.

The Lutheran approach to authority and ministry emerged in the thick of the early Reformation period. Luther's original theses marked a bold attempt to reform the faith of the church, a call to restore what he understood to be the heart of the gospel. In taking this step he challenged the magisterium's authority to be the "sole, qualified, living interpreter of the gospel," and he did not back down. Under attack from Rome, Luther understandably aligned himself with sympathetic political power in Germany for protection. But this political arrangement had consequences. When Luther realized, to his horror, that his challenge to the authority of the magisterium was spreading like wildfire among the rural poor and being embraced by interpreters with views at odds with his own understanding of the gospel, he helped shape a Protestant understanding of authority to avoid chaos among those who sought to reform the church. For Luther, divine authority rested in the gospel. The gospel, however, was both contained in Scripture and heard in the church where it is "rightly preached" and where the sacraments are "rightly administered." Right preaching and sacramental practice are carried out by those who have affirmed the gospel as outlined in the Protestant Lutheran confession(s), and who have been ordained to the ministry by others who had been ordained (either by Catholic or Protestant clergy, a process which assumed certain content regarding the meaning and role of ordained ministers).[9]

Thus a Protestant clerical order and authoritative structure emerged, closer and more accountable to the people than the Catholic clergy had been, especially as vernacular Bibles became available. But it was the educated clergy who were given authority for right interpretation of the gospel and a special sacramental role. Those in the Lutheran territories whose views appeared to be "against the gospel" were challenged, censured, or killed, and the Reformers appealed to the state, as the Roman church had done, to enforce right interpretation of the word of God.

In contrast, the Anabaptist movement, out of which the Mennonite denomination grew, ruled out (or had ruled out for them) the option of aligning themselves with friendly political powers in establishing or restoring "the true church." Luther and Melanchthon included Anabaptists among those whose views appeared to be against the gospel. For this reason, and because of the Münster Anabaptists' failed attempt to use political and military power to set up a "Christian" city, the ongoing Anabaptist movement could not embrace the model of a government-linked or state church. In addition, plain sense reading of the New Testament and desire to follow Christ in life led significant groups of Swiss–South German, North German, and Dutch Anabaptists to affirm nonresistance as part of the Christian ethic. Given this conviction, given their clear sense that Christian discipleship required intentionality (adult baptism) and discipline, and given their political and sociological reality, Anabaptist Mennonites needed to embrace an understanding of pastoral and church order and authority different from that of their Protestant and Catholic neighbors.

In the maelstrom of Luther's challenge to traditional authority, the Anabaptists clung to the freedom to practice faith unhindered by the authority of the wider church, and they were suspicious of calls for unity by those who represented religious and political power. For these radicals, the only true authority was the authority of God speaking through Scripture, interpreted in communities of those who chose to respond to God in Christ in faith and discipleship. The only Christ-like authority among humans seemed to be one that was freely given by or called out of a congregation or loose network of believers. To use more theological language: they recognized legitimate authority in the church as given by God or bestowed by the Holy Spirit. Under such circumstances, office in the church was assigned on the basis of charismatic authority, moral or spiritual authority, and the authority of expertise in valued skills (such as trustworthiness, ability to read Scripture and preach or to organize a church under persecution), rather than on the basis of right doctrine and right sacramental practice defined by a city council or state-supported order of ministry.[10]

Further, the authority of the office of ministry in the Anabaptist-Mennonite stream was initially tempered by a strong Radical Reformation suspicion of limiting definitive interpretation of Scripture to the clergy or to specific doctrinal formulations. Donald Durnbaugh in his work on the believers church described an aspect of this heritage when he wrote, "The view of the Reformers was that no preaching could be done unless it was performed by a pastor duly ordained by the state. They called Anabaptists 'hedge preachers' (*Winkelprediger*). Among the errors listed of the Anabaptists was that 'anyone who has a true faith may preach, even if no one has commissioned him: for Christ has empowered any and every man to preach when he said, "Go, teach all nations."'"[11]

Even as the office of ministry became institutionalized among Mennonites this perspective retained a voice, as is evident in the Ris confession (see note 10 below, on "conscience"). Although historian Arnold Snyder argues that the "pneumatic democracy" and anti-clericalism that marked the early Anabaptists did not last beyond the end of the sixteenth century, the impulse that undergirded them did not die out completely.[12] Selection of ministers and overseers by lot, for example, characterized the Swiss–South German American practice through the 1940s and was practiced by some U.S. General Conference Mennonite congregations at least until the late nineteenth century.[13]

True authority, defined initially as biblically based and Spirit led, then institutionalized in baptismal promises and covenantal ordination services, both established and placed limits on the authority of congregational members and their ministers. These three sources of authority (Scripture, Spirit, ordination) were sources of accountability for pastors, setting limits to their authority. The idea that baptism not only signified the acceptance of God's grace but also the pledge to engage in mutual address and discipline gave responsibility to but also placed limits on the authority of individual members of the church. However, an ecclesiology, polity, and ministry established on the basis of voluntary association was also inherently vulnerable in the face of divisive issues.

Historically Mennonites in some areas organized themselves with a strong congregation-focused polity, associating more or less loosely with a broader network or conference of congregations. Others placed more authority in the hands of district elders, overseers, or bishops, particularly in relation to issues of church discipline, where the community upheld and enforced the authority of such elders by attaching social stigma to an offender or by excluding an unrepentant sinner from community life. In both cases, however, disagreements among leaders about Christian belief—or more often, practice—

frequently resulted in splits within and among congregations or districts.[14] Because no state clout or overarching authoritative church structure backed up one side or another, the authority once offered to a leader of a group or the cooperation once enacted with a group of congregations could be quickly withdrawn.

This heritage continues to affect Mennonite churches in the U.S. and Canada. A continuum of differences in valuing the authority of the individual, the congregation, and the conference have been particularly visible in struggles about women in ministry and about homosexuality. Historically based ambivalence about the authority of the wider church has also marked Mennonite involvement in interchurch relations in the United States. While individuals have engaged in significant ecumenical conversation on behalf of the denomination, and cooperative relationships have existed at local levels, ecumenical conversation has not been a priority of the denomination. Mennonites have not joined either the National Council of Churches or the National Association of Evangelicals, although actions to become a member of the Canadian Council of Churches and an affiliate of the Evangelical Fellowship of Canada are pending at the next session of Mennonite Church Canada's annual assembly.[15] An area for growth for the Mennonite denomination in the U.S. and Canada is to develop our sense of belonging to the wider church.

Implications: pastoral authority and congregational responsibility

Democratic leadership and pastoral ministry

Given our experience with democratic political systems in the United States and Canada and the "democratic" form of our Mennonite church structures, it might be useful, or at least circumspect, to consider several ways in which democratic views of leadership might influence us.

For example, two different but widespread views of democratic leadership may unconsciously affect Mennonite pastors and church members. One is that the leader should represent the will of the majority of the people (congregation or conference) in carrying out the office of ministry; the other is that the leader should follow his or her conscience even when it contradicts the sense of the majority. Further critical attention to these views in relation to theological convictions may assist congregations and pastors in understanding and negotiating tensions.

I would also suggest that two of the primary legitimating sources of authority within a democratic system—office and expertise—need to be understood and embraced within a voluntary church. Office and expertise work together. Without the conferring of office, a leader has no representational authority. Without areas of expertise or at least competency, an office holder is not respected and cannot speak and act with authority.

Strengthening the notion of office has been one dimension of Mennonite theology of ministry in the past decade. I believe it is a helpful way of pointing particularly toward the representative authority of pastors. Once again, consideration of the representational role of democratic leaders might be instructive. Once installed in office, democratic leaders represent our cities, states or provinces, and nation to their own constituency and to those outside the boundaries of their political areas. They represent the constitutional and legal agreements and values that characterize that body. They represent the historical identity and practice of the area. And by virtue of their office, they are given unusual voice in interpreting this heritage and shaping its future.

Pastors also have a representational role. They represent the congregation to its members, to the wider church, and to the world. What they say and do and how they do it communicates something about the congregation, not only about the minister. But those who hold the office of pastoral ministry represent more than a specific body; they also represent God. At this point democratic and religious authority differ sharply. Also at this point Mennonites need to be theologically astute, because (at least in my view) a theology of ministry rooted in the Radical Reformation does not support the view that pastors represent *God* in a unique way. Ministers do not mediate God to others in a more significant or immediate way than is available to other Spirit-filled Christians. Mennonite pastoral ministers do not necessarily mediate forgiveness or acceptance by God more effectively than other Christians. Pastors are not more sacred than other members of the congregation. In fact, others in a congregation might embody the presence of God for individuals within or outside the congregation more profoundly than the pastor does at various times and places. In these ways the understanding of the office of ministry in Mennonite perspective continues to differ from the priestly office as understood by many in the Roman Catholic tradition.

What other members of the congregation *cannot* do is represent God *and* the congregation. Mennonite pastors carry a significant representational role because the church is much more than the individual pastor, and because the church represents or symbolizes a whole web of meaning, of congregations, and of practices with God as its foundation. Those who hold the office of pastor represent the congregation, the wider church, and God to members of the congregation and to those beyond.

While office is an important dimension of pastoral authority, the authority of expertise (competency) complements it. Expertise is particular to the individual pastor; different pastors have different areas of expertise. Pastors need to be minimally competent in a variety of areas, and when they handle these dimensions of ministry well, this competence appropriately strengthens their influence in the congregation. I would argue that a key factor in a congregation or conference deciding to bestow the office of pastoral ministry should be competence or relative expertise in critical reading of Scripture, of the central early theological beliefs and practices of the church which interpreted the gospel, and of the multiple global church traditions which developed them. This competence is of particular importance because other members of a congregation are not likely to share it; they in turn may be more competent than the pastor in reading and interpreting the cultural or social context in which the church is to live out its mission. Further, understanding the church's foundational convictions and its developing past is essential for the congregation's self-understanding and for discerning the leading of God in the practical situations they face.

Granting clear authority to the pastor as an interpreter of Scripture and teacher of the tradition of the church does not mean that the pastor decides what is right for a congregation to do in their current practice of faith. The pastor as expert in the "teaching authority" of the church has a distinct and limited role in the discerning work of the congregation as a whole. The pastor should be able to articulate with authority the core of faith (as understood in various ways) and explain why interpretations of the gospel developed as they did. He or she should be able to help the congregation evaluate these developments in order to identify the wisdom of various traditions and their failures, as a step toward better understanding our own faith and practices and to provide orientation for current decisions.

The congregation receives this teaching as well as other prophetic words, analyzes its own life situation and environment, and decides together what God may be calling the congregation to do in a particular time and place. One example of such a discernment process built on a consensus model is found in the book of Acts, culminating in the decision recorded in Acts 15. But other ways of making decisions in a democratic church may also respect both the hearing of tradition and the spontaneous prophetic spirit. What North American Mennonite churches may need to value and seek in the work of discernment is the competent voice of those who can help us receive and respond wisely to the common Christian tradition and varied denominational traditions of the church.

Authority, office, and expertise

The authority of office is temporary, but the authority of expertise is not. The model of "office" as defined above suggests that the authority of an office is linked to the holding and practice of that office. In this sense authority based on office is temporary, although it may well be conferred sequentially. This way of defining the authority of church leaders recognizes the temporal character of office-holding while preserving its significant representational character, that is, without reducing the office to a merely "functional" role.

This model of office further suggests that insofar as ordination is conceived as ordination to an "office," it is not properly understood as effective when the one ordained is no longer holding a pastoral office.[16] The authority of expertise or gift in pastoral ministry is a different matter, and its recognition by the church is often offered to people for life, whether or not they are active in a pastoral office. The authority of expertise in ministry as well as the authority of experience and character continue throughout healthy and righteous intellectual and spiritual life and may be recognized in the church apart from the holding of a specific office. One's *identity* as a pastor or minister may therefore remain subsequent to holding the office of pastor or minister, although the *authority* of pastoral office and administration do not.

Pastors with historical and interdenominational competence

Certain weaknesses accompany the strengths particular to the ecclesiology of the Anabaptist-Mennonite church in North America. Because this is so, congregations have special responsibility to call pastors with competence in two specific areas—ability to respectfully interpret the wisdom of the historical church in the process of looking toward the future, and commitment to and ability in relating to Christians of other denominations.

In a highly congregational church structure such as ours, there are not centralized criteria embodied in denominational procedures which determine who gets to be a pastor and who does not. Although ministers are structurally accountable to the people they serve, they are not structurally accountable to a wider denomination to be experts or even minimally competent in interpreting Scripture or the received teaching of the church. If the congregation does not value these abilities, they may be ignored. People in the congregation may need the wisdom of those with expertise in these areas in order to maintain their Christian identity and to know God truly, but they are not structurally accountable to take this wisdom into account. Further, people in the congregation may be morally accountable to Christian brothers and sisters beyond the congregation, but they are not structurally account-able except insofar as they wish to associate themselves with a conference of churches or with Christians from other denominational groups. The extent to which a congregation chooses to take into account other congregations or Christian traditions is essentially voluntary.

Given these realities, congregations ought to intentionally seek leadership that will address these weaknesses. First, congregations should ensure that their pastors are motivated, prepared, and supported to provide strong leadership in relating to Mennonites beyond the local congregation and in relating to other Christians, for the sake of the mission of the church. Such pastors need an ecclesiology that values and expects to be guided in its discernment and mission by the global Mennonite church and by the universal church, not only by the specific goals and dynamics of a local congregation. Second, congregations have special responsibility to ensure that their leaders can articulate the spoken "word and wisdom of the church," that is, provide perspective on why the church at various times in history interpreted Scripture or the gospel as it did and suggest how this theological work might be relevant in the congregation's own process of seeking the Spirit's leading in decisions regarding the future of the church.

For Mennonites to be prophetic within the larger church, we must lovingly engage it. And for Mennonites to be Spirit led, we must be open to the wisdom of God present in the memory and witness of the whole church. Both engagement with the larger Christian church and attention to its traditions are growing edges for many of our congregations, for many of our pastors, and for many of us who help shape the institutions that orient and form those who will lead the church into the future.

Notes

[1] Georges De Schrijver, "Hermeneutics and Tradition," *Journal of Ecumenical Studies* 19 (spring 1982): 45.

[2] Joseph Moingt, "Authority and Ministry," *Journal of Ecumenical Studies* 19 (spring 1982): 214.

[3] Leonard Swidler, "Demo-Kratia, the Rule of the People of God, or *Consensus Fidelium*," *Journal of Ecumenical Studies* 19 (spring 1982): 235.

[4] Swidler, "Demo-Kratia," 227.

[5] There is even ambivalence about the role or the authority of statements accepted in Mennonite denominational conference settings. A current example is the debate about the use of the Purdue and Saskatoon statements on sexuality, particularly the section on homosexuality. The debate addresses whether the position the statements describes truly "represented" the church, whether it simply reflects the views of representatives at a particular moment in time or articulates an ongoing "teaching position" for the church and its ministers, and whether it should serve primarily as a guide for ongoing congregational discernment or as a test of conference membership. Through an extensive consultative process the *Confession of Faith in a Mennonite Perspective* has achieved wider consensus as a document to serve as (1) a guideline for interpretation of Scripture, (2) a guideline for belief and practice, (3) a foundation for unity among churches, (4) an outline for instructing new members, (5) an updated interpretation of belief and practice for our time, (6) a help in discussing Mennonite belief and practice with other Christians and people of other faiths.

[6] Moingt, "Authority and Ministry," 206.

[7] Using Moingt's language of the "spoken word" for interpreting and evaluating Mennonite reality can obfuscate an important Anabaptist theological point. Lack of emphasis on "the authority of the spoken word which appeals to the memory and wisdom of the wider Christian church in interpreting the gospel" may be, as John Roth put it, "a natural or inevitable outcome of a theological tradition in which preaching is not considered a sacrament, and more emphasis is put on the *reception*

of God's word (through Scripture, spirit, discernment, teaching, etc.) than on the spoken word itself" (John Roth memo to Gayle Gerber Koontz, 27 August 2002). Roth's point should be kept in mind, but I would still argue that Moingt's basic point holds: As we interpret the meaning of the gospel for today, we need to attend *both* to prophetic local charismatic voices and to voices that appeal to the memory and wisdom of the wider Christian church.

[8] David Burrell, in a plenary address at the Believers Church Conference on "Assessing the Theological Legacy of John Howard Yoder," at Notre Dame University, Notre Dame, Indiana, March 7-9, 2002. Italics added.

[9] For example, *Baptism, Eucharist, and Ministry,* the ecumenical statement on the church and the ordained ministry notes that "it is especially in the eucharistic celebration that the ordained ministry is the visible focus of deep and all-embracing communion between Christ and the members of his body. In the celebration of the Eucharist, Christ gathers, teaches and nourishes the Church. It is Christ who invites to the meal and who presides at it. In most churches this presidency is signified and represented by an ordained minister" (*Baptism, Eucharist, and Ministry*, Faith and Order paper, no. 111 [Geneva: World Council of Churches, 1982], 22). The minister does not carry this representational role in the celebration of the Lord's Supper as clearly in the Anabaptist-Mennonite tradition. The grace of God in Christ is present through the Holy Spirit in the whole life of the community. Receptiveness to God's salvation through Christ is expressed in both worship (including the Lord's Supper) and discipleship—in the full life of the community— rather than especially focused in the congregation symbolically receiving the eucharist from a minister who represents Christ. At the same time, leadership ministry in the church is to be modeled on the service of Christ; in that sense, Menno can speak of those called to serve the church "in Christ's stead." (Quoted in Everett J. Thomas, ed., *A Mennonite Polity for Ministerial Leadership* [Newton, Kans., and Winnipeg, Man.: Faith & Life Press, 1996], 39.)

[10] The first concern of the article (no. 5) on "shepherds" in the Schleitheim confession (1527) is that they be "a person according to the rule of Paul," or a morally worthy person. They should also have "a good report of those who are outside the faith." The article makes no mention of doctrine. (In Howard John Loewen, *One Lord, One Church, One Hope, and One God: Mennonite Confessions of Faith,* Text Reader Series, no. 2 [Elkhart, Ind.: Institute of Mennonite Studies, 1985], 80.) Article 9 of the Dordrecht confession (1632), on the office of teachers and ministers in the church, begins by providing justification for the offices of various leadership ministries based on the pattern of Jesus and the New Testament church as well as the self-evident need for order. It then specifies both sound doctrine and a good reputation and report (godly example) as the most important criteria for leadership (Loewen, *One Lord, One Church,* 66). The Ris confession (1766/1895) also justifies offices of ministry on the basis of the practice of Jesus and the apostles and the need for good order, specifying that the church "look about for such men as are of good report, possessing the gift of the Spirit and true faith" (Acts 6:2-5) and

other essential characteristics (2 Tim 2:24-26; Tit 1:6-9). They should be chosen with prayer and "with the greatest possible unanimity (thus not doing violence to the rights common to the whole brotherhood, much less disregarding the same)" (Loewen, *One Lord, One Church,* 94). This confession outlines not only the holy responsibilities of the overseers and deacons, but also those of the church—to pray for, honor, kindly care for, and obey them, "yet in all this is the respect for their office and administration not to be in any wise binding upon the conscience, except in so far as their words and management are in accord with the Word of God . . . as the only rule of faith and life" (Loewen, *One Lord, One Church,* 97).

[11] Donald F. Durnbaugh, *The Believers' Church: The History and Character of Radical Protestantism* (New York: Macmillan Company, 1968), 233. Durnbaugh implied, of course, that this Anabaptist "problem" was actually a strength. The underlying issue of where authority lies remains.

[12] C. Arnold Snyder, *Anabaptist History and Theology: An Introduction* (Kitchener, Ont.: Pandora Press, 1995), 382-83. Snyder explains that as a tradition of textual interpretation developed, instead of looking to charismatic prophets and evangelists, congregations looked to bishops and elders (much as the early church had!). By the end of the sixteenth century, congregations had settled into their own distinctions of clergy and laity. Eventually the only true pastors were those commissioned or chosen by the elders and/or the congregation. This development made the priesthood of all believers "functionally obsolete." John Roth, however, suggests that this description is too strong. "Many Mennonite congregations up through the 1940s continued to select their leaders by use of the lot; a standard baptismal question (for men at least!) was whether you were willing to serve as a minister if your name came up in the lot. This is not functional obsolescence!" (John D. Roth, memo to author, 27 August 2002).

[13] The lot is noted as an option for selecting ministers in the first authorized document for ministry in the General Conference Mennonite Church, Berne, Indiana, 1893.

[14] See John D. Roth, "The Church 'Without Spot or Wrinkle' in Mennonite Experience," in *Without Spot or Wrinkle : Reflecting Theologically on the Nature of the Church*, ed. Karl Koop and Mary H. Schertz (Elkhart, Ind.: Institute of Mennonite Studies, 2000), 7-25. "Unlike their Catholic and Protestant neighbors," Roth wrote, "the Anabaptists did not have an episcopal hierarchy or a formal systematic theology to adjudicate conflicting interpretations of Scripture. In the absence of these authorities, the exercise of church discipline became an important means of defining group identity" (18).

[15] In the past few decades any movement toward joining these groups was deterred by the fact that until very recently membership in one excluded the possibility of membership in the other.

[16] Ordination could well be understood as an act of entrustment and certification that might be reactivated without further examination when someone is called to pastoral office in another setting.

5

The pastor as teacher

Perry B. Yoder

In my observation, the teaching role of the pastor is neglected in our churches. Several obvious factors account for this distancing of pastoral work from teaching. First, the bulk of the church's educational program takes place on Sunday morning when the pastor has other duties to attend to, including the sermon, conversation with congregants, and last-minute worship details. Second, apart from catechism, teaching is a responsibility that can easily be relegated to others, and in most congregations lay people carry responsibility for it. The education committee or commission normally has oversight for congregational education, including curriculum choice and staffing. Third, preparing to teach well takes time, and time is a scarce resource for most pastors.

The relative absence of the pastor in the educational life of the church is reflected in many seminary students' lack of enthusiasm for Christian education. For many people "Christian education" brings to mind work with children and youth, while pastors usually work with adults. Apparently this area of ministry can be safely neglected; the pastor has more important duties to perform and more central roles to fulfill.

The argument of this paper will be that the church's failure to understand the pastoral role as a teaching role is a serious conceptual flaw, with deleterious consequences for congregations and for the larger church. Those of us charged with educating people called to be Christian pastors need to give serious and sustained attention to preparing them to assume teaching responsibilities in the congregation. We need to foster understanding of the pastoral role as a teaching role.

I will begin consideration of the teaching role of the pastor by looking at its roots in the Old Testament. Then I will trace its development between the testaments. The biblical survey will conclude with a glimpse at the ministry of Jesus. Then I will offer reflections on how the pastoral role of teacher fits into the wider picture of what it means to shepherd the people of God.[1]

Biblical foundations

In teasing out the roots of teaching in the Old Testament, I will take a narrow view and examine the function of religious education and the religious educator in the community. With this perspective in mind, I begin with the questions "Where do we find the beginnings of the notion that leaders are to teach the sacred traditions?" and "Why was such teaching deemed necessary?"

These questions may seem strange or even silly. Of course the people must be taught the traditions of the faith. How else would they know them? But consider that in the Bible, commandments such as the Ten Words are addressed directly to all Israel and not just to the leaders or to a certain class who are then to teach them to the whole people. Even when Moses becomes an intermediary, he is just that. He is told the words that he is to speak to Israel. Scripture is addressed to the community. God's words are addressed to "you." In direct address all have equal access to God's instructions.

But this direct address only works for the first generation, for those who hear the words. New provisions need to be made so that subsequent generations in Israel will know the teachings of YHWH. These provisions are clear in Deuteronomy ("second law"). This repetition of the law is given prior to Moses' death for the next generation.

Instruction in the family

First, Deuteronomy includes provisions for instruction in the context of family life. Deuteronomy 6:4-25 is significant. Arranged in three sections, it begins and ends with exhortation to the Israelites to pass on God's instructions. The middle part, verses 10-19, warns against a materialism that will cut off the roots of faithfulness. The unit begins with the Shema, the basic declaration of Israelite faith: "Hear, Israel: YHWH is our God, YHWH alone; and you shall love YHWH our God with all your heart, and with all your vitality, and with all your strength."[2] This way of introducing the instructions that follow elevates them to a high status indeed.

Parents through recitation are to make their children aware of the teachings of God. "Recite them to your children and talk about them when you are at home and when you are away, when you lie down and when you rise. Bind them as a sign on your hand, fix them as an emblem on your forehead, and write them on the doorposts of your house and on your gates" (Deut. 6:7-9). Indeed, God's words are to be a constant subject of conversation in the family.

Second, this repetition and the practices that accompany it will lead children to ask questions. This eventuality is anticipated and addressed in the concluding section of Deuteronomy 6. When the child asks, "What are the statutes, laws and judgments that the LORD our God has commanded you?"[3] the parents are to be ready with the answer that their practice is grounded in God's grace. According to Deuternomy 6, home learning is not mere memorization or even socialization but is grounded theologically: because God has liberated us, we are faithful in our observance of God's instruction to us.

Communal instruction

Deuteronomy also makes provision for public, communal education. It stipulates a reading of the law every seven years. Through such community gatherings, the entire people becomes acquainted with the contents of Scripture. From a canonical point of view these public readings were evidently an important element of Israelite life, as seen in the fact that they were resumed by Nehemiah in the post-exilic period.[4]

Toward the end of the period of the Judean state and its temple, hints point toward the emergence of a special group that taught Scripture. In Jeremiah 8:8 the prophet refers, apparently, to a group who care for the *torah* ("instruction of God") and perhaps see to its preservation and publication. Jeremiah denounces them: "How can you say, 'We are wise, and the law *[torah]* of the LORD is with us,' when, in fact, the false pen of the scribes has made it into a lie?"

The attachment of torah or instruction to a group of "wise" people is novel, because usually in Jeremiah instruction is linked with the priests, as in Jeremiah 18:18. "They said, 'Come let us devise a plot against Jeremiah—for instruction shall not fail from the priest, nor counsel from the wise, nor oracle from the prophet. Come, let us strike him with the tongue, and we shall no longer have to listen to all those words of his.'"[5] This text reflects stereotypical responsibilities of the three groups: the priests are responsible for instruction, the prophets give oracles, and the wise give counsel.[6]

However, circumstances were changing in the time of Jeremiah. From the book of Kings we learn about the involvement of Shaphan, a member of the king's court, with the book of the law found in the temple. What is instructive for us is that the priest gives the scribe Shaphan responsibility for the scroll of the teachings. We would expect that if the priests were the ones who taught, Hilkiah would have kept possession of the scroll and sought an audience with the king in order to acquaint him with its contents. The role of the wise seems to be shifting—from duties involving statecraft and giving wise counsel and pragmatic instruction, to responsibility for the reading and preservation of sacred documents.

The book that was unearthed in the temple during the reign of Josiah is considered by most Old Testament scholars to have been Deuteronomy in some form. It is significant that the book of Deuteronomy, of all the books in the Torah, has an affiliation with the ideas and values associated with wisdom.[7] To give just one example, Deuteronomy 19:14 is a command against moving a boundary marker. Moving boundary markers is a concern of the wisdom materials, as seen in Proverbs 22:28 and 23:10 (cf. Prov. 15:25).

More generally, wisdom contains a certain universal humanism—a concern for all human life and especially for those less privileged. This concern is widespread in Deuteronomy, and the book's legislation seems intended to guard the welfare of those who may easily be taken advantage of. To cite some of the more obvious examples: released slaves were to be given wages when they were set free rather than being turned out empty-handed (Deut. 15:12-18; cf. Exod. 21:1-6); female slaves were to be released after seven years, just like male slaves (Deut. 15:12; cf. Exod. 21:7-11); female prisoners of war were protected (Deut. 21:10-14); and runaway slaves were not to be returned to their masters (Deut. 23:16-17).[8]

Given these two lines of converging evidence—Shaphan's involvement with the book of the law found in the temple, and Deuteronomy's connection with wisdom—we might see a new constellation emerging in Israelite society that formed the background for Jeremiah's denunciation of those who say, "We are wise, and the law [torah] of the LORD is with us."

With the destruction of the state and the temple, the two central and integrating institutions of the nation were destroyed. What would become the rallying point or points of Israelite identity? Deuteronomy's answer is that the instructions of God found written in the scroll of the law are defining for Israelite identity. As has often been remarked, Deuteronomy 13:1[9] marks the beginning point for an explicit claim by a written text for its own governing authority. In this passage we read first that the words of this law are not to be added to or subtracted from. A stable text is commanded and assumed. Second, in the following paragraph we find that a prophet who does wonders but teaches contrary to what is written in the law is not to be obeyed. A stable text trumps the prophetic word. A text is now positioned to become constitutive of a community that has been cut adrift from its traditional moorings.[10]

The book of Jeremiah portrays prophecy as a discordant and unreliable phenomenon. The prophets foretell different futures, and who can determine which prophets speak truth? Not even Jeremiah can distinguish true prophecy from false, as Jeremiah 28:1-12 illustrates. Even the law of the prophet found in Deuteronomy 18:22 is little help, because one cannot know whether the prophet speaks truth until the foretold event comes to pass. Those who guessed wrong about which prophet to trust find little consolation here! Jeremiah seeks to apply this rule only to prophecies of shalom, not to those of judgment (Jer. 28:9)—that is, to Hananiah's prophecies, but not to his own! The variety of prophetic words and tests for their veracity make it apparent that prophecy did not form a stable basis for judging what was God's word and what was not.[11]

A static written word, one that could not to be added to or subtracted from, would fit the bill, however. In any case, by the time of Nehemiah the tradition of oral prophecy had all but come to an end; God addressed the people more and more through the written word. So far so good. But with the rise of the written word as authoritative for the community, a new problem emerged. Few people had a copy of the Torah, few could read and study it, and perhaps not all could understand the meaning of what was read to them. Consequently, the role of the scribe/teacher became increasingly important, even central. The "reform" of Nehemiah and Ezra in the fifth century illustrates the centrality of the teaching role for the community.

The scribe is Ezra, a scholar of the Torah, as we learn from Ezra 7:10-12: "For Ezra had dedicated himself to study the Teaching of the LORD so as to observe it, and to teach laws and rules to Israel. . . . 'Artaxerxes king of kings, to Ezra the priest, scholar in the law of the God of heaven . . . '"[12]

Ezra's fulfillment of his teaching responsibilities is reported in Nehemiah 8. The reading and explanation of the law is followed by the celebration of the festival of booths and a renewal of covenant between the people and God. The returnees constitute themselves around the teachings of God as read to them by Ezra and as explained to them by the Levites.

In Nehemiah 8 the role of the scribes is twofold. First, they are to preserve the scroll of the teachings, or Torah, and to have it at hand to read to the people. Second, they are to explain the Torah so that the people can understand it. As texts and their interpretation become central for identity, so also teaching and explaining these texts become essential for the preservation of the community.[13]

One significant reason for the necessity of interpretation of the text is what David Halivni terms the "maculate Torah."[14] By this he means the text of Scripture as we have it today is not immaculate;[15] it has duplications, contradictions, and discrepancies. As proof of this claim, he points to the difference in the Ten Commandments as they are recorded in Exodus 20 and in Deuteronomy 5. And note the difference between the altar law in Exodus 20—where many altars are allowed—and Deuteronomy 5—where only one altar is allowed. The slave law in Deuteronomy 15 differs in significant and obvious ways from that in Exodus 21. Both cannot be practiced simultaneously. We must choose one or the other, or seek a harmony by combining aspects of both.[16]

The notion of a maculate scripture immediately raises two questions. Why does the Bible show evidence of being a human document? And second, how can such a document function as authoritative revelation for us? The Bible came to people fully within human history and addressed them in their particular situation. As incarnational revelation, it takes place within human history and shares in the contingencies of historicity and cultural particularity. The Bible comes to us in human clothing, in human language that made sense in a particular culture at a particular time and place.

But how can the Bible be revelatory for us, given its historicity and cultural embeddedness? The simple answer is that it needs interpretation. In fact, as we see from the example of Ezra, the biblical text has demanded interpretation from the beginning. The written teachings of God are too laconic, in the absence of explanation, to guide our life and thought. How does one obey the command "Honor your Father and Mother"? Jewish tradition addresses this need with the recognition of the oral Torah. At Mount Sinai, according to Jewish belief, God gave Moses both the written commandments and the oral Torah, the instructions about how to understand and carry out the teachings of the written Torah.

Jesus as a teacher entered into the discussion and shaping of the oral law within this tradition. For what cause may a man divorce his wife? For any cause, or only for certain specific causes? Jesus, at least in Matthew, agrees with those who argued on the basis of an interpretation of Deuteronomy 24 that adultery was the only legitimate cause for divorce. Or again, what happens if a person in desperate straits swears to God, for example, that if God spares his life he will give all that he has to God? Later he realizes that if he carries out his oath, he will not be able to provide for his parents and thus will break the commandment to honor father and mother. Jesus' answer is that people should not swear at all, a solution that will prevent making foolish vows. Yet Deuteronomy 10:20 commands us to swear by God's name!

Community, canon, commentary

We see in this scriptural tradition, beginning at least with Ezra, a threefold dialectic of community, canon, and commentary. Canon, the body of authoritative writings, demands commentary that explains how these writings are to be understood and practiced. Commentary is necessitated, first, by the text's language, terseness, and historical contingency. Second, its diversity and heterogeneity need explanation and understanding. Texts also need a community, because they are transmitted by a community and accepted as authoritative within a community.

When one of these three pieces—canon, commentary, or community—is missing, anomalies result and the community's vitality is compromised. When commentary is missing, all members of the community may interpret Scripture as they see fit, each understanding it as seems right in his or her own eyes. The outcome is what we see at the end of Judges—anarchy and the dissolution of the community. In Judges, the tribe of Benjamin was practically annihilated. Today interpretive anarchy may take the form of congregations going their own way without attending to better-informed and broader perspectives.[17]

The pastor's role as a teaching role

It is the task of the pastor as teacher to keep this three-cornered dialectic working. As teacher, the pastor instructs the community about its canon, its history, and its theology. As teacher, the pastor enables a congregation to discern a dynamic within the canon, to gain a historical perspective, and to understand their tradition in dialogue with their Scriptures. The canon then becomes not some ethereal "spirit of Jesus" or disembodied "ethic of neighborly love" or patchwork of proof texts, but teaching for how one lives a life of love for God and others. The pastor as teacher ensures that a congregation has an identity as a scriptural community.[18]

As teacher, the pastor has a privileged position at the hermeneutical table. Everyone can enter into the conversation about how a Scripture text should be understood and applied, but some interpretations are better founded than others. Some interpreters are in a better position than others to understand the text. Not all in Israel had a Torah scroll like Ezra did, nor did they all have time to devote to its study. Today, too, pastors should devote themselves to more study and reading than that for which the laity in their congregations have time or energy. By abandoning or ignoring this privileged position, pastors wittingly or unwittingly contribute to an interpretive Babel, and they forfeit a vital nurturing role. The pastor as teacher models a high regard for Scripture by taking its interpretation seriously. Such regard for the inspiration and authority of Scripture also means holding others accountable for less-than-rigorous understandings, ones perhaps based on hearsay, convention, or prejudice.[19]

Finally, the pastor as teacher embodies the role of commentary in the life of the community. Pastors bring fresh air to their congregations as they offer new understandings.[20] Through learning, the church grows and gains new life, released both from the death grip of unexamined tradition and from the threat of descent into anarchy.

Given the essential role of teacher for the identity and vitality of the community of faith, we may wonder why this role seems to be a low priority for most pastors. On the face of it this dynamic may seem strange and devoid of obvious explanation. How do we understand it? Perhaps it is not too much to suggest that pastors will not fill the role of teacher in the congregation easily and well until they see themselves as competent theologians, ethicists, and students of Bible.[21]

Notes

[1] I do not intend to cover the usual ground covered by books and articles falling roughly under the rubric of "Christian education."

[2] My translation. Unless otherwise noted, translations are from the NRSV.

[3] My translation.

[4] On the tradition of the public reading of the law, see James Watts, *Reading Law: The Rhetorical Shaping of the Pentateuch* (Sheffield: Sheffield Academic Press, 1999).

[5] *Tanakh: The Holy Scriptures: The New JPS Translation according to the Traditional Hebrew Text* (NJPS) (Philadelphia: Jewish Publication Society, 1999).

[6] For the function of the wise at court and more generally, see William McKane, *Prophets and Wise Men* (London: SCM Press, 1965)

[7] Moshe Weinfeld argued this thesis at length in *Deuteronomy and the Deuteronomic School* (Oxford: Clarendon Press, 1972).

[8] Hebrew versification; 23:15-16 (English).

[9] (Heb.); 12:32 (Eng.)

[10] For a recent discussion of Deuteronomy as the beginning of a canon, see Philip R. Davies, "The Mosaic Canon," in *Scribes and Schools: The Canonization of the Hebrew Scriptures* (Louisville: Westminster John Knox Press, 1998), 89-106. Davies's ardent skepticism leads him to place the beginning of the canonization process in the Persian period rather than in the late monarchical or exilic period. His three reasons for this dating include (1) a scribal class active in temple and palace, (2) an immigrant elite and the problem of identity, and (3) the existence of a "people" (79). Except for the second, these factors fit the time of Josiah just as well. Apparently it is necessary to posit an immigrant elite in order to place the processes in the Persian period. One could argue that a resurgence of nationalism in the period of Josiah better explains the need for identity definition and assertion.

[11] For the counterclaim that the Prophets were considered canonical along with the Law, see the arguments of Stephen B. Chapman in *The Law and the*

Prophets: A Study in Old Testament Canon Formation (Tübingen: Mohr Siebeck, 2000).

[12] NJPS.

[13] The written teachings of God become authoritative for the community only as they are understood and interpreted. It is not enough to hear or to read the text. This point is illustrated by Philip's conversation with the Ethiopian eunuch. The eunuch was reading from the prophet Isaiah, but he needed someone to explain the meaning of the words. This Philip was eager to do. Text and interpretation are bound together. Or to put it alliteratively, canon and commentary cannot be separated, for without commentary to make the canon understood, community will not emerge.

[14] David Weiss Halivni, *Revelation Restored: Divine Writ and Critical Responses* (Boulder: Westview Press, 1997).

[15] This terminology can be used playfully as well. The Christian tradition needed an immaculate conception, so that Jesus could be born without any human, sinful DNA. Many Christians today need an immaculate *reception,* so that the Bible is not marred by human transmission. Halivni, an Orthodox Jew, must wrestle with the humanness of the Bible, just as all Christians must wrestle with the humanness of Jesus. Without the human, there is no incarnation.

[16] The discrepancies and contradictions in the Torah make it improbable that the Torah promulgated by Ezra represented "the law of the land" undergirded by imperial power. On this point see Jean Louis Ska, "'Persian Imperial Authorization': Some Question Marks," in *Persia and the Torah: The Theory of Imperial Authorization of the Pentateuch,* ed. James W. Watts (Atlanta: Society of Biblical Literature, 2001), 161-82.

[17] One only needs to examine the varieties of interpretation offered in letters to the editor of *The Mennonite* to find a treasure trove of the ludicrous. Many begin with the assumption that the English text is the actual biblical text rather than a translation, and thus a commentary, on the actual text of Scripture. An English translation cannot serve as final arbiter of how a passage is to be understood.

[18] Donn Morgan in discussing Christian education writes, "Whatever else happens, we need to be in dialogue with scriptural values if the particularity of a Christian mandate for education is to be meaningful. The sages of ancient Israel in the post-exilic period were involved in the same type of dialogue, with the same issues at stake: identity, continuity, and mission" (*The Making of Sages: Biblical Wisdom and Contemporary Culture* [Harrisburg: Trinity Press International, 2002], 122).

[19] The past two decades have seen a significant shift in conceptualizing the pastoral role, from that of facilitator or servant-helper to that of leader or professional. Note, however, that in the areas of biblical interpretation, theological and ethical discernment, and historical perspective these concepts, apparently, do not apply. I believe that pastors should see themselves playing a professional leadership role as they expand perspective and deepen thought; as teachers their task is to increase the

congregation's understanding and broaden its horizons.

[20] In this regard this Jesus saying seems apposite: "Therefore every scribe who has been trained for the kingdom of heaven is like the master of a household who brings out of his treasure what is new and what is old" (Matt. 13:52). The expositor offers a blend of tradition and innovation.

[21] In shifting to a leadership model of pastoring, more emphasis has been placed on acquiring professional skills than on gaining truth and developing wisdom. Job 28 reminds us that there is a difference between technique and wisdom, and the former does not lead to the latter.

6

A New Testament model for ministry and leadership

Jacob W. Elias

In the Bergthaler Mennonite Church of my youth, our congregation was one of approximately ten congregations served by some twelve itinerant preachers who made the circuit about once every quarter. The *Ältester*, or presiding elder, made the rounds to all the congregations periodically to baptize those joining the church and to lead in commemorating the Lord's Supper. All the preachers were called from within the congregations and ordained to the ministry of preaching the Word. The *Ältester* was chosen from among the preachers and charged with responsibility for spiritual oversight and administration of the ordinances. Neither the preachers nor the *Ältester* got any formal training for their ministries. They may have received reimbursement for direct expenses but besides love gifts, mostly spontaneous, they were not supported financially.[1]

Responding to a relentless inner drive (already God's call to ministry?), I pursued an education through high school and university, thereby distancing myself from the cultural patterns prevailing in the church in which I had been raised. During my studies at the University of Saskatchewan in preparation for a projected high school teaching career, I participated in the life and worship of First Mennonite Church in Saskatoon. There Rev. J. J. Thiessen, the congregation's pastor and a respected leader in Mennonite conference circles, placed his hand on my shoulder and urged, "Jake, I want you to consider the ministry." The significance of that moment still helps sustain my sense of call to pastoral ministry, although I have spent only six years as a congregational pastor and many more years as a seminary professor and administrator.

As a student at Associated Mennonite Biblical Seminaries during the turbulent sixties (1965-68) I took courses in Bible, church history, theology, ethics, and the arts of ministry. Already in my first semester my wife, Lillian, and I also became involved in youth ministry, initially at Elkhart City Church of the Brethren. Then for two years we made ourselves at home in Broadway Evangelical Brethren Church in downtown South Bend, where I was invited to be an associate pastor with primary responsibility for youth, but with some general pastoral duties as well. In my campus courses and congregational ministries I had ample opportunity not only to "consider the ministry" but increasingly to own my calling to pastoral ministry and my identity as pastor.

When Mountainview Mennonite Church in Vancouver, B.C., extended the invitation for me to become their pastor, Lillian and I felt led by God to accept this call from the church. We experienced six marvelous years of challenge and growth in this dynamic urban congregation (1968-74). They eagerly welcomed and nurtured this young, still wet-behind-the-ears pastor. The church soon requested that I be ordained, and three months into my ministry Rev. J. J. Thiessen ordained me "to the full ministry." This meant that I was authorized not only to preach and exercise other leadership responsibilities within the congregation but also to baptize and lead in communion.

In subsequent discussions of how well AMBS prepared people for ministry during the formative 1960s and 1970s, I have often wondered: What kind of pastor was this twenty-seven-year-old Saskatchewan farm boy, recently graduated from seminary and now serving in a congregation in the heart of Vancouver? Among many other ministry moments I have often remembered a particular budget discussion during a church council meeting. I recall making a comment along these lines: "Here at Mountainview all of us are ministers. To make it possible for me to minister full time among you and in your behalf beyond the congregation, you provide financial support for my family and myself, so that I don't need to work for a living. Thank you for your support." I have recently asked myself whether this comment betrayed a "functional view" of ministry, a view rooted in a formation process at AMBS dominated by a paradigm emphasizing "the priesthood of all believers."[2] I have also wondered: To the extent that my ministry at Mountainview was faithful and effective, was this success due to the congregation's healthy respect for the "office" of ministry?

During the years when I was a student at AMBS, the Dean's Seminar was involved in enunciating a vision for ministry within the free church tradition and designing a curriculum to form pastors and other church leaders within it.[3] The article by John Howard Yoder, "The Fullness of Christ: Perspectives on Ministries in Renewal," was published within the year following my graduation from AMBS.[4] Its perspectives became part of the conversation that went on within the Dean's Seminar. Yoder's advocacy of a New Testament understanding of universal ministry rather than the "Protestant" model of the solo pastor seems to have been muted during my student years, or I was a dull and uncomprehending student.

Another ministry moment comes to mind. My conversations with the congregation prior to my being called as pastor included a telling comment by a member of the search committee: "What the church needs now is a spark plug." I realized that they wanted their pastor to get all fired up at regular intervals! In my elaboration of that metaphor I pointed out that a spark plug needs wires and battery and fuel and an entire infrastructure for the car to run, and in fact a car functions best when it has several spark plugs. It seems in retrospect that I must have been significantly shaped to envision a plural ministry based on the use of diverse gifts within the church for its common mission.

In marked contrast to some other graduates of AMBS during the 1960s and 1970s, I have always felt that I had been prepared well to begin ministry. Clearly I had a lot of growing to do. However, a functional or charismatic understanding of ministry never seemed to sidetrack me from my sense of calling to the pastorate or undermine my authority to fulfill my pastoral responsibilities. I was not familiar with the language of office to describe the representational character inherent in being a pastor, but I sensed that God and the congregation had called me to be a pastor and not just to do pastoral things among many other ministers in the congregation.

My assignment here is to reexamine the New Testament foundations for ministry and leadership. I engage this task within the framework of the AMBS mission "to prepare pastors, missionaries, teachers, evangelists, and other church leaders both to proclaim and to live according to the gospel of Jesus Christ, to minister effectively, and to equip other believers for their ministries."[5] Although I have not personally experienced the ambivalence about the pastorate that some of my AMBS-trained colleagues have felt, I share the desire for theological clarity and biblical faithfulness when envisioning the church and its leadership ministries for our time and place.

Charismatic ministries or official leadership?

In his summary of the features that recur within the diversity of the apostolic teaching and practice of ministry as reflected in the New Testament, John Howard Yoder identifies several "constants within flexibility." First he lists several features that definitely emphasize a functional understanding of ministry: multiplicity, plurality, diversity, and universality. His notation regarding universality includes a cryptic summary of them all: "No one is not a minister."[6] Yoder's summation also names some of the church leaders that appear in the New Testament. He describes these leaders by using functional categories. Among the common elements within the life of the New Testament church are "the constant need for the elder-bishop-pastor function of government in the local congregation" and "the constant need for the strategic teacher function maintaining the community's link with its past."[7]

Erland Waltner offers a different summary of ministry patterns in the New Testament. Because it is cited in the denominational document *A Mennonite Polity for Ministerial Leadership,* Waltner's summation has something of an official status:[8]

> 1. The organizational patterns of the government and ministry of the early church were dynamic and developmental rather than rigidly fixed. This is well illustrated in Acts 6 where organizational development came as a response to a real need.

> 2. The Christian ministry in one sense is the function of the entire church fellowship but in its practical administration calls for Christian leadership in carrying out many and varied functions. This calls for some kind of division of labor.

> 3. The Christian ministry finds its true nature and authority in Jesus Christ himself rather than in the Jewish community or in the chapters of Christian history.

4. It is difficult, if not impossible, to draw sharp lines of distinction between various kinds of ministerial offices simply on the basis of the biblical text.

5. The single bishop/elder in a congregation or in a given geographical locality appears to be a historical development rather than an originally instituted pattern of church government.

6. That the practice of ordination to ministerial offices, while not prominent in the New Testament, nevertheless has a clear biblical basis, includes prayer and the laying on of hands, and has a symbolic rather than a sacerdotal significance.

Yoder and Waltner clearly come out at different places, although they agree on some basic things. They both recognize that leadership patterns in the first-century church were evolving. Both seem to affirm a functional understanding of ministry, but Waltner is more open to the notion of ministry office. Ordination is perhaps the most obvious point of difference. Waltner affirms ordination as having a clear biblical basis (point 6 above). Yoder's summary makes no reference to ordination, but in a side note on this theme he calls for a moratorium on debate about the nature of ordination, adding: "If the current ecumenical discussion of baptism as universal ordination is more than whimsy, other ordination should be done away with."[9] In Yoder's view, therefore, the baptism of all members into the life and mission of the congregation is seen as being in tension, if not direct contradiction, with the practice of ordaining one individual or a few people for leadership in the church.

Debate about the nature of ministry and leadership in the New Testament and the implications for the contemporary church has, of course, also been active beyond Mennonite circles. The contours of the debate occurring in other denominations and ecumenically can be delineated using the sociological and ecclesiological categories of "charismatic" and "structured" leadership patterns. Discussion has often focused on whether the early church began as a charismatic community and then evolved for various reasons into a more structured institution with leadership offices, or whether charismatic and official ministries coexisted in the church from the early beginnings. Some scholars claim that a new consensus has emerged in this discussion,[10] but the debate among scholars and denominational leaders continues. My intention here is to offer a brief review of this ongoing conversation.

In the literature about patterns of ministry in the early church one can observe that writers who approach the biblical material with certain theological and polity assumptions happen to find these confirmed in the Scriptures. My digging in the literature reminded me that this phenomenon is not new. In his introduction to a book published in 1929, B. H. Streeter includes the following sardonic commentary on scholarly and ecclesiastical discussions about ministry: "For four hundred years theologians of rival churches have armed themselves to battle on the question of the Primitive Church. However great their reverence for scientific truth and historic fact, they have at least *hoped* that the result of their investigations would be to vindicate apostolic authority for the type of Church Order to which they were themselves attached. The Episcopalian has sought to find episcopacy, the Presbyterian Presbyterianism, and the Independent a system of independency, to be the form of Church Order in New Testament times."[11] Readers of the present essay and others in this collection will need to judge the extent to which I (or we) manifest the same tendency to find in the New Testament those understandings of ministry which fit one or more of our denominational patterns.

From charisma to office?

One influential reconstruction of early church life that has stimulated subsequent discussions of ministry and leadership emphasizes charismatic beginnings, followed by gradual evolution toward institutional structures of ministry. The particularities of these attempts at narrating the emergence of the early church are variously described. What follows is my attempt at a generic telling of this version of the story.

The first-century church sensed itself to be an eschatological community within which the relationships between people differed markedly from those that prevailed in the surrounding culture. All participants in the life of the church knew themselves to be equal members of the body of Christ, and all were recipients of the gifts inspired by the Holy Spirit for the good of all. Hence people in the nascent church had ministry roles to perform, as they were gifted and empowered by the Spirit, but there were no leadership offices in the church. In the course of time, however, the church moved from these egalitarian patterns of Spirit-inspired ministry to a reliance on the institutional authority of the bishops and the worldly structures of other offices of ministry. This regression into hierarchical leadership patterns came about because in the years following the deaths of the apostolic generation the church needed to address troubling heresies and schisms.[12]

To bring out some of the variety among those who see a linear development from charismatic to institutional ministries, I cite the work of several representative scholars. Rudolf Sohm lays out the story of the early church in a particularly vigorous way.[13] During the apostolic age, Sohm asserts, the church is a purely spiritual reality with Christ as the head, a community in which the Spirit bestows the needed gifts: "Where Christ is, there is the Church. The Church appears and works in *every* congregation of believers. Even where only two or three are gathered together in His name, there is Christ the Lord in the midst of them, and therefore all Christendom is gathered together with them, working with all its gifts of grace. *There is no need of any human priesthood.* There, in every congregation of believers, is the true Baptism and the true Lord's Supper, the full communion with Christ the High Priest and Mediator of all who believe on Him. *Still less is there any need of a legal constitution.* In fact, every form of legal constitution is excluded."[14]

According to Sohm, spiritual Christianity soon deteriorated into early Catholicism with its bishop and elders, its outward structures and rules: "The Church (*ecclesia*) is now no longer represented in every assembly of believers, but only in those assemblies presided over by bishops and presbyters. . . . The Church has changed, not merely her constitution, but her faith. . . . Dependence on outward organism, represented by bishop and presbyters, is the new law which has become binding on every Christian."[15] Sohm laments that, having been liberated from Jewish legalism through the grace of Jesus Christ, Christianity slipped back from grace to another form of law imposed by ecclesiastical doctrine and hierarchy.

In similar fashion, Hans von Campenhausen chronicles the slide of the church from a spiritual entity into a human social order. When the congregation abandons the freeing and life-giving work of the Spirit in favor of constitutional organization, a death has occurred. Speaking of Paul's view of the church, von Campenhausen says, "But, for Paul, the Church is not a human, natural entity, but a sheerly miraculous, transcendent phenomenon. The preaching of the Gospel is the only thing which calls to life the Spirit through which the congregation can become what it is. Christians have the Spirit of Christ. Because of this, spontaneity, obedience and love are in fact presupposed and required of the Church as, so to speak, the 'normal' thing. When the Church ceases to be spiritual, that is to say, when within her that which is normal for the world is exalted into a law, then in Paul's eyes she is dead."[16] Von Campenhausen observes, however, that in the course of time a system of elders emerged and official authority structures became established even in the Pauline churches. This transition is observable already in the Acts of the Apostles, and even more clearly in the pastoral epistles.[17]

One can find many similar and related reconstructions of the early history of the church and its leadership ministries. Bultmann notes that even as Jesus the proclaimer became the one proclaimed as the Lord of the church,[18] so the church as the fellowship of those being saved eventually was viewed as the institution imparting salvation through priestly administration of the sacraments.[19] In the social analysis offered by Gerd Theissen, the Palestinian Jewish phenomenon of itinerant charismatics supported by community sympathizers gave way in the Hellenistic society to the emergence of resident authorities who guided the church by means of a "love patriarchalism" kind of leadership.[20]

In the feminist liberationist hermeneutic of Elisabeth Schüssler Fiorenza, Jesus is revealed as one who teaches and models an egalitarian ethic, "a discipleship of equals." Schüssler Fiorenza notes that increasingly within the church, as evident already in the evangelists who wrote the Gospels and in Paul's letters, a leadership pattern characterized by patriarchal domination emerges. This imposition of patriarchy is especially evident in the household codes of Colossians and Ephesians and in the pastoral epistles written in Paul's name.[21]

Both charismatic and official ministries?

The other major rendition of the story of the first-century emerging church and its leadership ministries sees parallel rather than sequential developments. In this view, charismatic ministries and official leadership ministries operated side by side in the church from its earliest period. This way of telling the story does not decry a fall of the church from an initial charismatic high point to a worldly reliance on official leaders. Rather, the church from its beginnings benefited from both spontaneous Spirit-inspired ministry and more structured official leadership. The Holy Spirit empowered participants in the congregations to perform various kinds of ministries. Institutional leaders, energized by the same Spirit, exercised the authority of their office in behalf of the church.

These church offices are variously envisioned. James Tunstead Burtchaell proposes that the pattern of the Jewish synagogue with its presiding officer, elders, and assistants evolved into a threefold leadership structure in the church, of elders, a presiding elder, and deacons.[22] However, in the infancy of the church, it was often not these officers who actually led the local faith communities. Spirit-empowered apostles, prophets, and other activists inspired and moved the people by their proclamation and witness, while the officials presided: "Men and women known as apostles and prophets; men and women who carried no titles but whose activist zeal was accredited by the same divine fire: these were the ones to whom believers most notably deferred. The people who bore most powerfully in their persons the force of divine conviction and transformative impetus were people, who, without community screening or authorization, did God's work. They spoke with authority. But that does not mean that they presided."[23] Burtchaell argues that the existence of leaders in the early Christian community is taken for granted and therefore rarely noted; the zealous and inspiring activity of the prophets and apostles is the locus of the real action and excitement in the church.

R. Alastair Campbell challenges this judgment that the office of presiding elders in the early church is derived from the synagogue pattern.[24] He sees both within Judaism and in the Greco-Roman world that "in the ancient world *the elders are those who bear a title of honour, not of office, a title that is imprecise, collective and representative, and rooted in the ancient family or household.*"[25] "Elders" are therefore the respected heads of families. These seniors were also honored and respected in the house fellowship groups meeting in their homes. When house churches formed clusters or when they evolved into larger congregations, the household "paterfamilias" naturally became recognized as the overseer in the congregation or cluster as well.

What then was the relationship between these elders and the charismatic leaders that emerged in the life of the church? Campbell suggests an enlarged understanding of *charismata* as referring not simply to pneumatic manifestations but to any activity that contributes to the upbuilding of the community. He distinguishes in Paul's letters between two kinds of grace gifts: the all-inclusive *charisma*[G] which encompasses "Christian activity and ability evaluated by Paul as a gift of grace, whether it is regular and normal, or spontaneous and abnormal"; and *charisma*[P] which includes "paranormal, or pneumatic, or spontaneous activity, such as a sociologist of religion would describe as charismatic."[26] Campbell's opinion therefore is that the ministry of prophets, apostles, and teachers is preeminent over the ministrations of those who engage in ecstatic utterance or other extraordinary activity. Why? Because they edify the church.

Several additional studies have come out with comparable conclusions. Margaret Y. MacDonald sees the agenda in the Pauline letters moving from "community building" in the genuine Pauline letters, to "community stabilizing" in Colossians and Ephesians, to "community protecting" in the pastoral epistles. In each case, however, there are both charismatic and official ministries, with the latter gradually ascendant over the former.[27] Similarly Kevin Giles urges the recognition of both charisma and office in the church from the beginning: "In other words, *there is a ministry open to all*, and *a ministry given to a few*."[28] Although the passing of time and the division caused by heretical teachings led to the need for a more structured leadership (as evident in the pastoral epistles), the ministry offices are best seen "as a development of Pauline thought rather than as its antithesis."[29] According to Andrew D. Clarke, some Jewish and Hellenistic institutional patterns were taken over in the developing congregations. However, these leadership structures, which often privileged the wealthy and the powerful, were corrected by Paul and other apostolic leaders in the early church so that the life and relationships within the Christian community would conform to the way of Jesus.[30]

A New Testament model for ministerial leadership

When seeking to portray how ministry and leadership are envisioned in the writings of the New Testament, one is hard put to articulate conclusions that will satisfy the goal of providing solid biblical foundations and definitive answers to practical questions about ministry polity. A scholarly consensus does seem to have formed against the view that early church life gradually evolved from pure charismatic beginnings to a compromised institution dominated by authoritative officers in the church. Increasingly, scholars recognize that official and charismatic understandings of ministry coexisted from the beginning. The church, like the synagogue in Judaism and like voluntary associations in the Roman world, recognized formal and informal leaders in their midst. Within the church there were also spontaneous and charismatic movements of God's Spirit in the lives of individuals and within the gathered community.

So, what kind of normative guidance can one find in the New Testament on the question of ministry and on the issue of leadership for our day? To provoke further collective reflection about ministry and leadership among people who look to the New Testament for a theological framework and concrete guidance, I propose to focus on the one first-century model most abundantly accessible to us, namely, the pastoral model of Paul the apostle.

Some scholars look to the Gospel portraits of Jesus' life and ministry to see what he modeled and taught about service and ministry.[31] Many others have studied what Paul says about ministry and leadership. Some emphasize his earlier letters (the letters to Galatia, Thessalonica, Corinth, Philippi, and Rome);[32] others include the later letters, which are sometimes regarded as not directly from Paul himself (Colossians, Ephesians, the pastoral epistles).[33] Still others survey both the Gospels and the epistles with reference to ministry.[34]

However, what Paul and his heirs *say* about ministry and leadership is not our only point of reference. *How* Paul himself ministers and leads, as glimpsed in his letters, is also relevant to our question. I suggest that a potentially fruitful way of deciphering Paul's approach to ministry might be to look progressively at Paul the *person* in ministry, then at his ministry *practice*, and finally at what might be called the *performance* of his ministry.[35]

Paul as ministering person

Paul speaks of himself as a *person* in ministry by drawing on a variety of images and metaphors. Reflection on these self-descriptions leads to a portrait of this pioneer who planted churches and provided ongoing pastoral care by means of occasional letters addressed to them.

Paul draws on a cluster of family or kinship metaphors to refer to his relationship to the congregations. This family imagery is abundantly evident in his first letter to the church at Thessalonica. Within the relationship of mutuality made possible "in God the Father and the Lord Jesus Christ" (1 Thess. 1:1), all the members who make up the body of believers are a family. That Paul views the congregation as a family is indicated most clearly by his repeated use of *adelphoi*, "brothers and sisters" (e.g., 1:4; 2:1, 9, 14, 17). What then is Paul's relationship to the congregation? In 1 Thessalonians 2 he uses a particularly rich mixture of kinship metaphors, through which he projects his pastoral affection and encouragement toward these believers. As apostles of Christ, Paul and his partners Silvanus and Timothy could have come making demands; "yet we came in your midst as little children" (2:7).[36] When recalling their presence in the Thessalonian community, Paul and his partners portray themselves as childlike apostles!

The intimacy of this image continues into the next reminder of their conduct in Thessalonica: "As a nursing mother cherishes her own children so longing for you we were pleased to give you not only the gospel of God but also our own souls because you had become beloved to us" (1 Thess. 2:7-8).[37] Paul's role along with his partners Silvanus and Timothy, as apostles in the Thessalonian community, is compared to that of a nurturing mother who gives her children affectionate care.

Paul quickly adds yet one more family image, "like a father with his children" (2:11). Reminding the Thessalonians that he and his ministry companions had worked to support themselves while preaching the gospel in their midst (2:9-10), Paul expresses fatherly admonition and encouragement: "that you lead a life worthy of God, who calls you into his own kingdom and glory" (2:11-12).

The character of the apostle toward the congregation is therefore imbued with the tender family themes of vulnerability, nurture, and encouragement. In 1 Thessalonians 2:17, Paul even suggests that his hasty departure from Thessalonica has created an orphan, but it is he and not the congregation that is feeling bereft of parents![38]

Within the congregation as family, therefore, there is a special parental role for those providing pastoral nurture and care, but the relationship of mutuality continues among all the brothers and sisters in the Lord. In Paul's later letters he more often compares his relationship with the congregation to that of a father toward his children. For example, Paul is the nurturing yet firm father in 1 Corinthians 4:14-21. In Philippians he calls Timothy his son: "Like a son with a father he has served with me in the work of the gospel" (Phil. 2:22). And he identifies Epaphraditus as "my brother and co-worker and fellow soldier, your messenger and minister to my need" (2:25).

In Galatians, where Paul mounts the most vigorous defense of his understanding of the gospel, he slips into maternal imagery. Paul pleads with the congregation, "My little children, for whom I am again in the pain of childbirth until Christ is formed in you" (Gal. 4:19). Though Paul's later readers are not clear whether he pictures himself or the Galatian congregation as pregnant, the emotional impact is unmistakable. When reaching out to this congregation, whose waffling on theological and ethical identity issues deeply perplexes Paul, his outburst is a pastoral plea from a motherly heart.

Even the title "apostle," which is often seen as attesting Paul's authority to demand compliance from others, is qualified by an underlying subservience. Writing to house churches in Rome, Paul introduces himself first as "Paul, a slave of Christ Jesus, called to be an apostle and set apart for the gospel of God" (Rom. 1:1 NAB).[39] Similarly, in the beginning of Philippians, Paul and Timothy describe themselves as "slaves of Christ Jesus" as they address "all the holy ones in Christ Jesus who are in Philippi, with all the overseers and ministers" (Phil. 1:1 NAB).

Even in the Corinthian correspondence, where he finds himself pushed to defend his apostolic authority, Paul incarnates his calling in conformity to the weakness and the foolishness of the cross. It is as a weak and trembling evangelist (1 Cor. 2:1-5), as a prisoner of war being paraded down the streets of the conquering city (2 Cor. 2:14-17), as a battered and bruised jailbird (1 Cor. 4:8-13; 2 Cor. 4:7-12; 6:3-10), that Paul gives witness to the crucified and risen Christ. Therein lies his calling as apostle of Jesus Christ.[40] The character of the apostle is formed in this living relationship to God as made known in Jesus the suffering and triumphant Lord.

Paul's ministry practice

The general contour of Paul's pastoral *practice* can be glimpsed in his letters by looking especially at the verbs he uses to describe how he seeks to form and transform the communal relationships in congregations. Even a glance at a concordance will reveal that verbs of encouragement and exhortation[41] vastly outnumber references to commands in Paul's letters.[42] Expressions of thanksgiving abound, although as he begins his letter to the churches of Galatia Paul expresses perplexed astonishment rather than thanksgiving.[43] Also prominent are reminders that Paul knows that his primary calling is to preach the gospel and to invite individual and communal conformity to the gospel's claims.

When Paul acknowledges the ministry of others active as leaders within the congregations he addresses, he typically employs verbs and participles to describe what they do. In Corinth the members of the household of Stephanas "have devoted themselves to the service of the saints" (1 Cor. 16:15). Paul urges submission toward coworkers such as Stephanas, and he calls on the community to recognize such faithful service (1 Cor. 16:16-18). Similarly, in Thessalonica, Paul counsels support for their leaders, who are described in terms of what they do: "Respect those who labor among you and stand before you in the Lord and admonish you" (1 Thess. 5:12).[44] In the concluding chapter of his epistle to the Romans (Rom. 16:3-16), Paul extends greetings and affirmation to more than twenty local leaders in Roman house churches, both women and men. Their contribution is variously described, but a theme recurs: they are Paul's coworkers in the Lord. This chapter also opens with a commendation for Phoebe, a minister in the church at Cenchreae, who apparently delivered the letter to Rome. Paul says, "She has been a leader of many, and of myself as well" (Rom. 16:1-2).[45]

In sum, Paul's letters contain many more references to what congregational ministers and leaders do than to the names of offices to which they have been set apart and ordained. To be sure, Paul's letters, especially those addressed to Timothy and Titus, contain references to bishops, elders, and deacons.[46] And one should acknowledge that in occasional letters to congregations the absence of references to elders or other leaders does not prove that none existed; such leadership offices may have been assumed by both author and hearers.[47] However, the fact remains that the majority of Paul's references mention not the name of the office but rather the ministry functions which various people, including Paul and his apostolic coworkers, perform in and on behalf of the church.

Paul's ministry performance

What then can one say about Paul's ministry *performance* as evidenced in his pastoral letters? To address this question adequately one would need to follow the logic and inspiration of each of the letters that Paul addressed to specific congregations.[48] How does Paul's pastoral passion perform in Galatia and Thessalonica, in Corinth and Rome, in Philippi, Colossae, and Ephesus? Each of the congregations has its own culture and character, and each presents unique challenges for both local leaders and the itinerant apostle. Paul's letters to these congregations are certainly not carbon copies of each other; they speak to the particular dynamics and issues that surface at specific times in these various communities of faith.

What Paul's varied pastoral interventions in these letters to congregations have in common is a theological vision rooted in God's creative and redemptive activity in the past. The gospel that Paul preaches among the nations testifies to his conviction that God's grace, mercy, justice, and love have been climactically unveiled in Jesus Christ, especially through his faithfulness unto death on the cross, and his vindication in being raised from the dead. This gospel invites its hearers to respond in faith, love, and hope. Faith is at core a dynamic relationship of trust in the God who is made known supremely in Jesus Christ but also in the earlier narrative of call and promise and covenant and judgment and restoration within the Old Testament. Love is the law-fulfilling mercy and compassion mediated toward the broken world through the Holy Spirit–empowered community of faith and love. Such faith in God and such all-embracing love is modeled after and inspired by Christ's sacrificial love for all, including the enemy. When the faith community under the inspiration and empowerment of the Holy Spirit loves in that way, it gives powerful witness to God's reign of justice and peace, a reign already breaking into the present.

Within the suffering and the stresses of the present age, the community of faith and love manifests a living hope in God's reign, which is already here, yet still coming in greater fullness in the future. The community of faith in its life of worship, fellowship, and mission within the present age awaits the consummation of God's reign by living in light of God's assured future![49]

If this theological vision inspires Paul's pastoral interventions in the congregations within his circuit, what are the consequences for our discernment regarding ministry and leadership?

The pastoral leader, whether known as apostle (as in the case of Paul), or minister, or by another title, is called to the vocation of being a partner in the gospel of Jesus Christ.[50] Central to this calling or vocation is the mandate to participate with Christ as called and empowered servant-leaders affirmed and set apart by the community of faith for a ministry of proclamation and nurture and care. Pastoral performance entails participation with the gospel in a ministry of following Jesus' model of loving service. Women and men called to perform the privileges and responsibilities of this office therefore represent God, in worship and relationships and witness. As leaders who serve and servants who lead, pastors participate with Christ by sharing with their congregations the message of the Scriptures and the grand narrative of God's still unfolding future!

Notes

[1] Leonard Doell, *The Bergthaler Mennonite Church of Saskatchewan, 1892-1975* (Winnipeg, Man.: CMBC Publications, 1987), provides a historical survey of the development and character of this particular branch of the Mennonite church family.

[2] See Marlin E. Miller, "The Priesthood of All Believers," in *The Mennonite Encyclopedia* (Scottdale, Pa.: Herald Press, 1990), 5:721-22. Miller seeks to redress a prevailing misunderstanding regarding a presumed prevalent Anabaptist understanding of the universal priesthood of all members of the church.

[3] The results of the Dean's Seminar are summarized in Ross T. Bender, *The People of God: A Mennonite Interpretation of the Free Church Tradition* (Scottdale, Pa.: Herald Press, 1971).

[4] John Howard Yoder, "The Fullness of Christ: Perspectives on Ministries in Renewal," *Concern: Pamphlet Series for Questions of Christian Renewal* 17 (February 1969): 33-93.

[5] Mission statement, in *Growing in Ministry: 2002-2004 Catalog* (Elkhart, Ind.: Associated Mennonite Biblical Seminary), 4. This goal is the first of five.

[6] Yoder, "The Fullness of Christ," 85.

[7] Ibid.

[8] Everett J. Thomas, ed., *A Mennonite Polity for Ministerial Leadership* (Newton, Kans., and Winnipeg, Man.: Faith & Life Press, 1996), 34. *A Mennonite Polity for Ministerial Leadership* is a statement by a joint committee on ministerial leadership appointed by the Mennonite Church's Board of Congregational Ministries, and the Ministerial Leadership Services and the General Board of the General Conference Mennonite Church.

[9] Yoder, "The Fullness of Christ," 88.

[10] R. Alastair Campbell, *The Elders: Seniority within Earliest Christianity* (Edinburgh: T&T Clark, 1994); chapter 8 is entitled "Towards a New Consensus?" A response to Campbell is offered by Hermie C. van Zyl, "The Evolution of Church Leadership in the New Testament—A New Consensus?" *Neotestamentica* 32 (1998): 585-604. Both of these studies have interacted with the important scholarship done by James Tunstead Burtchaell, *From Synagogue to Church: Public Services and Offices in the Earliest Christian Communities* (Cambridge: Cambridge University Press, 1992). Burtchaell chronicles the Reformation-era challenge to an old consensus and the development of a nineteenth-century new consensus, which in turn provokes twentieth-century disputation and a resulting search for a new hypothesis.

[11] Burnett Hillman Streeter, *The Primitive Church: Studied with Special Reference to the Origins of the Christian Ministry* (New York: The Macmillan Company, 1929), viii; Streeter's italics.

[12] Catholic scholar Burtchaell, *From Synagogue to Church* (see especially chapters 2, 3, and 4) enunciates the contours of this composite story of the church, as developed by scholars during the nineteenth and twentieth centuries. Baptist scholar R. Alastair Campbell, *The Elders,* 1-19, offers a briefer synopsis.

[13] Rudolf Sohm's depiction of the church's early development is conveniently summarized in his *Outlines of Church History* (London: Macmillan and Co., Limited, 1931), 32-43.

[14] Ibid., 32; Sohm's italics.

[15] Ibid., 39.

[16] Hans von Campenhausen, *Ecclesiastical Authority and Spiritual Power in the Church of the First Three Centuries,* trans. J. A. Baker (London: Adam & Charles Black, 1969), 64.

[17] Ibid., chapter 5: "The System of Elders and the Beginnings of Official Authority."

[18] Rudolf Bultmann, *Theology of the New Testament,* vol. 1, trans. Kendrick Grobel (New York: Charles Scribner's Sons, 1951); see chapter 2: "He who had been the *bearer* of the message was drawn into it and became its essential *content. The proclaimer became the proclaimed*" (33); Bultmann's italics.

[19] Rudolf Bultmann, *Theology of the New Testament,* vol. 2 (New York: Charles Scribner's Sons, 1955); see chapter 10: "*The regulations of the Church all together become ordinances of divine law* and make the Church into an institution of divine

salvation" (110); Bultmann's italics.

[20] Gerd Theissen, *Sociology of Early Palestinian Christianity,* trans. John Bowden (Philadelphia: Fortress Press, 1978), 111-19. Critics have challenged Theissen's reconstruction as reflective of the view that what is normative for the church is not the radicalism of the itinerant prophets and evangelists, but the settled Hellenistic church with its established leaders; see Luise Schottroff, *Lydia's Impatient Sisters: A Feminist Social History of Early Christianity,* trans. Barbara and Martin Rumscheidt (Louisville: Westminister John Knox Press, 1995), 3-16.

[21] Elisabeth Schüssler Fiorenza, *In Memory of Her: A Feminist Reconstruction of Christian Origins* (New York: Crossroad, 1985); see especially chapters 4-8 for her depiction of the movement from Jesus' egalitarianism to the church's patriarchy.

[22] Burtchaell, *From Synagogue to Church;* see chapter 9, "A Conclusion," for a summary of his story of the emergence of leadership in the early church.

[23] Ibid., 350.

[24] Campbell, *The Elders.* Chapter 8, "Towards a New Consensus?" provides his summary.

[25] Ibid., 246; Campbell's italics.

[26] Ibid., 250.

[27] Margaret Y. MacDonald, *The Pauline Churches: A Socio-Historical Study of Institutionalization in the Pauline and Deutero-Pauline Writings,* Society for New Testament Studies monograph series, no. 60 (Cambridge: Cambridge University Press, 1988). "Ministry" is a subcategory within which MacDonald discusses the increasing institutionalization of the church at each stage; see 46-60, 123-38, 203-20.

[28] Kevin Giles, *Patterns of Ministry among the First Christians* (Melbourne, Australia: Collins Dove, 1989), 21; see chapter 1, especially 14-23; Giles's italics.

[29] Ibid., 23.

[30] Andrew D. Clarke, *Serve the Community of the Church: Christians As Leaders and Ministers* (Grand Rapids: Eerdmans, 2000).

[31] For example, David W. Bennett, *Metaphors of Ministry: Biblical Images for Leaders and Followers* (Carlisle, Cumbria, U.K.: Paternoster Press, 1993). Part 1 of his book deals with "terms used by Jesus for his followers." Part 3 is entitled "Following the master in church leadership today."

[32] Bengt Holmberg, *Paul and Power: The Structure of Authority in the Primitive Church As Reflected in the Pauline Epistles,* Coniectanea Biblica: New Testament series 11 (Lund: CWK Gleerup, 1978); Helen Doohan, *Leadership in Paul,* Good News Studies, vol. 11 (Wilmington: Michael Glazier, 1984).

[33] E. Earle Ellis, *Pauline Theology: Ministry and Society* (Grand Rapids: Eerdmans, 1989).

[34] Giles, *Patterns of Ministry,* attempts to survey the New Testament and the Old Testament roots of ministry patterns, and he includes developments beyond the first century. Also see David L. Bartlett, *Ministry in the New Testament,* Overtures to Biblical Theology (Minneapolis: Fortress Press, 1993).

[35] "Person, practice, and performance" are categories adapted from a working paper by Erick Sawatzky. They also correspond loosely to the way in which ancient rhetorical analysis focused on *ethos* (the personal character and values of the speaker), *pathos* (strategies for discerning and shaping the communal character), and *logos* (the logic or content of the tradition being transmitted reflectively and contextually.)

[36] Although the textual data strongly support the reading *nēpioi*, "little children"), all the translations render "gentle" (for *ēpioi*) on the premise that it fits better internally. For a defense of the translation "little children" instead of "gentle," see Jacob W. Elias, *1 and 2 Thessalonians*, Believers Church Bible Commentary (Scottdale, Pa.: Herald Press, 1995), 64-69. Cf. also Beverly Roberts Gaventa, "Apostles As Babes and Nurses in 1 Thessalonians 2:7," in *Faith and History: Essays in Honor of Paul W. Meyer*, ed. John T. Carroll, Charles H. Cosgrove, and E. Elizabeth Johnson (Atlanta: Scholars Press, 1990), 11:193-207.

[37] Again, translation from Elias, *1 and 2 Thessalonians*, 68-69. Cf. Beverly Roberts Gaventa, "Our Mother Saint Paul: Toward the Recovery of a Neglected Theme," *Princeton Seminary Bulletin* 17 (1996): 29-44.

[38] Elias, *1 and 2 Thessalonians*, 103-5.

[39] The NAB accurately translates *doulos* as "slave" (cf. NRSV: "servant," with footnote giving "slave").

[40] See Clarke, *Serve the Community of the Church*, 228-32, on this understanding of Paul as apostle.

[41] *Parakalō*, variously translated "encourage" or "exhort," occurs abundantly when Paul conveys pastoral counsel (e.g., Rom. 12:1).

[42] In Philemon 8, Paul indicates that although he is bold enough to command he prefers to appeal. *Enorkizō*, "adjure," is one of Paul's strongest verbs in this category, applied only in 1 Thessalonians 5:27 to advocate for inclusiveness within the community: nobody is to be excluded from hearing the message of this epistle.

[43] All of Paul's letters except Galatians (see Gal. 1:6) open with a "thanksgiving section" (see, e.g., 1 Cor. 1:4-9), which typically announces some of the major themes of the epistle.

[44] Translation from Elias, *1 and 2 Thessalonians*, 215; see also 215-19 and 227-30.

[45] Translations refer to Phoebe as "servant" (NIV), or "deaconess" (RSV), or "deacon" (NRSV), but the noun *diakonos*, when it refers to a male, is normally rendered "minister." The noun *prostatis*, which occurs nowhere else in the New Testament, is often translated "helper" (RSV, cf. NIV) or "benefactor" (NAB, NRSV), but the related participial form *ho proistamenos*, in 1 Thessalonians 5:12; Romans 12:8; and especially in 1 Timothy 3:4-5, 12, points to a ministry of leading or managing. For support of the translation given above, see Elias, *1 and 2 Thessalonians*, 230. Cf. also Ray R. Schulz, "A Case for 'President' Phoebe in Romans 16:2," *Lutheran Theological Journal* 24 (December 1990): 124-27.

[46] Philippians 1:1; 1 Timothy 3:2; and Titus 1:7 mention *episkopos*, literally "overseer" or bishop. Only 1 Timothy 5:1-2, 17, 19, and Titus 1:5 refer to *presbyteroi*,

"elders" (a term employed eighteen times in Acts). Much more frequent is *diakonos,* but in addition to the generic term for ministry or its more specific usage for some "practical ministries" (such as waiting on tables), this word occurs with reference to Christ himself (Rom. 15:8) and the state as God's servant (Rom. 13:4). For discussion of the *diakonia* word group in Paul's letters, see Clarke, *Serve the Community of the Church,* 233-45; and Giles, *Patterns of Ministry,* chap. 3.

[47] A point appropriately emphasized by Burtchaell, *From Synagogue to Church,* 187-89.

[48] For a letter-by-letter survey of situations being addressed by Paul's letters, an analysis of Paul's interaction with these issues, and an assessment of Paul's own leadership in these circumstances, see Helen Doohan, *Leadership in Paul;* and Colin G. Kruse, "Ministry in the Wake of Paul's Mission," in *The Gospel to the Nations: Perspectives on Paul's Mission,* ed. Peter Bolt and Mark Thompson (Downers Grove: InterVarsity Press, 2000), 205-20.

[49] In a manuscript still in process, tentatively titled "Remember the Future: The Pastoral Theology of Paul the Apostle," I seek to follow Paul's pastoral interventions in the lives of all of the congregations that he addresses.

[50] See Morna D. Hooker, "A Partner in the Gospel: Paul's Understanding of His Ministry" in *Theology and Ethics in Paul and his Interpreters: Essays in Honor of Victor Paul Furnish,* ed. Eugene H. Lovering and Jerry L. Sumney (Nashville: Abingdon Press, 1996), 83-100.

7

Ordination in the
King James Version of the Bible

Loren L. Johns

The question about whether or how it might be meaningful to talk about ordination from a biblical perspective requires that one address questions of definition and method. What exactly is ordination? Is it a biblical concept? What if what we call ordination in the church today is different from ordination as it was conceived or practiced in the Bible? Should we take our definitional cues from the Bible itself, or should we take what we "know" about ordination to the New Testament texts in order to see whether it is there?[1]

Such questions raise the even more foundational issue of our understanding of leadership and office. Behind the words we may or may not use for ordination, or the practices we may employ in installing and formally recognizing congregational leaders, lie questions about how our "offices" or understandings of pastoral ministry compare with those in the New Testament and whether New Testament patterns of ministry should determine today's church order. The latter question goes to the heart of the matter and represents a key issue in this book; the concept of ordination as a biblical and contemporary practice is but one small related issue.

Historically, the Mennonite church tradition has emphasized the priesthood of all believers while exhibiting some anticlericalism.[2] Some—especially those in the Old Mennonite tradition—have maintained that the biblical case for the rite of ordination is weak. In his study of "Mennonites and Ordination,"[3] Weldon Schloneger quotes several twentieth-century Mennonites who commented on the New Testament foundation for the practice. For instance, Paul M. Miller noted that ordination in the New Testament did not follow any prescribed order and that there was not much precision about how the term is used.[4] John Howard Yoder stated simply, "The New Testament is not clear about ordination."[5] In stronger words, Yoder noted, "There [are] . . . no grounds for seeing in the New Testament usage a clear conception of ordination as applying to some Christians and not to others."[6] Orlando Wiebe wrote, "There appears to be reason to believe that no attempt was made by Christ nor by the apostles to declare a permanent form of ministerial appointment or service."[7] The Mennonite Church study on leadership and authority similarly concluded in its report to the 1979 Mennonite Church General Assembly that "the New Testament does not give us a definite and detailed concept of ordination."[8] On the other hand, Erland Waltner could say that "the practice of ordination to ministerial offices, while not prominent in the New Testament, *nevertheless has a clear biblical basis.*"[9]

So what *does* the Bible have to say about ordination? In this essay, I will make some general observations about the use of the word *ordain* in three English translations of the Bible—the King James Version, the New Revised Standard Version, and the New International Version—and the words so translated in the original languages. Second, I will consider possible reasons behind the use of the word *ordain* in the King James Version in light of the seventeenth-century Church of England context. Finally, I will reflect briefly on some of the possible implications of the above for the church in the twenty-first century.

Biblical conceptions of ordination

One of the problems in considering a biblical perspective on ordination is the problem of determining what "ordination" is, biblically, in the first place. What Hebrew and Greek words mean "ordination"? The perhaps surprising answer is that actually none of them do—at least no technical term parallels the English technical term *ordination*.

In what follows I will lay out in some detail the biblical references to ordination and the words used in expressing it so that readers can study the evidence for themselves.[10] The word *ordain*, or *ordination*, occurs 19 times in the King James Version of the Hebrew Bible, 28 times in the New Revised Standard Version (with few of these in common), and 29 times in the New International Version, with a great deal of overlap between the NRSV and NIV. Of the 19 occurrences in the King James Version, only 17 translate a Hebrew or Aramaic verb, the other two being "supplied" to suggest the sense of the Hebrew text. These 17 translate 10 different Hebrew verbs and one Aramaic verb, most of which are common words meaning "to make" or "to do," "to put," or "to command." The 16 occurrences of *ordain* in the Septuagint (the Greek version of the Hebrew Bible) translate 11 different Greek verbs in those verses where a Greek equivalent exists!

Num. 28:6	עשׂה, *ʿśh;* γίνομαι, *ginomai*	
1 Kings 12:32	עשׂה, *ʿśh;* ποιέω, *poieō*	
2 Kings 23:5	נתן, *ntn;* δίδωμι, *didōmi*	
1 Chron. 9:22	יסד, *ysd;* ἵστημι, *histēmi*	
1 Chron. 17:9	שׂים, *śym;* τίθημι, *tithēmi*	
2 Chron. 11:15	עמד, *ʿmd;* καθίστημι, *kathistēmi*	
2 Chron. 23:18	—; —	
2 Chron. 29:27	—; —	
Esther 9:27	קום, *qwm;* ἵστημι, *histēmi*	
Ps. 7:13	פעל, *pʿl;* —	
Ps. 8:2	יסד, *ysd;* καταρτίζω, *katartizō*	
Ps. 8:3	כון, *kûn;* θεμελιόω, *themelioō*	
Ps. 81:5	שׂים, *śym;* τίθημι, *tithēmi*	
Ps. 132:17	ערך, *ʿrk;* ἑτοιμάζω, *hetoimazō*	
Isa. 26:12	שׁפת, *špt;* δίδωμι, *didōmi*	
Isa. 30:33	ערך, *ʿrk;* ἀπαιτέω, *apaiteō*	
Jer. 1:5	נתן, *ntn;* τίθημι, *tithēmi*	
Dan. 2:24	מנה, *mnh;* καθίστημι, *kathistēmi*	
Hab. 1:12	שׂים, *śym;* τάσσω, *tassō*	

When we look at *ordain* in the New Revised Standard and the New International Version, we see that most of the occurrences of the word in the Pentateuch (Genesis through Deuteronomy) are translated in the King James Version as *consecrate*. The word *ordain* is used by the NRSV and NIV in the following verses:

Exod. 28:41	מלא, *mlʾ;* ἐμπίπλημι, *empiplēmi*
Exod. 29:22	מלאים, *mlʾym;* τελείωσις, *teleiōsis*
Exod. 29:26	מלאים, *mlʾym;* τελείωσις, *teleiōsis*
Exod. 29:27	מלאים, *mlʾym;* τελείωσις, *teleiōsis*
Exod. 29:29	מלא, *mlʾ;* τελειόω, *teleioō*
Exod. 29:31	מלאים, *mlʾym;* τελείωσις, *teleiōsis*
Exod. 29:33	מלא, *mlʾ;* τελειόω, *teleioō*
Exod. 29:34	מלאים, *mlʾym;* τελείωσις, *teleiōsis*
Exod. 29:35	מלא, *mlʾ;* τελειόω, *teleioō*

Exod. 32:29   מלא, *ml'*; πληρόω, *plēroō* [NRSV only; NIV: "set apart"]

Lev. 7:37   מלאים, *ml'ym*; τελείωσις, *teleiōsis*

Lev. 8:22   מלאים, *ml'ym*; τελείωσις, *teleiōsis*

Lev. 8:28   מלאים, *ml'ym*; τελείωσις, *teleiōsis*

Lev. 8:29   מלאים, *ml'ym*; τελείωσις, *teleiōsis*

Lev. 8:31   מלאים, *ml'ym*; τελείωσις, *teleiōsis*

Lev. 8:33   מלאים, *ml'ym*; τελείωσις, *teleiōsis*

Lev. 8:33   מלא, *ml'*; τελειόω, *teleioō*

Lev. 16:32   מלא, *ml'*; τελειόω, *teleioō* [NIV only; NRSV: "consecrated"]

Lev. 21:10   מלא, *ml'*; τελειόω, *teleioō* [NIV only; NRSV: "consecrated"]

Num. 3:3   מלא, *ml'*; τελειόω, *teleioō*

Num. 28:6   עשה, *'sh*; γίνομαι, *ginomai*

2 Sam. 17:14 צוה, *swh*; ἐντέλλομαι, *entellomai* [NRSV only; NIV: "determined"]

1 Kings 1:36 אמר, *'mr*; πιστόω, *pistoō* [NRSV only; NIV: "declare"]

2 Kings 19:25 עשה, *'sh*; ἄγω, *agō* [NIV only; NRSV: "determined"]

2 Kings 23:5 נתן, *ntn*; δίδωμι, *didōmi* [NRSV only; NIV: "appointed"]

2 Chron. 2:4 —; — [No Hebrew or Greek word lies behind the NRSV's use of *ordained* here.][NRSV only; NIV: "ordinance"]

2 Chron. 22:7 —; γίνομαι, *ginomai* [NRSV only; NIV: "brought about"]

Ps. 8:2   יסד, *ysd*; καταρτίζω, *katartizō* [NIV only; NRSV: "founded"]

Ps. 65:9   כון, *kûn*; ἑτοιμάζω, *hetoimazō* [NIV only; NRSV: "prepared"]

Ps. 111:9   צוה, *swh*; ἐντέλλομαι, *entellomai* [NIV only; NRSV: "commanded"]

Ps. 133:3   צוה, *swh*; ἐντέλλομαι, *entellomai* [NRSV only; NIV: "bestows"]

Ps. 139:16 יצר, *ysr*; πλάσσω, *plassō* [NIV only; NRSV: "formed"]

Isa. 26:12   שפת, *špt*; δίδωμι, *didōmi* [NRSV only; NIV: "establish"]

Isa. 37:24   עשה, *'sh*; ποιέω, *poieō* [NIV only; NRSV: "determined"]

Isa. 48:5   צוה, *swh*; ἐντέλλομαι, *entellomai* [NIV only; NRSV: "commanded"]

Lam. 2:17   צוה, *swh*; ἐντέλλομαι, *entellomai* [NRSV only; NIV: "decreed"]

Lam. 3:37   צוה, *swh*; ἐντέλλομαι, *entellomai* [NRSV only; NIV: "decreed"]

Ezek. 28:13   נתן, *ntn*; τίθημι, *tithēmi* [NIV only; NRSV: "placed"]
Hab. 1:12   יסד, *ysd*; ἐλέγχω, *elenchō* [NIV only; NRSV: "established"]

We see here that a wide variety of Hebrew and Greek words lies behind the word *ordain* in the King James Version. The situation is not much different when we turn to the New Testament. If we exclude the uses of *ordain* in translating an inferior Greek text (2 Tim. 4:22 and Tit. 3:15), and the one place where it is "supplied," with no Greek verb behind it (Rom. 7:10), we see that the 20 remaining occurrences of the word translate fully 13 different Greek verbs: γίνομαι *(ginomai)*, διατάσσω *(diatassō)*, καθίστημι *(kathistēmi)*, κατασκευάζω *(kataskeuazō)*, κρίνω *(krinō)*, μετατίθημι *(metatithēmi)*, ὁρίζω *(horizō)*, ποιέω *(poieō)*, προετοιμάζω *(proetoimazō)*, προορίζω *(proorizō)*, τάσσω *(tassō)*, τίθημι *(tithēmi)*, and χειροτονέω *(cheirotoneō)*! Such a variety of Greek words calls into question whether "ordination" was a New Testament concept at all.

The King James Version uses a form of *ordain* in the following verses:

Mark 3:14   "And he [Jesus] *ordained* [ποιέω, *poieō*] twelve, that they should be with him, and that he might send them forth to preach." [NRSV and NIV: "appointed"] ποιέω usually means "to make" or "to do."

John 15:16   "Ye have not chosen me, but I have chosen you, and *ordained* [τίθημι, *tithēmi*] you, that ye should go and bring forth fruit." [NRSV and NIV: "appointed"] τίθημι usually means "to put" or "to place."

Acts 1:22   ". . . beginning from the baptism of John, unto that same day that he was taken up from us, must one be *ordained* [γίνομαι, *ginomai*] to be a witness with us of his resurrection." [NRSV and NIV: "become"] γίνομαι usually means "to happen" or "to become."

Acts 10:42   "And he commanded us to preach unto the people, and to testify that it is he which was *ordained* [ὁρίζω, *horizō*] of God *to be* the Judge of quick and dead." [NRSV: "ordained"; NIV: "appointed"] ὁρίζω usually means "to define" or "to set limits to."

Acts 13:48   "And when the Gentiles heard this, they were glad, and glorified the word of the Lord: and as many as were *ordained* [τάσσω, *tassō*] to eternal life believed." [NRSV:

	"ordained ; NIV: "appointed"] τάσσω usually means "to arrange" or "to put in place."
Acts 14:23	"And when they had *ordained* [χειροτονέω, *cheirotoneō*] them elders in every church, and had prayed with fasting, they commended them to the Lord, on whom they believed." [NRSV and NIV: "appointed"] χειροτονέω usually means "to elect" or "to choose" and means literally, "to stretch out the hand," whether in voting or in the laying on of hands.
Acts 16:4	"And as they went through the cities, they delivered them the decrees for to keep, that were *ordained* [κρίνω, *krinō*] of the apostles and elders which were at Jerusalem." [NRSV and NIV: "reached" (the decisions)] κρίνω usually means "to judge" or "to decide."
Acts 17:31	"Because he hath appointed a day, in the which he will judge the world in righteousness by that man whom he hath *ordained* [ὁρίζω, *horizō*]; *whereof* he hath given assurance unto all *men*, in that he hath raised him from the dead." [NRSV and NIV: "appointed"] ὁρίζω usually means "to define" or "to set limits to."
[Rom. 7:10	"And the commandment, which *was ordained* [—] to life, I found *to be* unto death." [NRSV: "promised ; and NIV: "intended"] No Greek verb lies behind the King James Version's use of *ordained* in this verse.]
Rom. 13:1	"Let every soul be subject unto the higher powers. For there is no power but of God: the powers that be are *ordained* [τάσσω, *tassō*] of God." [NRSV: "instituted"; and NIV: "established"] τάσσω usually means "to arrange" or "to put in place."
1 Cor. 2:7	"But we speak the wisdom of God in a mystery, *ordained* [προορίζω, *proorizō*] before the world unto our glory." [NRSV: "decreed ; and NIV: "destined"] προορίζω usually means "to decide beforehand."
1 Cor. 7:17	"But as God hath distributed to every man, as the Lord hath called every one, so let him walk. And so *ordain* I [διατάσσω, *diatassō*] that they which preach the gospel should live of the gospel." διατάσσω usually means "to arrange" or "to put in order."
Gal. 3:19	"Wherefore then *serveth* the law? It was added because

of transgressions, till the seed should come to whom the promise was made; *and it was ordained* [διατάσσω, *diatassō*] by angels in the hand of a mediator." διατάσσω usually means "to arrange" or "to put in order."

Eph. 2:10   "For we are his workmanship, created in Christ Jesus unto good works, which God hath *before ordained* [προετοιμάζω, *proetoimazō*] a preacher, and an apostle, (I speak the truth in Christ, *and* lie not;) a teacher of the Gentiles in faith and verity." προετοιμάζω usually means "to prepare beforehand."

[2 Tim. 4:22   "The second epistle unto Timotheus, *ordained* [χειροτο-
(postscript)   νέω, *cheirotoneō*] the first bishop of the church of the Ephesians, was written from Rome, when Paul was brought before Nero the second time." χειροτονέω usually means "to elect" or "to choose" and means literally, "to stretch out the hand," whether in voting or in the laying on of hands.]

Titus 1:5   "For this cause left I thee in Crete, that thou shouldest set in order the things that are wanting, and *ordain* [καθίστημι, *kathistēmi*] elders in every city, as I had appointed thee." καθίστημι usually means "to take someone somewhere" or "to appoint."

[Titus 3:15   "It was written to Titus, ordained [χειροτονέω, *cheiroto-
(postscript)   neō*] the first bishop of the church of the Cretians, from Nicopolis of Macedonia. χειροτονέω usually means "to elect" or "to choose" and means literally, "to stretch out the hand," whether in voting or in the laying on of hands.]

Heb. 5:1   "For every high priest taken from among men is *ordained* [καθίστημι, *kathistēmi*] for men in things *pertaining* to God, that he may offer both gifts and sacrifices for sins. καθίστημι usually means "to take someone somewhere" or "to appoint."

Heb. 8:3   "For every high priest is *ordained* [καθίστημι, *kathistēmi*] to offer gifts and sacrifices: wherefore *it is* of necessity that this man have somewhat also to offer. καθίστημι usually means "to take someone somewhere" or "to appoint."

Heb. 9:6   "Now when these things were thus *ordained* [κατα-σκευάζω, *kataskeuazō*], the priests went always into the

| | first tabernacle, accomplishing the service *of God*. κατασκευάζω usually means "to prepare" or "to construct." |
| Jude 4 | "For there are certain men crept in unawares, who were before of old *ordained* [μετατίθημι, *metatithēmi*] to this condemnation, ungodly men, turning the grace of our God into lasciviousness, and denying the only Lord God, and our Lord Jesus Christ. μετατίθημι usually means "to change someone's [or one's own] position," whether literally/physically, as in "to transfer," or metaphorically, as in "to change one's mind." |

In contrast to the King James Version, the New Revised Standard Version and the New International Version use the English word *ordain* to translate a narrower range of Hebrew and Greek words. *Ordain* in the NRSV translates only six different Hebrew words, and seven different Greek words. By far the Hebrew most often translated *ordain* in the NRSV is מלא, (*ml'*; or its nominal form), which means, "to fill." One understanding of ordination was often expressed through the idiomatic phrase, "to fill the hand of" (see Exod. 28:41; 29:9, 29, 39; Lev. 8:33; 16:32; Num. 3:3; 1 Kings 13:33). When mention is made of the "ram of ordination," the Hebrew phrase means literally, "ram of fillings." However, in the Septuagint, the Greek word most often translated *ordain* or *ordination* is τελειόω (*teleioō;* or its nominal form), and the equivalent phrase to the Hebrew Bible's "ram of fillings" is "ram of τελείωσις *(teleiōsis),*" or "ram of perfection."

The interests of King James I and the Church of England

When King James I undertook to produce a unified translation of the Bible, he did so in the context of seventeenth-century England, with all the privileges of power and position at work in the nation and in the Church of England. While the King James Version was "new" in the sense that it did not exist before, the preface indicates that the purpose of the translators was not to create a new translation from scratch, but rather to revise the earlier translations in order to eliminate the alternatives and produce just one accepted standard version.[11] In practice, the King James Version was based primarily on the Tyndale and Geneva Bibles and the Rheims New Testament.[12] According to Jack Lewis, James wanted to produce a new translation so that the whole church would be bound to "it alone, and [to] none other." He wanted to adjudicate the various readings of the other versions in such a way that his version could "not justly . . . be excepted against."[13] His primary interest was to impose order and peace on a divided church.

Such implied interests in order and authority can hardly be missed in the first and next-to-last paragraphs of the preface:

> Great and manifold were the blessings, most dread Sovereign, which Almighty God, the Father of all mercies, bestowed upon us the people of England, when first he sent Your Majesty's Royal Person to rule and reign over us. For whereas it was the expectation of many, who wished not well upon our Sion, that upon the setting of that bright Occidental Star, Queen Elizabeth of most happy memory, some thick and palpable clouds of darkness would so have overshadowed this Land, that men should have been in doubt which way they were to walk; and that it should hardly be known, who was to direct the unsettled State; the appearance of Your Majesty, as of the Sun in his strength, instantly dispelled those supposed and surmised mists, and gave unto all that were well affected exceeding cause of comfort; especially when we beheld the Government established in Your Highness, and Your hopeful Seed, by an undoubted Title, and this also accompanied with peace and tranquility at home and abroad.

> And now at last, by the mercy of God, and the continuance of our labors, it being brought unto such a conclusion, as that we have great hopes that the Church of England shall reap good fruit thereby; we hold it our duty to offer it to Your Majesty, not only as to our King and Sovereign, but as to the principal Mover and Author of the work: humbly craving of Your most Sacred Majesty, that since things of this quality have ever been subject to the censures of ill meaning and discontented persons, it may receive approbation and patronage from so learned and judicious a Prince as Your Highness is, whose allowance and acceptance of our labors shall more honor and encourage us, than all the calumniations and

hard interpretations of other men shall dismay us. So that if, on the one side, we shall be traduced by Popish persons at home or abroad, who therefore will malign us, because we are poor instruments to make God's holy Truth to be yet more and more known unto the people, whom they desire still to keep in ignorance and darkness; or if, on the other side, we shall be maligned by self-conceited Brethren, who run their own ways, and give liking unto nothing, but what is framed by themselves, and hammered on their anvil; we may rest secure, supported within by the truth and innocency of a good conscience, having walked the ways of simplicity and integrity, as before the Lord; and sustained without, by the powerful protection of Your Majesty's grace and favor, which will ever give countenance to honest and Christian endeavours against bitter censures and uncharitable imputations.[14]

King James had a marked dislike, even hostility, toward the Geneva Bible with its marginal notes. James clearly wished to displace this Bible, with its implicit and explicit challenges to the "divine right of kings."[15] In its place, James wanted with his version to "reinforce the image of the king as the political and spiritual leader of his people. The unity of king, Bible, and church would ensure the unity of the English people."[16] Alister McGrath suggest that as it turned out, the most significant factor in the ultimate success of the King James Version "appears to have been the fact that it was associated with the authority of the monarch at a time when such authority was viewed positively."[17]

The implied interests in the position of the king and in properly authorized lines of accountability in the hierarchical church and government of England clearly visible above suggest that the word *ordain* may have been chosen to support the interests of hierarchy and office in that ecclesiastical and political context.

Analysis of the biblical and historical evidence

What does this brief survey of the biblical and historical evidence suggest? First, the sheer variety of words translated *ordain* or *ordination* in the King James Version underscores the fluidity of the concepts and practices that lie behind what we have learned to call ordination. To ordain was to make or put or appoint or institute or decree or establish or choose or lay hands on or put in place—something like that. I suspect that John E. Toews is right when he says that "ordination for ministry through the laying on of hands as practiced in the church is without biblical foundation" and that "there is no biblical linkage of personal call to ministry and ordination through the laying on of hands, as often practised in the Protestant Church."[18]

Second, the evidence could suggest that not only was there no common *practice* or *form* of ordination in the Bible but also that there was no common *conception* of ordination. Any defense of ordination must be made on theological, ecclesiological, and/or practical grounds, since no facile appeal to biblical precedent or to a New Testament theology of ordination stands up under scrutiny. Whether the modern practice of ordination cannot be aligned with Anabaptist-Mennonite theology insofar as it inevitably "sacerdotalizes" pastoral ministry, as Toews claims, is another matter.[19]

Third, the historical evidence may suggest that the defense of "office" (vs. functionalism) in the free church traditions has unwittingly perpetuated the political and theological interests of the Church of England by way of the King James Version even as its defenders were unaware of them. While political and theological interests are not inherently bad or to be avoided, they function most constructively when they are acknowledged and thus open to some scrutiny.

Finally, these observations demonstrate that any attempt to develop or articulate a biblical theology of ordination cannot proceed on the basis of any English translation of the text. Careful reference to the original languages is beneficial in most cases, but required by the evidence itself when dealing with "ordination."

It is outside the scope of this essay to pursue one final historical question that deserves attention in its own right. One would expect that the use of the one word *ordain* to translate many varied Hebrew and Greek verbs and concepts influenced the polity and practical theology of English-speaking churches in the West from the seventeenth through the twentieth centuries. But did increased dependence upon the King James Version by a historically *German*-speaking people bring with it a changing view of ordination? It would not be surprising if it did.

Notes

[1] This question is not intended to be rhetorical. The former procedure often lies implicitly behind the task of New Testament theology, sometimes with the assumption that New Testament theology and practice—once properly identified and understood—should simply be adopted by the modern church. The latter procedure *can* be an exercise in using the Bible to buttress whatever practice is current, or it can reflect the necessity of interpreting and reapplying biblical thought and practice for an ever-changing historical context.

[2] For a treatment of the history and nature of anticlericalism in one part of the Anabaptist-Mennonite tradition, see the essay by Karl Koop, "Worldly Preachers and True Shepherds: Anabaptist Anticlericalism in the Lower Rhine," pages 24-38 in this volume. While anticlericalism often accompanied an emphasis on the priesthood of all believers, the latter does not necessarily entail the former.

[3] Weldon Schloneger, "Mennonites and Ordination," May 12, 1980, Student Papers File, Associated Mennonite Biblical Seminary.

[4] Paul M. Miller, *Servant of God's Servants* (Scottdale, Pa.: Herald Press, 1964), 27.

[5] John H. Yoder, "The Fullness of Christ," *Concern: Pamphlet Series for Christian Renewal* 17 (February 1969), 61.

[6] John H. Yoder, "The Fullness of Christ," 61.

[7] Orlando Wiebe, "The Commissioning of Servants in the Church," (paper presented at the Mennonite Brethren Churches study conference on The Ministry: Men and Media, Buhler, Kans., March 5-6, 1970), 9.

[8] *Leadership and Authority in the Church*, Mennonite Church General Assembly 1979 Study Report, 79.

[9] Everett J. Thomas, ed., *A Mennonite Polity for Ministerial Leadership* (Newton, Kans., and Winnepeg, Man.: Faith & Life Press, 1996), 34; italics added.

[10] I would like to acknowledge and thank my former copastor, David E. Mishler, who collaborated with me on an earlier form of this essay.

[11] On this point, see "Publication of the King James Bible (1611)," in *Christian History: The 100 Most Important Events in Church History*, Issue 28.

[12] Ibid.

[13] Jack P. Lewis, "Versions, English," in *The Anchor Bible Dictionary*, ed. David Noel Freedman (New York: Doubleday, 1992) 6:823-24, 6:832-33.

[14] "Preface," *The Holy Bible: King James Version* (Oak Harbor, Wash.: Logos Research Systems, Inc., 1995).

[15] See Alister McGrath, *In the Beginning: The Story of the King James Bible and How It Changed a Nation, a Language, and a Culture* (New York: Anchor Books, 2001), esp. 141. See also David Neff, "A Translation Fit for a King," *Christianity Today* (October 22, 2001), 37-39, 75.

[16] McGrath, *In the Beginning*, 171.

[17] Ibid., 289.

[18] John E. Toews, "Toward a Biblical Theology of Leadership Affirmation: Rethinking the Meaning of Ordination" (Benjamin Eby Lecture at Conrad Grebel University College, Waterloo, Ont., November 7, 2003), forthcoming in *Conrad Grebel Review*. I recommend Toews's provocative biblical, historical, and theological study of ordination as a means to further consideration of these issues.

[19] Toews argues that how a church selects and affirms its leaders must ultimately be based on its particular ecclesiology. And an Anabaptist-Mennonite ecclesiology requires the desacramentalization of appointment to ministry, along with the eschewing of any notions of status and power, tax benefits, ordination for life, and/or distinctions between clergy and laity.

8

The pastor as prophet

Ben C. Ollenburger

It is far from obvious whether an essay with the title "The pastor as prophet" has anything to say. If it does say something, it may thereby simply beg the question whether we should in any case consider pastors as prophets or whether pastors should be prophets. "Begging the question" is a logical fallacy (in the classical terms of formal logic, the fallacy of *petitio principii*). Analogously, an essay titled "The pastor as pugilist" would beg the question—the question of whether being a pugilist falls somehow within the role or office of pastor. English speakers in North America having become lazy with respect to our language, we tend now to equate begging a question with merely suggesting or provoking one. But I mean to be precise. Hence, I mean seriously to ask whether we should in any case consider pastors as prophets. To answer that question, without begging still others, requires that we share an understanding of what or who pastors are, and so also prophets. I begin with pastors.

How we understand the *pastoral* office

Mennonites, like other Christians, have tended to believe that ministry is the work of the whole church and the calling of all its members. Some Protestants, including often Mennonites, have spoken in this regard of "the priesthood of all believers." In the Reformation period and immediately afterward, when Lutherans coined the phrase, it made a particular kind of sense: believers did not require a cleric, a priest, to mediate between them and God. Later, the phrase came to serve as a kind of slogan for the dispersal of ministry, and hence the gifts of ministry, across the church. Drawing especially on the Pauline letters, some have taken this slogan to mean that neither ministry nor any specific set of ministries may be especially and officially, much less permanently (sacramentally), concentrated in any one person or cadre of people in the church or within a congregation.

On this understanding, of course, there can be no talk of "the pastor," in case we should assign that term or title the meaning it normally has in English. The Mennonite polity manual of 1996, perhaps evincing some discomfort with the term, ascribes to it a vacuous definition: "Pastor. A term commonly used to designate the spiritual leader of a congregation."[1] Not every pastor is a congregation's spiritual leader, of course, and the reverse is also true. Indeed, over most of their history in Europe and North America, Mennonites have refrained from speaking of their ordained ministers as pastors. (I am aware of exceptions.) The term was sometimes regarded as alien: Lutherans had pastors, just as Catholics had priests, but Mennonites had neither.[2] Perhaps some part of this reticence derived from a strong belief that ministry is the work of the whole church and the calling of all its members.

For whatever reasons, Mennonites came recently to embrace the term *pastor*. But how shall we understand that term? In its proffered definition, the Mennonite polity manual again fails adequately to guide: "In this document, it [the term pastor] is more often used to describe a 'shepherding' function of a minister (i. e., *pastoral ministry*)."[3] In other words, when aiming to speak precisely the manual refers to pastoral ministry—that is, to one of the functions of a minister. It thus raises at least three questions: (a) whether "a minister" is a pastor; (b) whether *pastor* designates only a set of functions qualifying ministry; (c) whether pastoral ministry is equivalent to "shepherding" (whatever that may include). It fails, then, in guiding us toward a shared definition of *pastor*.

In this regard, the polity manual may simply reflect a host of uncertainties and disagreements among Mennonites. But it seems evident that Mennonites tend to have in mind, not only a set of functions, but what we may properly call an "office": the office of pastor. Since the authors of this volume serve as seminary faculty, it would be appropriate to cite as authoritative another seminary-authored document, *Ministerial Formation and Theological Education in Mennonite Perspective*. It defines the pastoral office thus:

> The term "office" refers to the common characteristics
> and specific responsibilities of a particular ministry and
> to the way it is ordered in relation to other ministries in

the church. . . . The office of pastoral ministry will normally include particular responsibility for leading congregational worship, preaching and teaching, providing pastoral care, administration (in the sense of giving guidance in the congregation's ministry and mission as a whole), helping to call forth and nurture the ministries of others in the congregation, and cultivating good relations with other congregational and conference bodies. With the responsibilities of the office also come appropriate authority and standards of accountability.[4]

Whether or not this definition is in every respect adequate, I propose to use it in this essay as a shared understanding of what we mean by *pastor*. That is, a pastor is someone who holds or exercises, or has been entrusted with or ordained to, just this office. While it aims to embrace the conviction that ministry is the work of the whole church and the calling of all its members, this definition separates one "particular ministry" as distinctively pastoral and as embodying or constituting an office. Such "official" authority, responsibilities, and accountability as may pertain to a pastor—to any pastor—will do so by virtue of that office, and not, for example, by virtue of personality, charismatic endowment, education, or conviction. Presumably, those would be considered as qualifications *for* the office, but they do not define it.

What, if anything, in this understanding of the pastoral office would give rise to or permit consideration of the pastor as prophet? No answer suggests itself immediately. More to the point, none is possible apart from a shared understanding of *prophet*. To that matter I turn next.

How we understand *prophetic* witness

As it turns out, Mennonites seem to share an understanding of what it means to be a prophet, or of what it means to be prophetic. A quick search of articles and documents in the *Canadian Mennonite Encyclopedia Online* provides confirmation.[5] The article "Social Gospel" says that Walter Rauschenbusch "was a lonely prophet" in his campaign for social justice and against an exploitive capitalist system in the U.S. A document from 1961, "Christian Witness to the State," describes the church's "prophetic witness" as just that—witness to the state.

The 1989 document "Nonresistance" defines prophetic witness as "social service and witness in the wider world, even . . . political activism." The article on "Socio-political Activism" cites Menno as a prototype of "prophetic witness to the state" because of his opposition to capital punishment, among other things. "A Christian Declaration on Capital Punishment" (1965) similarly cites "the prophetic commission given to the church" as the basis for the church's appeal to Parliament in opposition to capital punishment and in favor of the rehabilitation of offenders. The General Conference's "Justice and the Christian Witness" (1983) speaks of "prophetic protest."

In all of these cases, to be prophetic is to bring Christian convictions, especially convictions about social (in)justice, to bear critically, and sometimes also constructively, on an arena—the state, the wider world, a government—outside and distinct from the community of faith. We need not here debate the adequacy of this implied understanding of church and world or church and state. Our question concerns the pastor as prophet, and thus the relation of the pastoral office to the understanding of prophecy and of prophets, or of being prophetic, that we seem to share.

To put it bluntly, no such relation is evident. We understand the pastoral office in terms of congregational ministry, in its relation to other ministries, and in its relation to other congregations and conference bodies. The pastoral office is one that is definitively in and to and for the church. On the other hand, we understand prophets or prophecy or prophetic witness to be definitively otherwise—to and for and against the world. This does not deny that acting prophetically or bearing prophetic witness falls within the church's calling, or that a pastor may (or that pastors often do) lead a congregation in the exercise of this calling and the bearing of this witness. I mean only to observe that being a prophet, as we commonly understand that term, falls outside our understanding of the pastoral office. If this is so, then the title of this essay does indeed beg the question; being a prophet is no part of being a pastor.

This essay would end both prematurely and unhelpfully if the conclusions reached so far were its final word. Obviously, they are not. In what follows I will suggest that our evidently shared understanding of prophecy is inadequate, and that a biblical reconsideration may help to enrich our understanding of the pastoral office.[6]

Prophets and prophecy in the Bible

The Old Testament

The Bible, and especially the Old Testament, portrays prophets acting in a dazzling variety of ways, some of them unsuitable as a model for pastors. Saul, for example, "stripped off his clothes, acted as a prophet before Samuel, and fell naked all day and all night" (1 Sam. 19:24).[7] Elijah famously executed his rivals, the prophets of Baal (1 Kings 18:40). By way of contrast, the prophet Miriam led in celebratory song and dance, while Huldah provided authoritative interpretation of a newly recovered book of the covenant (2 Kings 22:8-20).[8] In none of these cases was prophecy addressed to someone outside the community of faith—outside Israel. Indeed, among the defining characteristics of prophecy in the Old Testament is its focus on *Israel*.[9] Even when prophets issued oracles against foreign nations or their rulers, their proclamation was on behalf of Israel as the people of God. More properly, but at the same time, their proclamation was on behalf of Israel's God. Here, then, we meet another defining characteristic of prophecy: prophets spoke for God and at God's initiative.

These two characteristics of Old Testament prophecy—it (1) addressed Israel (2) on behalf of God—are most in evidence in what I shall call the prophetic canon: the books from Hosea through Malachi.[10] True to our common understanding, social justice is a pervasive concern in the prophetic canon. Social *in*justice constitutes one of two reasons the prophets routinely cite for God's judgment on Israel; the other is idolatry—the worship of or trust in something or someone other than YHWH. These reasons often flow together: Israel's self-reliance, their trust in themselves or in some ally, constitutes the kind of rejection of YHWH in which oppression of the poor flourishes. In other words, Israel practices idolatry to sanction injustice (Jer. 7:9-11).

The reverse is also true (Isa. 1:10-31; 2:6-9; 5:1-9; 7:1-17; 22:8b-14). The prophetic canon attests a radical theocentricity, which demands the singular veneration of YHWH in every sphere of Israel's existence. Its violation brings judgment—unavoidably, but not automatically. Judgment remains both God's decision and God's action. However, judgment is not the only theme in the prophetic canon. Its theocentricity comes to even clearer expression in the prophets' promises regarding Israel's future beyond judgment. The singular cause of this future is once again God, and the reasons behind the promises lie, in this instance, entirely within God's own self (Hos. 11:8-9). So too does the initiative lie entirely with God, to the extent that salvation even precedes the repentance it will provoke (e.g., Ezek. 36:25-28; cf. 18:30-32).[11]

In the preceding paragraphs I have made some broad generalizations about the content of prophetic proclamation. As important for our topic are some of its formal qualities, of which I also offer generalizations. For example, much of the prophetic canon consists of poetry. Prophets, as the prophetic canon represents them, were powerful poets, able to exploit and—this may be more significant—to expand the expressive potential of the Hebrew language. Indeed, the prophetic canon is itself a monumental work of literary imagination and artistry.

However, the prophetic imagination was not free-floating; it drew on a rich store of tradition, which gave prophetic proclamation much of its power. Prophets were thoroughly familiar with, even as they formed or reformed, Israel's traditions. Isaiah's reference or allusion (in chapter 51) to traditions of Abraham and Sarah, creation, exodus, and Zion, in unprecedented combination, is stunning.

Further, then, prophets were interpreters; by way of their poetic-literary creations, they engaged in the often striking interpretation of Israel's traditions, its situation, and even of other prophets.[12] In all of this—in their poetic, literary artistry; in the power of their imaginations; in their appropriation and reformation of Israel's traditions; in their interpretation even of earlier *texts* (cf. above, on Huldah)—prophets were theologians. The prophetic canon presents prophets as visionary theologians, who proclaimed what Israel did not expect and often did not want to hear: the word of God.

Zechariah, in chapters 1–8, provides an excellent example. These chapters address a dispirited Judean community that was dominated by Persian imperial power and given to doubt God's promises.[13] Drawing on earlier prophetic texts, especially Isaiah and Jeremiah; adapting symbols from popular culture; and even borrowing imperial forms of speech, Zechariah's artistically crafted visions and oracles, and his sermon (chaps. 7–8), *create* for the Judean community a world reordered—the *real* or *true* world, open to a future that YHWH is bringing to pass. Zechariah envisions a world in which YHWH, not Persia's emperor, is "Lord of the whole earth" (4:14). In *this* world, the Judean community can live in the hope and practice of *shalom* (the term occurs in Zech. 6:13; 8:10, 12, 16, 19). It remains to be said and emphasized that Zechariah attributes everything envisioned and proclaimed, imagined and crafted, to God's own initiative: "the word of the LORD of hosts came to me" (7:4).

The New Testament

Zechariah, like others in the prophetic canon, was the ambassador of a contested sovereignty.[14] The same was true of Christian prophets. Zechariah represented YHWH's highly contested sovereignty over the whole earth, indeed to God's cosmic reign (Zech. 1:7-15; 6:1-8; cf. Gen. 1:1). Christian prophets, most of them anonymous, represented—they were among the ambassadors of—the highly contested sovereignty of Jesus Christ, which is to say of "God's reign in Christ."[15] As Paul describes it in Ephesians, through God's design and act Christ is sovereign over the whole earth and his reign is cosmic (Eph. 1:10, 20-22).[16] Paul himself was among those prophets (who were also teachers) as a leader of the church in Antioch, the first *Christian* church (Acts 13:1; 11:26). In Ephesians, Paul associates God's elevation of Christ to sovereignty "in the heavens" (Eph. 1:20-22) with the traditional grant of gifts when a new king acceded to the throne (4:8; cf. Ps. 68:18). In this case the gifts were spiritual (Eph. 4:3-7) and distributed in the church. Among these "gifts" were prophets and pastors, literally *shepherds*, who were also teachers (4:11).

Paul includes in the same verse (Eph. 4:11) apostles and evangelists among Christ's gifts to the church. In 1 Corinthians 12:28, Paul again speaks of leadership in the church and assigns priorities: "God has appointed in the church," he says, "first apostles, second prophets, third teachers" (v. 28a). To this ranked list of divinely appointed leaders Paul adds a set of spiritual endowments and responsibilities: "*then* deeds of power, then gifts of healing, assistances, leaderships [KJV: governments], various kinds of tongues" (v. 28b). The first part of the list, thus (also like Ephesians 4), concerns categories of spiritual leaders and the second part concerns various gifts, capacities, and responsibilities—all of whom and all of which God appointed in the church.

Paul's concern in 1 Corinthians 12 is with the church's unity, grounded in its Spirit-inspired confession of Christ's contested sovereignty: "Jesus is Lord" (v. 3). Paul insists that the Spirit's provisions include every member of the body, so that each member is an essential part of the whole. In that respect the Spirit is egalitarian in its distribution of gifts. But the church's unity is differentiated: not all have the same gifts, and some of God's "appointments" have a relative priority: apostles, prophets, and teachers.

Unity is also Paul's concern in Ephesians, including in chapter 4. The church's Spirit-enabled unity is both corporate—"in the bond of peace"—and confessional: "one body and one Spirit, . . . one hope, . . . one Lord, one faith, one baptism, one God and Father of all" (4:3-5). Apostles, prophets, and evangelists, so also pastors-*teachers*, were given on behalf of that unity. Threatening the church's unity and threatening the gospel—threatening the faith—is the church's susceptibility to faddish *teachings* or doctrines (4:14). Prophets and pastors (who are also teachers) alike are given for (a) "equipping the saints for the work of ministry," and (b) "building up the body of Christ;" so that the body may "attain to the unity of the faith and the knowledge of the Son of God"—to "maturity," in other words (4:12-13).

"Building up" the church remains Paul's concern in 1 Corinthians 14, where prophets and the gift of prophecy figure centrally. In this chapter Paul focuses not on church leadership but on worship. In chapter 12, he had distinguished prophecy from speaking in tongues; in chapter 14, he reinforces that distinction, using the criterion of "building up" or edification (1 Cor. 14:3, 4, 5, 12, 17, 26). Prophecy here serves the same ends, building up the body in faith, as do prophets in Ephesians 4:11.

Prophecy remains a spiritual gift—it comes by revelation—but in 1 Corinthians 14, Paul lays extraordinary stress on thinking (v. 20, twice), on disciplined judgment or thoughtful evaluation (v. 29), and on engagement of the mind (vv. 14, 15 [twice], 19; cf. v. 23!). Hans von Campenhausen concludes: "For Paul prophecy always means the power of moving and convincing speech, which as such is inevitably practiced with the aid of 'reason,' and likewise makes its appeal to the lively rational judgment of the audience."[17]

But prophetic speech is properly convincing, and the audience's judgment properly rational, in dependence on a specific criterion: the gospel, or in other words, the apostolic faith. In Romans 12:6 Paul insists that prophecy must be "according to the analogy of faith," hence in proportion to *the* faith: "the faith" that Paul teaches (Gal. 1:23); "the word of faith that we preach" (Rom. 10:8); "the faith of the gospel" (Phil. 1:27). As Thomas W. Gillespie puts it: "In Romans 12:6b prophecy is (1) drawn into the orbit of gospel proclamation, and (2) subjected to the standard provided by the content of this message. Just as faith (*fides quae* [what faith believes]) corresponds to the kergyma, so also prophetic speech must demonstrate its appropriateness in relation to 'the faith of the gospel' (Phil 1:27)."[18]

As in the Old Testament's prophetic canon, prophets in the New Testament (1) addressed the community of faith (2) on God's behalf—as ambassadors of a contested sovereignty: God's reign in Christ. Like their Old Testament counterparts, and if we take the book of Revelation as an example (Rev. 1:3), Christian prophets exploited the resources of their language and their own artistry in service of their proclamation. They proclaimed both judgment and salvation. They were interpreters of tradition, of the church's situation, and of Scripture: the book of Revelation interprets the Old Testament by way of proclaiming God's sovereign and contested reign in Christ. And thereby they were theologians: the first Christian theologians (Gillespie). Insofar as they built up the body of Christ through their words, enabling the ministry of the whole church (Eph. 4:12), they were pastoral theologians (Acts 15:22-23, 32).

Conclusion

We began with the question whether we should in any case consider pastors as prophets or whether pastors should be prophets. I have argued that, given our prevailing understandings of both the pastoral office and of prophets, we would have to conclude that we should not. But I have tried also to show that our prevailing understanding of prophets and prophecy—of being prophetic—requires revision if it means to be biblical. Does this biblical understanding, as I have sketched it, then accord with our understanding of the pastoral office? It certainly does so if, or to the extent that, we understand this office to embrace the gift and art of proclaiming and teaching the Word of God—of using any and all linguistic, artistic, literary, and intellectual resources in the interpretation of the church's tradition, its situation, and its Scripture to build up the body in the faith—as ambassadors of God's contested sovereignty and as pastoral theologians. In this case, our understanding of the pastoral office is enriched. However, I would offer three caveats.

First, neither pastors nor others in the church have the capacity to make themselves prophets. Prophecy comes by God's initiative or not at all (Deut. 18:20). Being a prophet or acting prophetically does not attach to any office. Genuine prophets, and genuinely prophetic words or actions, are typically recognized and affirmed after the fact. None of those in the prophetic canon refer to themselves as prophets. In the early church, false prophets were common (1 John 4:1). Prophecy and testing the spirits go together.

Second, then, "the pastor as prophet" places considerable responsibility on congregations, especially the responsibility of "testing the spirits." As we saw above, this includes the capacity for assessing any sample proclamation, whether it accords with "the faith of the gospel." Ministry is the work of the whole church and the calling of all its members. As part of its collective ministry, a congregation has theological responsibilities.

Third, prophecy may take various forms. Miriam the prophet led in song and dance. In the temple, musicians were to *prophesy* with the lyre, the harp and cymbals; Jeduthun "prophesied with the lyre in thanksgiving and praise to YHWH" (1 Chron. 25:1, 3).

Whatever forms they may employ, prophets proclaim the contested sovereignty of God. The church confesses that the principal instrument of this sovereignty is the cross. When a pastor, at God's initiative, summons the congregation away from its (and the pastor's) perennial and serious temptations to believe and to act contrary to "the word of the cross" that rules the church; when a pastor refuses the emoluments of other wisdoms that would rob the cross of its power (1 Cor. 1:17); when a pastor leads a congregation in embracing the foolishness and sovereignty of the word of the cross—the gospel— as the power of God (1 Cor. 1:18), the pastor is a prophet. No question.

Notes

[1] Everett J. Thomas, ed., *A Mennonite Polity for Ministerial Leadership* (Newton, Kans., and Winnipeg, Man.: Faith & Life Press, 1996), 137.

[2] The aforementioned polity manual offers some of the terms and titles Mennonites have used for ordained ministers (ibid., 35-61).

[3] Ibid., 137; quotation marks and italics in the original.

[4] *Ministerial Formation and Theological Education in Mennonite Perspective*

(Elkhart, Ind.: Associated Mennonite Biblical Seminary, 1992), 3-4 (reprinted in this volume as Appendix 1; see page 241). Marlin E. Miller was the principal author of this section. The polity manual, while avoiding the term *office,* offers a similar description (Thomas, *A Mennonite Polity,* 78). Interestingly, whereas *Ministerial Formation* defines *administration* as overall congregational guidance, *A Mennonite Polity* defines it as "administration of the ordinances" (78).

⁵ http://www.mhsc.ca/index.asp?content=http://www.mhsc.ca/mhsc/projects.htm

⁶ Stanley Hauerwas makes similar but different points, in "The Pastor As Prophet: Ethical Reflections on an Improbable Mission," in *Christian Existence Today: Essays on Church, World, and Living in Between* (Durham: Labyrinth Press, 1988), 149-67.

⁷ Quotations of biblical texts generally follow the NRSV; where a rendering differs, as here, the translation is my own.

⁸ An earlier scholarly judgment held this "book" (of the covenant or of the law) to be at least roughly equivalent to Deuteronomy. We will not go amiss imagining that to be the case.

⁹ "Israel" here serves for the community of faith in the Old Testament, without differentiating between the two states, Israel and Judah.

¹⁰ Excluding Lamentations and Daniel, which fall among the Writings in the Masoretic (Hebrew) canon; in it, Hosea–Malachi constitutes the "Latter Prophets," and Joshua–2 Kings, excluding Ruth, the "Former Prophets."

¹¹ Paul Joyce, *Divine Initiative and Human Response in Ezekiel* (Sheffield: JSOT Press, 1989); Amy L. Barker, "Unveiling the Mystery: Divine Initiative and Human Responsibility" (unpublished paper, Associated Mennonite Biblical Seminary, 2002).

¹² Hauerwas, "Pastor As Prophet," also emphasizes prophets as interpreters.

¹³ For detailed exposition see my commentary on Zechariah in the New Interpreter's Bible (Nashville: Abingdon Press, 1996), 7:733–840; and "Zechariah's Vision of Mission and Peace—the Reign of God: An Inquiry into Zechariah 1–8," in *Beautiful upon the Mountains: Biblical Essays on Mission, Peace, and the Reign of God,* ed. Mary H. Schertz and Ivan Friesen (Elkhart, Ind.: Institute of Mennonite Studies, 2003), 99-122.

¹⁴ I borrow the concept from Richard John Neuhaus, who wrote of pastors as "ambassadors of a disputed sovereignty," in *Freedom for Ministry* (San Francisco: Harper & Row, 1984), 60.

¹⁵ Ibid., 61.

¹⁶ Questions about the authorship of Ephesians need not occupy us here.

¹⁷ *Ecclesiastical Authority and Spiritual Power in the Church of the First Three Centuries* (London: Black, 1969), 189.

¹⁸ *The First Theologians: A Study in Early Christian Prophecy* (Grand Rapids: Eerdmans, 1994), 61.

9

Pastors and the church's witness in society

Ted Koontz

Church and society: A historical context

Within the broad range of Christian traditions, Mennonites have typically been seen, and have seen themselves, as comparatively against, withdrawn from, or critical of the larger society or culture.[1] As a sect, they have usually been content to run the society of the church and have been less involved in running the society outside it. Compared to those within the churchly traditions of Christianity, Mennonites have seen God's work in history as less directly connected to the outcomes of political, economic, and military struggles of states.[2] The focus in the Mennonite context has been more on bearing witness to the coming reign of God by seeking to live here and now, within the society of the church, according to the vision of that reign.

Mennonites' view of the church as a separated society within the larger society resulted partly from seeing the church not as an all-inclusive, territorially defined organization but as a voluntary, disciplined body consisting of those who have chosen Christ and his way. It also resulted from persecution; denied full participation in the life of the larger society, Anabaptists retreated for the sake of their survival to the margins of society. And it resulted from some particular—and peculiar—understandings of what it means to accept Christ and his way. Most notable, in terms of generating tension with the larger society, were their refusal to bear arms and to swear oaths of loyalty to rulers. In many intolerant political contexts these factors combined to make substantial parts of the Mennonite family a wandering people, moving from place to place in search of a safe haven in which to live and practice their faith. This sociological experience of being a pilgrim people, not being at home, not being full citizens, and not completely trusting their powerful hosts reinforced a sense of distance from the larger societies in which they sojourned.

Church and society in Canada and the United States

Many Mennonites in North America still occasionally feel substantial separation from the world. In recent times, I have experienced this separation most sharply in the ways we have felt called to respond to the events of September 11, 2001, and the war in Iraq—responses at odds with those of many of our friends in the wider society. Yet these experiences of sharp separation are no longer the norm but the exception. They come as a shock in the context of our usually comfortable relations with our societies.

Our theological and experiential heritage of separation[3] in many ways does not fit the recent and current experience of Mennonites in North America. We have been tolerated, accepted, sometimes even lauded by our societies, for our disaster relief work, for example. We have become citizens, given the right (some would say the duty) to participate in political processes. Most of us vote, and some hold public office. Some of us have (not for the first time) become wealthy, part of the economic elite, and most have become comfortable. Many are highly educated and provide leadership in social service and educational institutions. Most of us no longer live in relatively isolated communities, and we count many people outside our faith community as coworkers, acquaintances, and friends.

In short, in significant ways we have made ourselves at home in Canada and the United States. We seldom, if ever, contemplate the need to migrate in order to practice our faith. And not only have we made ourselves at home; we have been welcomed to do so. Our nations have not pushed us to the margins but have embraced us as citizens. These changes are substantial, and for the most part I am grateful for them. I believe that a society that accepts people like us is a better society than one that does not. And I have no desire to live as a refugee.

Yet our current context poses challenges. I want to explore one such challenge here: how we appropriate, modify, or reject an understanding of our relationship to the wider society that seems wrong descriptively (we are no longer as separate as our tradition suggests) and perhaps is wrong normatively (should we really be as separate as the tradition seems to suggest?).

A second look at church and society

On more careful consideration, it is apparent that no church is ever completely separate from society, nor is it (unless it has sold out) completely at home in society. Different churches at different times choose different places to establish limits regarding their participation in society. For example, pacifists typically say no to fighting in wars, but cannot—unless they emigrate, or are jailed or executed—avoid all participation in their nations' war efforts. Nonpacifist Christians, at their best, say no to some kinds of fighting, and to all fighting in some wars, but say yes to some fighting in others. Although their views on divorce and remarriage have changed, most North American Christians agree on the permanence and sanctity of marriage, something that puts Christians in tension with a significant portion of our society. How countercultural a group's decisions seem depends on the behaviors their society expects.

In short, no Christian group's response to culture is all-or-nothing. We do not uncritically accept or reject culture as a whole. Rather, we accept parts of our society's culture (driving on the right side of the road, for example), reject other parts (pornography, for example), and debate others (the increasing acceptance of homosexuality, for example). And because our societies are pluralistic, we frequently find some people in "the world" who share some of our convictions. The lines between church and world are often not cleanly drawn.

We do not treat our culture as a monolith, to be accepted or rejected in its entirety. Nor should we. We are not called to be for or against culture; we are called to exercise discernment. We need to engage in discerning what in society is for and what is against the values of God's reign. We should not to seek to be against culture for its own sake. Because we are for God's reign, we need to use that loyalty as a measure of what in our culture we should be for, and what we are against.

How does this approach differ from that of other Christian groups? Mennonite tradition should cause us to be more wary of accepting the norms of societies than the traditions of Christendom would lead us to be. But the difference is one of degree, not of kind. The common task of all Christian groups is discernment. While I am convinced that our task (and problem)—discernment—is fundamentally that of people in other Christian traditions, I also believe that our inherited wariness about assuming the rightness of cultural norms is a valuable resource for us, for other Christians, and for our societies.

In comparison to other societies where we have lived, much about our North American societies represents a modest movement toward God's reign. Examples include freedom of religion, toleration of conscientious objection, freedom to participate in the larger society as citizens, educational and economic opportunities, governments somewhat more accountable to the population. Because of these good developments, we could easy become simply grateful for our society, uncritically "for" our culture.

While we should be grateful for the ways our societies inch toward the values of God's reign, our wariness about conflating society's values with those of God's reign should keep us mindful of the ways our culture's values hinder God's reign. Examples from the U.S. include: treatment of native peoples and racial minorities, welfare policies that undermine rather than undergird stable families, pursuit of individual satisfaction encouraged at the expense of family and social goods, enormous and growing economic disparities that undermine human dignity and (especially internationally) human survival, valuing American lives far above the lives of others (seen in our conduct of recent wars), valuing the wealth of stockholders above the well-being of people, entertainment that assumes sexual restraint and marriage should not be taken seriously, advertising that tells us that a new car or a new perfume will provide fulfillment, and the arrogance of power and righteousness that pervades political life in the United States—an arrogance that appropriates to itself godlike prerogatives. Some of these examples may apply in Canada, while others do not.

Our societies are diverse. In them we hear different voices on these matters. Yet many of the dominant voices contradict fundamental aspects of the Christian faith. We seldom hear about humility; loving our neighbors, let alone our enemies; self-sacrifice, except that of soldiers dying for their country; the dangers of mammon; the centrality of commitment even if it is costly; repentance and forgiveness, rather than tolerance at best and self-righteousness as worst; generosity and sharing instead of hoarding or spending on oneself; the need to look at God's world with eyes open to the needs of others, rather than just to our needs, or our nation's.

Pastors and moral discernment in congregations

If this analysis is accurate, a critical task of the church in its relationship to the wider society is an internal task. It is the task of moral discernment, of sorting out the values, messages, technologies, and practices that emerge within our societies, of seeking to determine which are in harmony with God's reign and which oppose it.[4] This discernment must also include determining what kinds of initiatives would be helpful within our societies; that is, the task is not only reactive.

This internal task of discernment may seem self-evident: how can we live in society and witness to it with Christian wisdom and integrity unless we have explored the implications of the gospel for the issues we face? Yet this internal work is often left undone, leaving us to respond reflexively, uncritically, to issues around us. How much serious moral reflection have we done as churches on matters of health care access and ethics, or uses of the Internet? Sometimes in not doing the task of discernment, we assume an almost automatic criticism of developments in our society; perhaps more frequently we assume an almost automatic acceptance of them.[5] Conscious discernment is an essential step in determining whether to be for or against culture, or where to be amid the variations and complications on the continuum between these extremes.

While such discernment is finally the work of the church as a whole, pastors play a crucial leadership role in it, as in other aspects of the church's life. This leadership role is most evident in the preaching and teaching functions of pastors. Perhaps the clearest way to define the calling of pastors in this regard is to call it *prophetic*. Pastors carry the special responsibility, duty, burden, and joy of being God's messengers.

Pastors exercise this role first and foremost in relation to the church. That is, the first task of the pastor as prophet is to bear God's message to God's people. To these prophets is given in a special way (though not the only or the ultimate way) the task of studying the gospel message, holding it before congregations, and exploring its implications for our life in, and witness to, society. Pastors are to connect the Christian message with the events and issues of the day, to suggest—perhaps indirectly by simply expositing a pertinent text, or perhaps quite baldly—the implications of the Christian gospel for the important issues facing people in the congregation and the society. The primary work of the pastor as prophet is to bring the Word to our attention in a way that makes it lively and relevant to the issues we face.[6]

This prophetic leadership is crucial if the church is to engage its surrounding culture critically (analytically, carefully, and thoughtfully, rather than reflexively). At the same time, it is the duty of gathered Christian believers to do the work of discerning. That is, pastors often initiate the discernment process and certainly should carry substantial weight in it, but discernment ought ultimately to be the work of the gathered community.

Pastors and the church's lived alternative

Authentic discernment of God's Word will, until God's reign fully comes, result in communities and individuals whose lives differ from their neighbors' in some significant ways. Not in all ways, of course, and not for the sake of being different, but because accepting God's grace, seeing and embracing God's vision for humankind, will make a difference in how we live. These lived differences, even apart from explicit efforts at witness to society, are critical to the churches' relation to and witness in society.

Two sets of biblical images describe how this witness happens. The images of a city on a hill and of a lamp on a lampstand illustrate witness that happens simply because of the visibility of what is seen. Simply by its nature, without special effort, it stands out, is seen, and bears witness. Examples of such witness might include not flying the national flag in Mennonite schools and churches; welcoming immigrants into our congregations; or more dramatically, wearing special clothing and maintaining a distinct way of life, as the Amish do.

In contrast, the biblical images of salt and leaven describe a witness made not by standing out, but by blending in. This common form of Christian witness and service includes the way people run their businesses, attend conscientiously to their tasks as employees, love their children, and care for their neighbors. In doing simple things in ordinary life in ways that are shaped by faith, Christians can be a powerful witness to and influence in society. This form of involvement can also shape society's institutions, as seen in Mennonite mental health professionals' impact on reshaping their field, or in the way

Mennonites' work in transformative justice has begun to permeate the criminal justice system. Christians who accept leadership in public life also follow this blending-in model.

Both of these models have strengths and dangers that cannot be explored here. The models differ significantly, yet they are similar in that the witness arises directly from our being, from who we are, rather than from our speaking. The role of the pastor with respect to these forms of witness is to nurture our being, helping us become people who live the gospel from the center of who we are, people who cannot help but witness because our character has a Christian shape. This pastoral role of shaping Christian character applies at the level of Christian communities corporately as well as to individual believers.

Pastors and the church's public witness

In addition to these forms of witness that arise from Christians' way of being, the church witnesses by speaking. But the word spoken by the church to the society has integrity and power only to the degree that it is accepted and lived by the members of the church. Perhaps the most frequent criticism of churches' efforts to speak to public policy questions in Washington is that the fine words spoken by church representatives are not matched by what political leaders know of church members' convictions and actions.[7] Thus, an intimate connection exists between the discerning process, the actual life of churches and members, and their explicit public witness. If they are to have credibility, public pronouncements must be integrally related to the church's life.

When churches are clear about what should be said in public, their pastors are their natural spokespeople, because our society assumes that it is pastors who represent their churches, and perhaps God, to society at large. This task of speaking on behalf of the church, of framing the message of the church for the listening society, is another part of the prophetic work of pastors.

How we frame these messages is important. I would counsel pastors speaking on behalf of churches to speak their first language, that of Christian faith and theology, rather than trying to adopt directly the language of public policy. Pastors and their churches are experts in understanding and attending to the language of Christian faith. They are not experts in the language of public policy and have no special standing when they enter into policy debates using that language. The primary witness in this context should be to the values and perspectives derived from faith in Jesus Christ, and should be spoken in this language. If translation is necessary, I'd suggest that normally someone other than the pastor do it.[8]

Conclusion

The matters discussed here are complex and controversial. My aim is not to settle the issues in one short essay, but to invite further reflection both on the relationship of church and society more generally, and on the role of the pastor in this context more specifically. Clearly, in North America Mennonite pastors play critical roles in the lives of our congregations, despite differences in understandings of their roles and their office. My hope is to foster discussion of one aspect of the larger question of how to understand and articulate what we mean by *pastor*.

Notes

[1] H. Richard Niebuhr in his famous book *Christ and Culture* (New York: Harper & Row, 1951) developed his typology of Christian perspectives on relations with the wider culture. He associates Mennonite perspectives with the view he labels "Christ against Culture." See Charles Scriven, *The Transformation of Culture: Christian Social Ethics after H. Richard Niebuhr* (Scottdale, Pa.: Herald Press, 1988); and Glen H. Stassen, D. M. Yeager, and John Howard Yoder, *Authentic Transformation: A New Vision of Christ and Culture* (Nashville: Abingdon Press, 1996), for criticisms of Niebuhr's arguments on this matter. In this essay I use the terms *society, culture,* and *world* synonymously, although for many purposes it is important to distinguish them.

[2] The distinction between *church* and *sect* as analytical, descriptive terms is made most influentially by Ernst Troeltsch in *The Social Teaching of the Christian Churches* (New York: Harper & Brothers, 1960).

[3] It is worth noting that there are significant differences within the Mennonite traditions North American Mennonites have received and developed, differences, for example, among various Mennonite "denominations," among Mennonites of varying cultural/national origins (Dutch/Russian vs. Swiss/South German vs. a wide variety of newer ethnic backgrounds), and differences between Canadian and U.S. Mennonites. Yet, when compared with other Christian traditions, Mennonite groups' commonalities warrant more emphasis than the differences.

[4] Even this is a vast oversimplification, of course. Many—perhaps most— practices, technologies, etc., are a mix of positive and negative. Consider the Internet, for example.

[5] The stance (accepting or rejecting) toward developments in our culture seems to vary with the differing theological, political, and ideological orientations of members and congregations; it often runs (uncomfortably, for me) close to the liberal/conservative fault lines in our society. This tendency itself is likely a powerful testimony to our acculturation into different parts of North American societies.

[6] See Ben Ollenburger's essay in this volume, "The Pastor As Prophet," pages 118-28.

[7] See for example, Keith Graber Miller, *Wise As Serpents, Innocent As Doves: American Mennonites Engage Washington* (Knoxville: University of Tennessee Press, 1996.); and Allen D. Hertzke, *Representing God in Washington: The Role of Religious Lobbies in the American Polity* (Knoxville: University of Tennessee Press, 1988).

[8] An example of my effort to speak to an issue of public debate (war) in a public setting from a specifically Christian theological perspective is found in Terry Nardin, ed., *The Ethics of War and Peace: Religious and Secular Perspectives* (Princeton: Princeton University Press, 1996).

10

"For God so loved"

Mary H. Schertz

The day after my father died, the two events being forever linked in my mind, a tragic incident took place at a factory in Goshen, Indiana. Robert Wissman, an employee of the firm, shot seven coworkers, killing the plant manager, and then killed himself. On that wintry December afternoon of carnage and terror, and in its aftermath, two Associated Mennonite Biblical Seminary graduates played key roles in ministering to the needs of the community. Clair Hochstetler is a chaplain at Goshen General Hospital where the wounded were taken. He not only provided immediate pastoral care for them and their families but also organized a team of twenty-nine other pastors to work with those affected by the tragedy in the days following the incident. Before the factory reopened he and another pastor conducted a spiritual cleansing for the facility and the workers, an experience about which Clair says, "The depths of hell and the heights of heaven were touched." Finally, after the cleansing, he was unable to shake an urgent inner nudge to contact Wissman's mother, an act of compassion that led to his involvement in Wissman's funeral service.[1]

Meanwhile, across town, Teresa Dutchersmith, a pastor of Faith Mennonite Church, realized that Robert Wissman and his mother and brothers were her backyard neighbors. Following a leading of the Spirit, she also went to introduce herself and visit the family. Out of that act of compassion a relationship developed that led to Teresa's officiating along with Clair at the Wissman funeral service at a local funeral home. During the difficult and sensitive service, she assured the family, "In the weeks ahead, anger, blame and suspicion may be directed at you, Bobby's family. But that won't separate you from the love God has for you through Jesus."[2]

At the seminary where Clair and Teresa received their training for ministry, we as their faculty expressed our gratitude, our respect, and yes, even our pride in how these former students had conducted themselves. And we expressed faint surprise. Surprise not because our students had comported themselves with such excellence—we expected no less!—but surprise because the community had turned to Mennonite ministers to lead them in such a time, and furthermore, had recognized and named the significance of that leadership. We normally think of ourselves as training ministers for the church, not the public arena. But in this crisis, rampant with fear and blame, Mennonite ministers led the community through the valley. Our faculty surprise was a telling mark of where we as a denominational seminary are with respect to the question of ministry as public service.

Our denominational reluctance to understand public leadership as part of ministry is no doubt rooted in the complex history of our ecclesiology and spirituality. Malinda Berry, yet another AMBS alum, suggests additionally that the problem is in essence a failure of love, a failure that is also rooted in our sociology, a consequence of privilege. She writes:

> The Civil Rights Movement was all about struggling for Black liberation. All that organizing and agitating was about more than getting the right to vote or sit down at a lunch counter in the South. It was about redeeming the soul of a nation. As Mennonites, we tend to think it is folly to presume that our nation has a soul and that it can experience God's redemption. But when you are an African American or other disenfranchised member of the society, you have to believe such a thing is possible if you are going to live fully. The alternative to this view of the state is nationalism, and its limitations are obvious.[3]

In this proclivity to look inward rather than outward, to be content with private oratory and public silence, we Mennonites are hardly alone. Since the civil rights movement, clergy involvement in the public forum has been mostly evident in the dubious contribution of the political far right. In a survey conducted by Auburn Seminary's Center for the Study of Theological Education, a university dean made this poignant comment: "Clergy are not public leaders. They don't convene the forums for public conversation, and they're not in the forefront of articulating issues. . . . Religious leaders in this town helped lead the civil rights movement. . . . I don't know what the issue is, but if it came up today, those religious leaders do not appear to be at the table, and they certainly are not leading the conversation."[4]

The Auburn Center study and the actions and words of these AMBS graduates may have an important message about "the heart of the matter" for us as Mennonite theological educators. What these younger leaders seem to be showing us and telling us is that we do not have to fail in love this way. Despite a theology of ministry that lacks a concept of public service, they are acting and speaking not only as the leaders of the church but as leaders in the public arena. They are acting and speaking not only as people concerned for the soul of the church but also as people concerned for the soul of the nation. As we as a people of God stand at the threshold of this new century, can we afford to follow our historical proclivities, the tendencies of our ecclesiology? Is God perhaps calling us to rethink our relationship to the world as we ponder just what a minister of the church should be, know, and do? Is God perhaps calling us to love the world in a new way?

The shepherd of the flock

In the Mennonite denomination generally and also at AMBS, we have tended to think of the pastor as a shepherd of the flock. The metaphor of 1 Peter 5, with its warning about the roaring lion prowling outside the fold, exerts a strong pull on our ministerial imagination. Pastors are caregivers for the congregation; they spend their time and energy ministering to those who have made a decision to be a part of the body of Christ, and to their families. Certainly, mission and outreach have been an integral part of that ministry—both from the perspective of the pastor and from the perspective of a congregation as a whole. But that mission and outreach have been concentrated on gathering in: gathering the unchurched into the congregation, gathering the lost into the body of Christ. We have thought and done less in the realm of going out, of meandering the highways and the byways to serve in ministry with those outside the walls of our church buildings as the need arises.

The nurture of the congregation and the mission to the lost are indeed vital concerns of the church. But what I want to suggest here is that in order to minister effectively in the church, and in order to fulfill the mission of the church to the lost, the pastor must also have a sense of public responsibility, a love for the world. Our theology of ministry should not only make room for but should mandate that sense of responsibility. I believe that the vitality of what we do and say on the village square has a direct bearing on the integrity of our lives within our houses of God. We should emulate Paul, who in defending himself before King Agrippa could say that "none of these things has escaped [the king's] notice, for this was not done in a corner" (Acts 26:26). Our formation of ministers ought to incorporate an expectation that public service and participation in public discourse is the norm rather than the exception. We ought to inspire our pastors in training to consider their important roles as lovers of their communities and their nations.

Coming out of the corner

It is tempting, upon recognizing a gap in our own tradition of theology and service, to reach for help from some other tradition. The Catholic idea of parish, for instance, might have something to offer us in its sense of the congregation's geographical terrain, and in the priest's responsibility for all who live in that area, whether or not they come to church. Perhaps we need to look again, more empathically, at the Lutheran version of a two-kingdom theology. Perhaps even the "moral majority," despite its selfish politics, has something to offer in its bold assurance that Christians should speak to national and community issues from a faith perspective.

I believe, though, that a concept of the ministry as public service, if it is to have authenticity and integrity, must grow out of our own Mennonite ecclesiology and our own Mennonite spirituality. I also believe that—despite the seeming disinterest in the *world* sometimes fostered by our tradition of nonconformity and our emphasis on the visible church—just such a ministry as public witness and service is integral to Anabaptist-Mennonite ecclesiology and spirituality. Finally, I believe that the public arena needs and would benefit from Anabaptist Mennonite pastors who offer a perspective on its concerns and participate in its discourse about our common life in the world God created.

In formulating a theology of ministry that includes concern for the welfare of the city, we might well draw upon our longstanding and excellent tradition of service more generally. Despite our entrenched notions about separation from the world, not being conformed to the world, oriented to the church rather than the world, we have not escaped or avoided responsibility in the world. Natural disasters, wars and the people they displace, famines and epidemics have, at least in the last hundred years, aroused us from our internal preoccupations to become involved in meeting needs. People all over North America and around the world can testify to the work of Mennonite Disaster Service and Mennonite Central Committee. Less obviously, but significantly, people locally and globally can testify to the aid they have received from Mennonite congregations who have responded to needs in the fields of mental health, day care, and housing, among others.

What is necessary for a theology of ministry as public service is to extend our exemplary response beyond crisis and material need. I think we need a broader and more sustained public presence and voice, a willingness to get involved in the problems, celebrations, and discourse of our communities when no particular crisis demands our attention. In those activities we have had little involvement, and what participation we have had has sometimes been questioned, debated, or simply denounced as "worldly."

One source of that criticism lies in a division among us about where our true obedience lies. We can hardly ask Mennonite pastors and other church leaders to take a public role with confidence if we as a people are not sure we should be involved in public life. Defining ministry as not only ministry with, in, and to a congregation but in, with, and to a community and a world is not possible until and unless we are willing to work toward resolution of our insecurity about how we relate to the world.

An issue of the Mennonite Central Committee *Washington Memo* dealt with Mennonites' differing views of the nation. Although these views have been expressed many times over the years in greater depth and detail, the memo's concise formulations are useful. The issue posed the question in terms of kingdom(s) and ethic(s). Lois Barrett represented the "two kingdoms/one ethical standard" view, and Lindsey Robinson represented the "two kingdoms/two ethical standards" view.

Barrett claims that the standard of behavior that God requires of the church is also the standard that God has for nation states. The way of Jesus is the way that "organizations, systems, governments, and powers should be called to move." Furthermore, the "only Christian nation is the church of Jesus Christ."[5] Barrett's view, one shared by many Mennonites, allows for and even demands a witness to the state, a voice in the public forum. But the aim of the witness is to draw the state into the church, to unite all under the sovereignty of Christ. This time-honored view does not envision a participation in the activity of the state for the sake of the soul of the nation. It does not envision a ministry in the state for the sake of that state's well-being and vitality.

Lindsey Robinson represents another view of the state. He is no less opposed to war than Barrett. But he believes, in contrast to Barrett, that while Jesus' teaching and example prohibit Christians from participating in war, the state has a responsibility to maintain order and protect its citizens from those who seek the state's destruction. The New Testament ethic of love and nonviolence is not for all people everywhere. The state, composed of nonbelievers, is ordained by God for certain civic responsibilities, including the use, if necessary, of lethal violence.[6] There is a place for public witness in this view of the state. Speaking to the leaders of the nation, encouraging them to find less violent ways to resolve issues, and reminding the state of its God-ordained responsibilities are legitimate avenues of Christian witness. But the state is essentially without soul—our witness is to check its proclivities toward excess rather than to nurture its spirit.

At the seminary in Elkhart, the ethos of the faculty lies somewhere within these two views, with a larger allegiance to the two kingdom/one ethic position (Lois Barrett is, after all, on our faculty), in part because of the lingering and pervasive influence of John Howard Yoder. But I am unsure that either of these two views is helping us be true and faithful in our pastoral obedience for the time and place where we find ourselves. What these two typical Mennonite views both lack is a concern for the welfare of the soul of the nation itself, to use Malinda Berry's term. Neither of the two views envisions a participation in the activity of the state for the sake of the soul of the state. The question for ministry is whether either of these views is adequate for the challenges that lay ahead for the church of the twenty-first century.

God so loved the world

A better way might be to think of one kingdom, one church, and two modes of obedience. Ulrich Luz, in the conclusion of his commentary on the Sermon on the Mount, considers the questions of praxis in ways that I find helpful in thinking about Mennonite ministry as public service. In his view, "For the evangelist Matthew there is no understanding of the Sermon on the Mount which is separated from praxis."[7] This statement fits well with a traditional Mennonite understanding of the Sermon on the Mount, yet Luz is critical of Anabaptist interpretations of the sermon, as well as those of other Reformers. The Reformed tradition has, in its refusal "to make the Sermon on the Mount the vision and standard for a future shape of the *church,* "become "saltless salt."[8] But the Anabaptist model of practicing the sermon, he charges, has led us "for the sake of the purity of the gospel, to limit the Sermon on the Mount to the Christian's inner realm and to leave secular responsibility to others."[9]

In Luz's opinion, a true reading of the Sermon on the Mount would call not only all churches but also all communities to demonstrate obedience to the will of the Father. That statement is remarkable—not unlike some of the more radical things Mennonites have said, but with a crucial difference. As a denomination we have seen the world as a bleak place, a godless place. We have seen it as a mission field and considered ourselves responsible to bring the light of Christ to it, our message of salvation being its only real hope. That view may have impressed upon us our responsibility, given us a sense of urgency, but it is not quite the truth. At least as Luz sees it, and in this I think he is more biblical than we have been, the truth is that God is already active in the world, loving it, providing for it, offering grace, and holding out hope. As the church, we need to be alive in the world, discerning God at work and joining in as partners. In the church, as the church, believers working together with God can build the body of Christ strong and true. That is our direct obedience and a worthy, honorable purpose. In the world, believers can work together with nonbelievers wherever we discern God at work. That is our indirect obedience and also a worthy, honorable purpose.

What we as a denomination have failed to grasp, our seminary graduates have nevertheless sometimes glimpsed. God is in love with the world, with its towns, counties, states, nations. The world has a soul. It is created by God and God is in love with it. The Bible witnesses to this reality time and time again, from the beginning in Genesis to the eschaton in Revelation. The vision is of a world created by God where people love each other and worship God. The biblical story is nothing less than the narrative of this often unrequited, neglected, tromped-upon, undeserved, but forever freely offered love.

The idea of pastor as community leader stretches us beyond our comfort zone. For the shepherd of the flock to also be the orator and actor for the will of the Father in public life in our villages and cities is a notion that seems fraught with danger. To begin to love the world as God does and to minister in it as Jesus did will require some perceptual adjustments. God's reality is messier than we would like. The church cannot quite so neatly be equated with God's kingdom. The world cannot quite so neatly be characterized as bleak and godless.

We fear losing focus, losing the purity of our witness, losing our distinctiveness as the people of God. We get caught in the timeless tension between holiness and love. Perhaps there is no human way of living with the tension without losing our balance. Perhaps we are doomed, as the collectives of faith known as denominations, to fall onto one side or another of that uneasy partnership.

But on the other hand, perhaps not. Perhaps the unfaithfulness for which most of us are culpable is not trying hard enough to be both holy and loving as God is holy and loving. I suspect that if we are to claim a public response to public affairs as part of our God-given responsibility as pastors, we may need to honor a particular relinquishment. We may need to let go of the notion that we know what holiness and love are. We may need to take courage in hand and dare to step out into the world that God loves, the world in which the holy one is at work, and see what happens to us as pastors in the world. Our truest nonconformity may not be in withholding ourselves from the world but in loving it as God loves it.

Such a loving and public pastoral role in community life will necessarily take on as many shapes and colors as there are Mennonite pastors willing to assume it. One grace of the pastorate, although we have not always recognized it, is the wealth of styles that individuals bring to their call. There is no single kind of pastor, no one personality that must fulfill that role. But there are characteristics of Mennonite pastoral leadership, well-honed pastoral gifts among us, for which our communities are quite literally dying.

Peace and justice

Other denominations and even our own communities are often frustrated by our lack of public leadership on issues of peace and justice. I was at the Catholic-Mennonite dialogue at St. John's University in Minnesota in July 2002. There our Catholic brothers and sisters said repeatedly that they are looking, sometimes in vain, for witness out of the breadth and depth of our experience with conscientious objection to war and making peace. It is difficult for them to understand why we have not been more vocal, more present, either in ecumenical discussions about these topics or in the communities in which we serve. Why aren't we sharing what we have learned over the centuries about living and articulating the peace witness? Why do we need to be asked? Why do we wait for invitations to speak and be present?

Community as community

I admit that I hesitate, in light of our history of church splits over the years, to claim that we have anything much to offer our political and social communities about community. But perhaps that is exactly why we must begin to speak, write, and act in behalf of the communities in which we live, the communities for which we care and in which we have a stake. The ecclesial fractures in which we have participated, to which we have contributed, and by which we have been wounded may be one of the gifts we have to offer our civic communities. Ecclesial fractures are not good, any more than suffering is good. But to be honest about our failures, while honoring in word and deed our commitment to community despite the odds, might well be the most powerful witness we can make to a world hungry for human connection and meaningful relationships.

It is no surprise that the work of peace and justice and the work of community are frequently one and the same. Those of us in the historic peace church tradition know only too well that nonresistance, nonviolent resistance, and pacifism are not universally embraced. On the other hand, violence in our schools is a problem with which most parents are concerned. Crime on the streets, gangs, drugs—all the civic problems that form the content of political speeches—are communal problems to which a peace and justice perspective can and should speak. Environmental issues, the quality of our water and food supplies, are also common concerns and concerns which we as people of peace and justice, people of community, people of Christ, can address.

Joy and light

Last, but by no means least, in our public ministries we can be people of joy, characterized by that certain lightness of being of the people who belong to the kingdom of God. The text that my father chose for his funeral sermon was the passage in which Jesus says he came that we might have life and have it abundantly. The day his pastor preached from this text in honor of my father, the church was full not only with the people of the church but also with the people of the community—neighboring farmers, car mechanics, our mail carrier. Their presence was a witness to the way he lived out his verse, in joy and light.

Clair Hochstetler, in addition to being a chaplain, is a clown and a juggler. He sees his work, in both roles, as leading people to the heart of God.[10] The God in love with the world came to us in Jesus so that we might have abundant life, and share it with the world that is the object of God's love.

Advent 2002

The evening of the first anniversary of my father's death and the tragic factory shooting in Goshen was dark and gloomy, as only evenings in northern Indiana can be. I drove along back country roads enjoying the Christmas lights, despite their liturgical incorrectness and the fact that they sometimes reflect a crass commercialization of Christ's birth. But as I turned on Benham Avenue and drove past the seminary, all was dark. My beloved chapel sat huddled with its back to the world, no light visible. It is such a sacred and joyous place for me, a place where I have been embraced with a warm and passionate spirituality. My truest home, it breathes with a richness that I take utterly for granted, but that sometimes still, after all these years, renders me mute with awe, gratitude, and the raw assurance of God's presence.

That dark Advent evening, however, it seemed to project something less than the abundant life to which my father's life was a witness. I wanted to turn it around and light it up, to let it embrace

Benham Avenue with the kingdom reality I knew it held within it in extravagance.

I long for the day when we can turn and embrace the world, loving it as God loves it and opening ourselves to ministry as public service.

Notes

[1] Leanne Phillips, "Hospital chaplain looks for hope in crisis," *The Goshen News,* December 15, 2001.

[2] Steph Davis, "'Person who did this terrible thing—was not Bobby,'" *The Elkhart Truth,* December 12, 2001.

[3] Malinda Berry, "On Racism, Mennonite Politics, and Liberation (Words We Don't Like to Hear)," *Vision: A Journal for Church and Theology* 3 (fall 2002): 23.

[4] Elizabeth Lynn and Barbara G. Wheeler, "Missing Connections: Public Perceptions of Theological Education and Religious Leadership," *Auburn Studies* 6 (September 1999): 7. For continued debate of the topic, see also *Theological Education* 38, no. 1 (2001), an issue devoted to "Public Character in Action: Patterns and Possibilities."

[5] Lois Barrett, "Does God Have Two Standards?" *Washington Memo* 34, no. 5 (September-October 2002), 6.

[6] Lindsey Robinson, "God's Purpose for the State," *Washington Memo* 34, no. 5 (September-October 2002), 7.

[7] Ulrich Luz, *Matthew 1–7: A Commentary* (Minneapolis: Augsburg Fortress, 1989), 456; Luz's italics.

[8] Ibid., 457.

[9] Ibid., 459.

[10] Phillips, "Hospital chaplain looks for hope," December 15, 2001.

11

The pastor as healer

Willard M. Swartley

A key concern in pastoral ministry these days is whether the identity of the pastor rests primarily in the office or in the function of the pastoral role. Put another way, how does pastoral identity develop, from the nascent stage to full-orbed self-understanding? Does it develop from conferred authority by church leadership or by doing deeds of ministry? Or is it as a result of spiritual formation that one becomes a pastoral person, and is so recognized by the congregation and the church and society more broadly? This matter in not easily resolved, but it seems likely that a vital interplay of these factors is at work in making a person a pastor.

On this and other dimensions of pastoral ministry the patterns and understandings of the early church are instructive. Carl Volz's study, *Pastoral Life and Practice in the Early Church,* helpfully presents the profile of the pastor. It shows clearly the many dimensions of the office and task.[1] Volz's section on pastoral life is especially illuminating. He refers to a brief treatise, *Pastoral Rule,* by Gregory I, bishop of Rome. After listing the necessary virtues of the pastor, Volz sums up Gregory's emphasis: "A pastor whose life does not embody his teaching cannot expect any parishioner to take his advice seriously."[2] Drawing from contributions in the *Didascalia Apostolorum* (c. 200-225), and by Jerome and Chrysostom, Volz writes: "The pastoral vocation included the ontological dimension—that is, [the pastor] was called to be someone as well as to do some things, . . . to represent Christ to the people, and as Christ's representative, to exemplify Christlike virtues."[3] Gregory believed practice of spiritual disciplines is necessary to achieving this goal; he held that spiritual formation is as important as what the pastor does in ministerial duties of service to the people.

Against the background of attempts to understand the pastoral office and pastoral tasks, it is useful to consider an aspect of the pastoral identity in the early church that we rarely speak of now in shaping pastoral leaders, the identity of healer. Granted, God is the ultimate healer, and people are healers only derivatively, as they represent the divine healer. But even this point has had low profile in pastoral formation, except perhaps in the formation of pastoral counselors.

New Testament foundations

One of the few agreements among historical Jesus scholars, in their spate of publications in the last third of the twentieth century, is that Jesus performed miracles of healing and exorcisms. A third of Mark's Gospel is devoted to this theme, and Luke also accentuates it.[4] But the issue is even deeper, for it involves Jesus' identity. In his mission to herald God's reign come and coming, he did not simply do the work of healing; his identity was that of a healer. Because he was what he was as the visible reflection of God his Father, he did these deeds and commanded his disciples to do the same (Matt. 9:35–10:1; Mark 3:14-15; 6:7-13; Luke 9:1-6; 10:5-11, 17). The Gospel narratives present this ministry as intrinsic to the gospel and to Jesus' identity and mission. When John the Baptist sought assurance that Jesus was the one expected, whose coming John announced, Jesus' answer establishes his identity by pointing specifically to his deeds of healing (Luke 7:18-23).

Two features of New Testament Scripture compel us to regard this healing ministry as an endowment not limited to Jesus as God's Son, or as a power intended only for the apostles. First, the texts cited above clearly indicate that Jesus commanded the healing ministry. The Great Commission, which we have understood to apply to Jesus' followers in all ages, instructs his disciples to "obey everything that I have commanded you" (Matt. 28:20). Second, the book of Acts demonstrates that the disciples did in fact continue this ministry, and that it was a major factor in the growth of the early church. Peter's healing at the Beautiful Gate of the man lame from birth, recorded in Acts 3–4, set the course of action for the disciples after Pentecost. The healing manifested the power of "the name of Jesus."

In Acts Luke sums up Jesus' ministry as "preaching peace" and going about "doing good and healing all who were oppressed by the devil, for God was with him" (10:36-38). Striking also is Luke's portrayal of the power of the gospel mission as victory over magic, sorcery, and demonic power in the context of opposing spiritual realities of the Greco-Roman world.[5] The four key stories are Philip's and then the apostles' encounters with Simon Magus in Samaria (chap. 8); Paul's encounter with Elymas the magician in Salamis, Cyprus (chap. 13); Paul's exorcism of a spirit of divination in a slave girl in Macedonia (chap. 16); and the gospel's confrontation of sorcery and magical arts in Ephesus (chap. 19). The first three encounters occur as the kingdom gospel is presented in a new geographical area, and the last episode in Ephesus is a grand finale to Paul's missionary work before he heads for Jerusalem. Luke uses these dramatic encounters as structural markers in the gospel's advance. They show that the gospel presents sovereign claims of a sovereign Lord, and other rival magical powers that cater in healing must give way before the gospel of Jesus Christ.

Healing and exorcism need to be distinguished from each other. Healing is the broader term; exorcism is a specific form of healing. In the biblical narrative and in the early church (of the second to fourth centuries) the two regularly occur together, as in the description of Philip's ministry in Samaria in Acts 8:7.

In Paul's letters healing is identified as one of the gifts of the Spirit *(pneumatikoi)*. In 1 Corinthians 12:8-10 Paul mentions both healing *(charismata iamatōn)* and discernment of spirits *(diakriseis pneumatōn)*. The summary of his discussion (vv. 28-30) refers twice to the gift of healing, but the gift of discerning the spirits is not mentioned. While Acts narrates healing miracles of Paul, Paul himself does not mention them in his letters. He does speak of his own infirmity, which he identifies as "a messenger of Satan to torment me." He "appealed to the Lord about this" three times, but the Lord's answer was "My grace is sufficient for you, for power is made perfect in weakness" (2 Cor. 12:7-9). This passage shows that healing does not occur in all cases, even for an apostle. This datum is especially surprising because Paul understands the affliction to be linked to an attack by a messenger *(angelos)* from Satan. In Philippians 2:25-27 Paul mentions Epaphroditus, who had been "so ill that he nearly died." Then Paul says that "God had mercy on Epaphroditus." Paul does not mention miraculous healing but seems to imply a natural process of recovery.

These glimpses into sickness and healing in Paul's letters are significant because they temper the many New Testament reports of miraculous healings with another reality, that of the ordinary experience of sickness or affliction that does not yield to miraculous cure. Nonetheless, Paul's reference to "works of healing" as a charism in the church that serves the health of the whole community, taken together with the witness of the Gospels, Acts, and the early church, leads us to regard healing ministries in the church as an important dimension of ministry and pastoral leadership in the congregation.

The New Testament text most frequently used for ongoing healing ministry in the church is James 5:14-15: "Are any among you sick? They should call for the elders of the church and have them pray over them, anointing them with oil in the name of the Lord. The prayer of faith will save the sick, and the Lord will raise them up; and anyone who has committed sins will be forgiven." This text has provided the basis for the church's practice of various forms of healing ministry. It is instructive to take a brief historical look at these practices of the church.

Historical considerations

Among the many sources in the church fathers that speak of the healing ministry of the church are several from Irenaeus and Origen. Denouncing the Gnostics, Irenaeus (120-200 C.E.) writes, "For they can neither confer sight on the blind, nor hearing on the deaf, nor chase away all sorts of demons. . . . And so far are they from being able to raise the dead, as the Lord raised them, and the apostles by means of prayer, and as among the brotherhood oftentimes when necessity has arisen."[6]

Later Irenaeus speaks of the gifts of grace given to the disciples and the church, by which some drive out evil spirits, others "heal those who are sick by laying on of their hands and make them whole."[7] Again he notes that healing is a mark of the true church; the leaders of the Gnostic sects lack such powers. Unlike the Gnostic heretics, Christ's true followers have the name of the Lord Jesus Christ, who lived among humans as a human and who made all things; the true church also possesses the gifts of the Spirit.

Origen (185-254 C.E.) defends Christian belief against the pagans by pointing to healing and exorcist powers in the faith community: "There are still preserved among Christians traces of the Holy Spirit which appeared in the form of a dove. They expel evil spirits and perform many cures and foresee certain events according to the will of the Logos. . . . The name of Jesus Christ can still remove distractions from the minds of men, expel demons, and also take away diseases."[8]

Others associated with the healing tradition in the early church are Gregory Thaumaturgus ("wonder-worker"), whose work is described by Basil and Gregory of Nyssa. Martin of Tours was also known for his many healings.[9]

Exorcism played an important role in the early church. Everett Ferguson observes, regarding the early church's missionary success in the first three centuries, that "the most notable mark of the early church was its ability to deal with the spirit world in the Roman Empire. . . . I am persuaded that an important factor in the Christian's success in the Roman world was the promise which it made of deliverance from demons."[10]

Peter Brown in his study of the age of Augustine concurs that "from the New Testament onwards, the Christian mission was a mission of 'driving out' demons. Martyrdom, and later asceticism, was a 'spiritual prize fight' with the demons. The bishop's office was 'to tread down Satan under his feet.' Full membership of the Christian Church, by baptism, was preceded by drastic exorcisms. . . . The Church was the community for whom Satan had been bound: his limitless powers had been bridled to permit the triumph of the Gospel; more immediately, the practicing Christian gained immunity from sorcery."[11]

Ferguson further observes that the early church fathers regarded Jesus' death and resurrection as the defeat of Satan.[12] "By reason of . . . baptism," Irenaeus writes, "Christians are delivered from the power of demons and have been identified with Christ." Precisely on this point the early church knew what we have forgotten. In many parts of the early church Christians regarded baptism as a person's exorcism. People came to the gospel from paganism, from being under the spell of the demons of the pagan religions. In the rite of baptism demon powers were expelled.

Alan Kreider's recent study confirms this portrait. Concurring with Ramsay McMullen, Kreider says that exorcism was the chief factor in conversion to Christianity; it was power over evil spirits that attracted people from the pagan world. Kreider cites many sources from the fathers, including an account of an exorcism reported by

Origen, who notes that "things like this lead many people to be converted to God, many to reform themselves, many to come to the faith."[13]

Along with the miracle tradition of healing in the early church, another equally significant tradition of care for the sick and dying flourished. Even the harshest critics of the early church admired its care of the sick and the poor, including those left on the streets to die. The church developed a massive "social security" program; in C.E. 251 the church in Rome had 1,500 widows and poor people on its roll for support.[14] This tradition represents the ongoing task and ordinary reality of the church's healing mission.

During the Medieval and Reformation periods the healing and exorcist ministries became more liturgical in expression, and continued to be practiced in some parts of the Western and Eastern churches.[15] The waning of the earlier spiritual vitality and the institutionalization of Christianity contributed to this shift toward a sacramental approach to healing ministry, although the charismatic element was never entirely lost.

Thomas Aquinas's understanding of healing reduced it to a natural process.[16] The Enlightenment and the rise of modern science made the church's healing ministry even more quiescent. Only recently, partly under the influence of pentecostal and charismatic traditions, has healing again risen to prominence in the church. This change is evident in virtually all traditions, from Roman Catholic to evangelical. As N. T. Wright writes, "Recent times have seen a remarkable resurgence of a whole range of healing ministries. Twenty years ago, I doubt if you could have found a single book on, say, the healing of memories. Today there is likely to be a whole section in the average Christian bookshop, bringing together insights and experiences from an astonishingly wide range of people—monks, psychiatrists, lay workers, Orthodox, and Roman Catholics as well as Protestants and evangelicals."[17]

The present challenge

What is the import of this brief review of healing in the New Testament and church history for the identity and role of the pastor today? I doubt that search committees ask prospective pastors whether they are healers. Congregations in conflict may want leaders who can aid healing, and those who seek counseling for emotional wounds may need ministers able to bring healing, but I suspect that the question "Are you a healer?" rarely surfaces in interviews of pastoral candidates.

Illness is present in almost every congregation almost all the time, and many prayer requests during sharing time in our Sunday services are for those who are ill. But still our pastors are not known primarily as healers of physical or mental illness. In fact people seeking help with emotional problems are often referred to pastoral counselors and psychiatric centers. The gap between the early church leader as healer and the primary identity and role of pastors today beckons us to assess this matter theologically and pastorally.

It is true that more congregations today conduct services for healing than was the case thirty years ago. At the end of Sunday morning worship every six weeks or so the pastors and elders of my congregation offer anointing and prayers of healing to anyone who comes forward. At our churchwide assembly in 1993 I led a seminar on healing with Duane Beck, our pastor at Belmont Mennonite Church, and the room was filled to capacity with two hundred people. In that session we learned that the congregations represented were addressing healing in a variety of ways, including a twelve-step healing group, a men's group taking up study and discussion of healing, a women's retreat on the healing dimensions of prayer, a Sunday morning sermon series on healing, mediation efforts focused on healing, Stephen ministries, a Sunday evening anointing service, and anointing the sick.

A biblical theology to guide a healing ministry

On occasions when I have presented Bible studies on healing to pastors, it has become evident to me that they are involved in healing ministry and want to learn more about it both theologically and practically. What follows are seven theses that I believe describe a biblical theology capable of guiding us in the ministry of healing.

God intends shalom and community for humanity, but sin and Satan are at work against us and against God's intentions for us.

We live in a marvelous, mysterious world created by God. We know that this world has been made by an awesome God who enthralls us with vast stretches of space containing innumerable galaxies, and with the intricacies of DNA. Day by day we experience delights to the eye, ear, smell, taste, and touch, and when life is functioning normally we say, "Yes, this world is very good." When all is well we experience health, and we claim it as a gift from God.

But when illness strikes, we may feel abandoned by God. We may pray for healing, and sometimes we do not know how to pray. Sometimes our prayers are miraculously answered, but often they are not—not in the way we would like. We may have doubts about God's good world and wonder who or what else is playing in this drama of history to subvert health.

God is God, and we are weak, mortal, frail creatures.

Biblical creation theology declares that humans are *adam*, made from the ground *(adamah)*. Our health is therefore linked to the earth, and we must accept our mortality and finitude. Wanting to be "like God" and thus denying or evading our mortality perpetuates the error of the fall. As a result of our human disobedience, we resist letting God be God. Humans fail to accept their creaturely dependence upon God as creator. Accepting our creaturehood is an essential part of human health.

The psalms emphasize this dimension of our human existence. Psalms 90 and 103 acknowledge that human life is frail and brief. In Psalm 39 the psalmist tells God, "Let me know how fleeting my life is. . . . I am your passing guest, . . . like all my forebears (vv. 4b, 12b)." The logic of these verses appears to be that since the psalmist is a sojourner, it is imperative that God "hear my prayer . . . that I may smile again, before I depart."

Illness puts us in a quandary before God, because it interrupts and challenges our experience of God's good world.

The psalms especially lead us in voicing our cries to God in the face of this distressing disruption of our experience of God's world as good. At least a dozen psalms, in part or in full, fit into this thematic category. The best known healing psalms are 6, 30, and 88. These psalms bare the soul to God in prayer. As C. S. Lewis said, "I pray because I need to. I pray not to change God but to change myself." Similarly, in these psalms the psalmist cries to the Lord because he needs to; there is no other to turn to. Medical resources were rare, and not recognized as a source for healing. Rather, God was the healer (Exod. 15:26).

In Psalm 30 the healed person is free to praise and thank God in an unhindered way. The psalm traverses three stages of experience: original shalom (v. 6), the disorientation of sickness and cry for help and healing (vv. 2, 8-10), and restoration to "new life" in which "you have turned my mourning into dancing, . . . so that my soul may praise you and not be silent" (vv. 3, 10-12).

In our suffering God is not absent but is present in love.

These four voices from Scripture enunciate a positive function of suffering: From Jeremiah we learn that all sufferers are not sinners; some are suffering saints. From Habbakuk we learn that some sufferers are worshiping saints. From Job we learn that the righteous sufferer is a friend of God. And from Isaiah we learn that a sufferer can also be a savior. At the deepest level, suffering can endear one to the heart of God, for God hears the cry of the sufferer. These lines from *Shadowlands*, a film about C. S. Lewis, express it well: "God's love includes the gift of suffering"; "pain is part of the happiness; it's all in the deal."

Jesus is healer-savior and leads us in faith and prayer.

In *Jesus, a New Vision,* Marcus Borg seeks to sketch a historical portrait of Jesus. He writes that "during his lifetime [Jesus] was known primarily as a healer and exorcist. People flocked to him, drawn by his wonder-working reputation, as the gospels report again and again: 'they brought to him all who were sick or possessed with demons. And the whole city was gathered together at the door'; as a healer, 'His fame spread, and great crowds followed him'; 'People came to him from every quarter.'"[18]

In some cases in the Gospels faith plays a significant role in a healing. For example, the woman whose hemorrhaging is cured alone of all the people in Mark's Gospel is commended for her faith. Her faith contrasts to the disciples' lack of faith (4:40) and the unbelief of those in Jesus' hometown (6:1-6). Bounded by this segmental inclusio of no faith, the response of the woman is thrown into bold relief. In some other healings also, faith is called forth by Jesus either from the one to be healed or from those attending to the infirm person.

Are Jesus' healings "faith healings"? An answer to this question is not simple, because our modern conceptions of the relation between the physical/material worlds and the spiritual worlds do not mesh well with those of people in the first century. The matter is further complicated by Calvinist and Arminian differences over the origin and nature of faith. If faith is seen as an act of the human will, conjured up by human effort, then no, the healings are not faith healings. If faith is seen as gift of God apart from the gospel message that awakens faith, then the answer is again no, the healings are not faith healings. But if faith is seen as openness to divine presence in humble trust, then yes, these are faith healings. For then it is Jesus himself whom the believing one embraces as mediating the divine presence, and the power for healing is free to do its work. The issue of faith in the Gospels is intertwined with acceptance of Jesus as messianic revealer of the kingdom (compare, for example, Mark 6:1-6 and 5:34-36).

This connection between faith and acceptance of Jesus as messianic revealer of the reign of God also provides a context for valuing miracles as a ministry of the church. Miracles do not happen in accord with some formula of human faith. Rather, miracles are given, as bestowals of the kingdom's presence exalting Jesus Christ. For those whose views of reality are not fenced in by rationalistic walls that separate the material from the spiritual, an openness to the presence of the spiritual may, and because God is gracious, often will be answered by special signs of the kingdom—wonders, mighty works, call them miracles, if you will—which point to Jesus Christ as God's mender of creation. Prayer, inspired by Spirit-power and in the name of Jesus, connects us to the God from whom all blessing flow. Hence, prayer is essential if one is to have a disposition open to God's healing as sign of kingdom presence. Prayer also provides empowerment to endure suffering in hope of the ultimate healing.

The Spirit too is healer and is the divine pledge of complete healing.
A key New Testament perspective is that believers share in the sufferings of the present aeon. Indeed, all creation has been groaning, waiting with eager longing for God's final redeeming, healing work in behalf of those bearing the Christian hope. God's children await the redemption of their bodies (Rom. 8:18-23), which correlates with God's defeat of the last enemy, death (1 Cor. 15:26, 57-58).

The redemption of the body is based on the central Christian belief of resurrection from the dead. In uniting with Christ's death and resurrection in baptism, believers receive the Holy Spirit as a down-payment for final redemption. As long as this temporal tension is a part of our salvation, we share in the groaning and sufferings, waiting in hope. As Christiaan Beker puts it, "In their own bodies, Christians live existentially the tension of their present uncompleted existence in solidarity with an unredeemed creation, and they must therefore yearn for the consummation of the resurrection, which is nothing but God's triumph over the power of death that poisons his creation."[19]

From the perspective of suffering and hope we encounter distinctive features of a Christian approach to health: our personal health is seen within the larger context of Christ's work in a mending of all creation. The gift of the Spirit is our experiential participation in the overlap of the ages. It is a source of empowerment from the standpoint of God's final healing of all things.

The church is called to be God's face of healing in this world.

Our mission is to mediate the healing power of God, Christ, Spirit through prayer and exercise of faith. Among the activities of the church that convey healing power are prayers of healing, including anointing with oil; participating in the eucharist or Lord's Supper; identification with the cross and resurrection; proclamation of the Word; use of heart-language and cultivation of open relationships; celebrating feasts and festivals together; and offering each other warm hellos and goodbyes, including the kiss of peace.

Conclusion

In light of the biblical foundations for ministries of healing,[20] the church's historical practices of healing, and a contemporary ethos that values healing ministries, seminary educational and formation programs ought to foster the identity of pastors as healers. Preparation for pastoral ministry should include a clear and adequate biblical and theological basis for healing ministry and a good grasp of the experiences of the church, East and West, in its healing efforts. These biblical and historical pieces should be integrated into the regular M.Div. pastoral program as well as into the pastoral care and counseling program that prepares people for chaplaincy roles. Indeed this emphasis might be regarded as an organizing center for a seminary curriculum, because healing was so much at the heart of Jesus' own ministry. Healing in the Gospels is synonymous with salvation, and thus it represents the very purpose of ministry: to bring people God's salvation through Jesus Christ, to make them whole.

Notes

[1] Carl A. Volz, *Pastoral Life and Practice in the Early Church* (Minneapolis: Augsburg Fortress, 1990). Another helpful book is *The Pastor: Readings from the Patristic Period,* ed. Philip L. Culbertson and Arthur Bradford Shippee (Minneapolis: Augsburg Fortress, 1990).

[2] Volz, *Pastoral Life,* 87.

[3] Ibid., 89; Volz's italics.

[4] See my work in *Israel's Scripture Traditions and the Synoptic Gospels: Story Shaping Story* (Peabody, Mass.: Hendrickson Publishers, Inc., 1994), 85-87.

[5] See Susan Garrett, *The Demise of the Devil: Magic and the Demonic in Luke-Acts* (Minneapolis: Augsburg Fortress, 1989), for detailed study of the gospel's encounter with magic and the demonic in Luke-Acts. See also her treatment of the many dimensions of Satan's work in her study of Mark, *The Temptations of Jesus in Mark's Gospel* (Grand Rapids: Eerdmans, 1998).

[6] *Adversus haereses* II.xxxi.2, quoted in Reginald Maxwell Woolley, *Exorcism and the Healing of the Sick* (London: Society for Promoting Christian Knowledge, 1932), 14.

[7] *Adversus haereses* II.xxxii.4; in Woolley, *Exorcism,* 15.

[8] *Contra Celsum* I.lxvii; cf. vii.4.

[9] Some of the secondary sources for further research on healing in the early church are Morton Kelsey, *Healing and Christianity: A Classic Study,* 3rd ed. (Minneapolis: Augsburg, 1995), 125-56; Ronald A. N. Kydd, *Healing through the Centuries: Models for Understanding* (Peabody, Mass.: Hendrickson Publishers, Inc., 1998), 70-81. An older work, Evelyn Frost, *Christian Healing: A Consideration of the Place of Spiritual Healing in the Church of Today in the Light of the Doctrine and Practice of the Ante-Nicene Church* (London: A. R. Mowbray, 1940), is also helpful. Sources that document the continuing healing tradition in Eastern Orthodoxy are: John T. Chirban, ed., *Health and Faith: Medical, Psychological, and Religious Dimensions* (Lanham, Md.: University Press of America, 1991); and Stanley Samuel Harakas, *Health and Medicine in the Eastern Orthodox Tradition* (New York: Crossroad, 1990).

[10] *Demonology of the Early Christian World* (New York and Toronto: Edwin Mellen Press, 1984), 129.

[11] Peter Brown, "Sorcery, Demons and the Rise of Christianity: From Late Antiquity into the Middle Ages," in *Religion and Society in the Age of Saint Augustine* (New York: Harper and Row, 1972), 136.

[12] For Irenaeus, e.g., "Christ's victory over the devil (is) the key motif in developing his doctrine of the atonement" (Ferguson, *Demonology of the Early Christian World,* 124). The preaching of the gospel is a means of defeating the

demons. It brings the victory of Christ to bear upon the oppression here and now, and releases humans from Satan's tyranny.

[13]Alan Kreider, *The Change of Conversion and the Origin of Christendom* (Harrisburg: Trinity Press International, 1999), 17.

[14] For more on this topic, see my article, "Mutual Aid Based in Jesus and Early Christianity," in *Building Communities of Compassion,* ed. Willard M. Swartley and Donald B. Kraybill (Scottdale, Pa., and Waterloo, Ont.: Herald Press, 1998), 21-39.

[15] Here I refer to two important sources on connecting exorcism with baptism: Henry Ansgar Kelly, *The Devil at Baptism: Ritual, Theology, and Drama* (Ithaca: Cornell University Press, 1985), a study of the history of the rites from the early church into the modern period; and Murad Saliba Barsom and Athanasius Yeshue Samuel, "The Sacrament of Holy Baptism according to the Ancient Rite of the Syrian Orthodox Church of Antioch" ([Hackensack, N.J.]: A. Y. Samuel, 1974).

[16] But during mass at the end of his life, December 6, 1273, Thomas Aquinas experienced something that shifted his focus and spiritual understanding: "I can write no more. All that I have written seems like so much straw compared to what I have seen and what has been revealed to me."

[17] N. T. Wright, *Bringing the Church to the World* (Minneapolis: Bethany House Publishers, 1992), 132-33.

[18] Consecutively, Mark 1:32-34, Matthew 4:24, Mark 1:45; Marcus Borg, *Jesus, A New Vision: Spirit, Culture, and the Life of Discipleship* (San Francisco: Harper San Francisco, 1987), 60.

[19] *Suffering and Hope: The Biblical Vision and the Human Predicament* (Philadelphia : Fortress Press, 1987), 17.

[20] A thorough recent study of the biblical contribution is the work of John Wilkinson, a theologian and medical doctor who spent his life as a medical missionary and is now a Senior Fellow in the Royal College of Physicians of Edinburgh: *The Bible and Healing: A Medical and Theological Commentary* (Edinburgh: Hansel Press, and Grand Rapids: Eerdmans, 1998).

12

The pastor as spiritual orienteer

A pastoral theology approach

Arthur Paul Boers

I am still coming to grips with having exchanged the pulpit for a seminary lectern. Some of the happiest moments of my life and some of the hardest happened in my sixteen-plus years as a pastor. At times, I could not believe that not only was I permitted to do so many awesome, holy, and fun things, I was even paid to do them! At other times, I fulfilled responsibilities for which no payment could ever be enough.

One of the hardest moments of my ministry, and one of the richest, was accompanying a nine-year-old child and his family in the last hours of his life. He had just had one more open-heart surgery. Church members, family, and friends kept vigil together for thirty-six long hours before he died. It was intense, and many of my skills were called on all at once. Grabbing only a little sleep here and there, I felt dazed at times. Clarity about what I was doing was vital. I wish I had been that clear more often in my ministry.

Such clarity is a theological task. I have had a love-hate affair with theology. In high school I was interested in theology. I grew up in a church tradition that is theologically oriented. Ironically, a theological issue was a big reason that I was dissatisfied there: I could not accept what I was taught and told about predestination.

In university I majored in philosophy, fascinated with learning how to think and analyze. But I eventually grew tired of the seemingly endless hair-splitting and intellectual games. I liked Marx's critique: "Philosophers have interpreted the world. The point is to change it."

Later, I came to Associated Mennonite Biblical Seminary. By then I was leery of theology as well, which often seemed like philosophy: endless debates that never led to action. For me, as a peace activist, the point was to change the world.

But Marx's quote leads to questions. How does one know what to change if one does not understand the world? How does one know where to go without diagnosing what is wrong and what needs to happen? How can one act without careful reflection?

After seminary I did not plan to be a pastor, but I was called nonetheless. Perhaps I should have paid attention to what the church of my childhood taught about predestination and providence! As a pastor, my ambivalence about theology was problematic. I was not always sure what I was doing or why. I am embarrassed to admit that I did not seriously reflect theologically on being a pastor until after I had earned three seminary degrees and been a pastor for more than a dozen years. My D.Min. work challenged me to think more systematically and theologically as a pastor.

As a result, I grew dissatisfied with Mennonites' apparent lack of appreciation for theology. I looked for more substantial theological discourse, not just for the sake of my pastoring but for the sake of the church. I worry when we leave it to individual congregations to work on such huge questions as who participates in communion, whether unbaptized people should be welcome at the table, and the place of homosexuals among us. Not all congregations—or pastors, for that matter—are equipped to address these issues. And too often our discussion focuses only on whether the process is good and whether we are therapeutically appropriate. Process is important, as is psychology, but I am not content to have such important issues decided solely on such bases.

So I have almost come full circle in my journey with theology. In reclaiming a love for theology, I do not reject action. Rather, I have found a way to combine them. Thus pastoral theology is an ideal discipline for me. It blends my fascination for action and ministry with reflection on the church's ministries. Pastors need such theological reflection.

Spiritual theology

In the theologically inclined church where I was raised, every other Sunday we heard: "'You shall love the Lord your God with all your heart and with all your soul, and with all your mind.' This is the greatest and first commandment. And a second is like it: 'You shall love your neighbor as yourself.' On these two commandments hang all the law and the prophets" (Matt. 22:37-40).

This central Gospel text says that one way of loving God has to do with how we use our minds, an essential aspect of theology.

Another central Gospel text, Jesus' Great Commission, also alludes to the importance of theology when it enjoins "*teaching* [new disciples] to obey everything that I have commanded you" (Matt. 28:19-20).

I am partial to what is sometimes called spiritual theology. It is concerned with meaning and relationship in such a way that all areas of one's life and being are related and integrated.[1] Spiritual theology has to do with how to live the Christian life; it includes prayer, spiritual direction, and theological reflection "so that all of [one's] thinking becomes prayerful."[2] Spiritual theology deals with our most basic yearnings. One pastor describes our fundamental neediness in terms of three "longings [that] haunt us: the desire for triumph over death; the desire for meaning; and the desire for intimacy" with God and others.[3] Augustine famously summed these up in the prayer "Our hearts are restless until they find their rest in Thee."

Spiritual theology incorporates intellectual disciplines, yet is broadly concerned with the Christian life, spirituality, and faithfulness. It was the church's first theological approach, was predominant until the early Middle Ages, and still predominates in Eastern orthodoxy where "the title 'theologian' has been reserved for those mystics who go most deeply into the wisdom of God."[4] Eugene Peterson laments the sundering of theology: at first "there was no split between living the Christian life and thinking about it. But then the rise of scholasticism and the polemics of the reformation came about and the two became separate. The systematic theologian became an academic and the spiritual theologian became the chaplain."[5] In the twelfth and thirteenth centuries, emerging scholastic theology "moved . . . away from theology conceived as a commentary on the sacred page and an introduction to the experiential knowledge of the divine mystery. The personal assimilation of the mystery of the faith was gradually replaced by a theology that fostered a critical understanding of the doctrinal content of the faith."[6]

Spiritual theology does not displace, downplay, or disregard other theological approaches, but keeps them in perspective. "Knowledge must become subservient to that wisdom whose beginning resides in the fear of the Lord."[7] As John Macquarrie warns, such wisdom does not rule out scholarship: "From the days of the church at Corinth, there have been instances of spirituality . . . gone astray through exuberance. Spirituality needs understanding . . . that theology supplies. A theology without spirituality would be a sterile academic exercise. A spirituality without theology can become superstition or fanaticism or the quest for excitement."[8]

I am not objecting to academic theology; I am making a case for a broader take on theology. Spiritual theology "refuses to separate the study of theology from the personal transformation of the theologian," "emphasizes the spiritual and ethical character of the quest for God" as "growth in theological knowledge must go hand in hand with moral and spiritual growth." Without being anti-intellectual, it "rejects the primacy of thought, and asserts a necessary unity of mind and heart in the quest for God."[9]

A practical benefit of spiritual theology is that it fits postmodern priorities and concerns about spirituality, meaning, and experience. Kenneth Leech, calling for a renewed spiritual theology, says that overcoming the gulf between spiritual and academic theology is "one of the most urgent tasks of Christian theologians and pastors today."[10]

Anabaptists, we often hear, are not creedal. We have not produced many systematic theologies either. While more praxis-oriented, our emphasis on personal devotion and practical obedience nevertheless resonates well with spiritual theology.

Spiritual theology is *pilgrimage.* Theology is not done in a vacuum or an ivory tower (although such places have their uses, even in theology). As a pastor, I saw again and again how experience shapes people's theology, affecting even their ability to hear, receive, or understand theology. Little wonder that Frederick Buechner claims that "all theology, like all fiction, is at its heart autobiography."[11] Anabaptists take experience seriously. Testimonies are important. When people join us, they are more likely to be pressed to articulate their relationship with God than to subscribe to certain creeds. This was true of my entry into the Mennonite church, and for all my love of theology, true for all those I pastored into our faith as well.

Spiritual theology is about *relationship* with God. As John Macquarrie writes:

> We can know God only in the way that we know other beings, that is to say, by communion or communication at a personal level. . . .
>
> Thus theology includes prayer and is even, in some respects, a kind of prayer itself. It is not surprising that

> such great theologians as Augustine and Anselm slip
> naturally from speaking *about* God to speaking *to* [God],
> and we experience no awkwardness in this transition.[12]

Various church fathers "were mystics, poets, and visionaries rather than academics or theoreticians: their theology was inseparable from . . . visionary insight and . . . intense prayer."[13] Anabaptists (like other evangelicals) insist on the importance of paying attention to our relationship with God.

Spiritual theology is itself a *spiritual discipline.* Macquarrie writes, "The heart of theology is deep meditation on the . . . Christian faith. . . . Christian truth is not something that we make up but something that is given to us in the acts of God in Israel, in Christ and in the Church. The theologian meditates and ponders deeply upon the given of God's revelation, though he or she has also the *task* of interpreting and applying it."[14] As a spiritual discipline, it is more akin to *discernment* than to science. Anabaptists value spiritual disciplines and discernment more than intellectual expertise.

Spiritual theology is *corporate* in nature. Macquarrie notes, "The theologian is . . . a member of the Body of Christ with the special function of expounding, interpreting, and sometimes criticizing the faith of the Church in a given situation. The business of theology, even in its critical function, is to bring to expression the faith of the people of God, not merely the opinions of the individual theologian, though, of course, the theologian's individuality will not be lost in the process. But theologians can perform their work only as they participate in the community."[15] Anabaptists believe that God is known in the community of believers, and that God works through that community. We resist individualistic interpretations of the faith.

Spiritual theology stresses *practical faithfulness*, discipleship, living out one's convictions. Anabaptists would agree that "it is in love of one another that we see most perfectly . . . the character of the Godhead, and it is in love shown forth among human beings that we come closest to the imitation of the divine life."[16] Mennonites often quote Hans Denck, a sixteen-century forebear—and mystic!—who wrote that "no one knows Christ except one follows him in life."

Spiritual theology emphasizes *doing justice*: "Hallowed be your name, your kingdom come, your will be done, on earth as in heaven" (Matt. 6:9-10). "Revelation and liberation go together."[17] We know

God in *doing* justice (see, e.g., Jer. 22:15-16).[18] Anabaptists strongly emphasize working for God's reign and believe this means working on behalf of the oppressed, rejected, alienated, and neglected.

Spiritual theology is marked by *humility in approaching God.* Macquarrie reminds us that "God, the Holy and Ultimate Reality . . . is not a subject-matter that can be subjected to scrutiny, manipulated, made the matter for an experiment."[19] Original Testament spirituality urged against naming, portraying, or describing God. "Gregory of Nyssa used over forty different words to speak of this incomprehensibility. However much we may attempt to speak of [God's] nature, God remains unutterable, unfathomable, the unsearchable depths of reality."[20] Augustine observed, "If you think you have understood, it is not God."[21] Anabaptists have had a prevailing intuition of humility in our views. Many prefer not to be polemical about convictions and remain respectfully open to learning from others. We are reticent of speaking too adamantly about what we believe, and we often resist forceful preachers.

Finally, spiritual theology calls for *ongoing change, metanoia,* learning, and even repentance. A pastor associates this lifelong transformation with Jesus' words commending becoming like children: "As our vision . . . deepens and expands, we are forced to unlearn things. . . . In the realm of the spirit we have to become a child if we are to see the world once again with any wonder."[22] Jesus' counsel to be childlike, simple, and humble is central for Anabaptists in our conviction about our need for ongoing growth. St. Benedict called this change conversion of life. As Gregory of Nyssa said, "To find God is to seek [God] incessantly."[23]

Spiritual theology in an Anabaptist perspective holds promise for wholeness and growth in our unfolding relationship with God. What then might it say about ministry, about pastoral theology?

Looking for a theology of ministry

I entered the pastorate reluctantly and hesitantly. Over the years, I struggled to know what a pastor really is. Sometimes I tried to be one of the gang in the pews. Sometimes I modeled my ministry on community organizing or activism. At other times, social workers were my role models. Some pastors see themselves primarily as pastoral counselors, group facilitators, or even CEOs.

Mennonites struggle with how to speak about ministry and leadership. According to the recent *Confession of Faith in a Mennonite Perspective,* "Christ calls all Christians to minister to each other in the church and on behalf of the church beyond its boundaries."[24] The ministry of those called by God to be ministers or pastors is *representational,* "not to relieve the other believers of responsibility, but to *represent* Christ and the church in the congregation *and* on the church's behalf in the world."[25]

The Bible offers many metaphors for ministry leadership,[26] as do modern authors. Implications can be derived, for example, from Avery Dulles' classic church models: hierarch in institutional church, mystic in mystical communion church, priest in sacramental church, preacher in herald church, (suffering) servant in servant church.[27] Carnegie Samuel Calian spells out a number of ministry styles—servant-shepherd, politician-prophet, preacher-teacher, evangelist-charismatic, builder-promoter, manager-enabler, liturgist-celebrant—but finally proposes "grass-roots theologian."[28] Donald E. Messer suggests five paradoxical images: wounded healer, servant leader, political mystic, enslaved liberator, practical theologian.[29]

William H. Willimon sees in some suggestions—"'wounded healers and living reminders' (Henri Nouwen), 'sacramental persons' (Urban Holmes), 'symbol bearers' (John Westerhoff), 'the clown' (David Switzer)"—a "frantic search for some attribute that somehow makes pastors unique."[30]

These images are all about a small slice or aspect of what a minister does or is. In my pastorates, different models were important, but none entirely captured what it means to be a pastor. Priests conduct rites, but do they administer? Manager-enablers administer, but do they help someone die well? Counselors care for others, but do they preach? Preachers preach, but do they pray?

Mennonite approaches

William H. Willimon and Stanley Hauerwas—two United Methodists deeply informed by Anabaptism—are suspicious of clericalism: "Church history is full of examples of how theologians attempted to give isolated credence to the clergy."[31] Willimon points out that many—if not most—things pastors do can often be performed better by more skilled or gifted lay people.[32]

Since the 1960s, many Mennonites played down pastoral leadership. Erick Sawatzky's essay details that phenomenon. Billed as Anabaptist renewal, such egalitarianism (according to John Esau) in fact had much to do with "political, cultural, and sociological realities of the modern era."[33] Various Mennonite theologians concerned with training pastors (including Marlin Miller and Marcus Smucker) discovered both through historical scholarship and contemporary experience the need to better understand the pastoral office.[34]

Several Mennonite suggestions have emerged in recent years. Esau said that ministers *represent* Christ or even "the triune God."[35] Claiming the mantle of God's representative, however, feels like elitist clericalism. I do not believe it is convincing terminology in our contemporary church.

One of my teachers, Marcus Smucker, proposed "incarnational presence." The pastor's role is "to 'incarnate' the presence of God to those with whom I sojourn and to speak to God in behalf of others."[36] There are things I like about this. It connects well with an observation by another of my mentors, Henri J. M. Nouwen: "What else is ministry than witnessing to the [the One] whom 'we have heard, and we have seen with our own eyes; . . . watched and touched with our hands' (1 John 1:1)? Ministry is the manifestation in our own person of the presence of Christ in the world. . . . This means much more than speaking and acting in the Name of [the One] who came to us long ago. It means that our words and actions themselves become a manifestation of the living Christ here and now."[37]

But I have reservations. Smucker intends his metaphor to be active, but "presence" terminology can feel passive. Furthermore, "incarnational presence," like "representational role," speaks in lofty, unfamiliar terminology that may not connect with people in the pews.

Pastoring as spiritual orientation

Eugene Peterson calls for a paradigm shift from pastors as program directors to pastors as spiritual directors.[38] Spiritual direction is "paying attention to God, calling attention to God, being attentive to God in a person or circumstances or situation."[39] "Direction" may sound authoritarian (indeed, it often has been throughout the history of its practice), but it can simply mean directing attention to God.

For spiritual theology the term *spiritual direction* has promise but also limitations. It is largely associated with other (primarily liturgical) Christian traditions, even if it is now faddish. (It remains to be seen how long the spiritual direction movement will last.) It has an unfortunate "I-you" feel (i.e., "*I* direct *you*.") It too often is private, individualistic, and disconnected from the church. I find it disturbing how many spiritual directors hang out their shingle as if they were private practice therapists.

Nevertheless, pastoring, like spiritual direction, could be entirely summarized as "directing attention to God." Preaching, teaching, worship leading, praying, and visitation are all intended to help people pay attention to God. Counseling, pastoral care, and administration also direct people's attention to God. Pastoral ministry directs attention to God. "Almost all of what a pastor does, even the seemingly little things, especially the little things, can be opportunities to orient us toward God."[40] Thus all pastoral acts and ministerial duties are—or should be—judged and evaluated by whether they turn, orient, or direct attention to God.[41]

Turning attention to God happens not just once a week on Sunday or only in church. True worship means people will also turn toward God in all of their lives and activities. Hauerwas and Willimon have characterized prayer as "bending our lives toward God" or "bending our wants toward what God wants."[42] All of this is in the spirit of Romans 12:1-2: "I appeal to you therefore, brothers and sisters, by the mercies of God, to present your bodies as a living sacrifice, holy and acceptable to God, which is your spiritual worship. Do not be conformed to this world, but be transformed by the renewing of your minds, so that you may discern what is the will of God—what is good and acceptable and perfect."

The language of directing to God has promise. It is not elitist: people in the pew can understand paying attention, turning, or being oriented toward God. It is biblically and theologically rich language. Turning is an important term in the Bible. In the Original Testament, people were sometimes distracted from God by turning aside or away (*natah, sur*). Similarly the Original Testament equivalent of repentance (*shub*) means either turning away from evil and sin or turning toward God. The New Testament *epistrepho* has a similar sense (Acts 11:21; 14:15). There are also biblical themes. Walter Brueggemann, reflecting on the Psalms, has written fruitfully on the Christian life as one of moving from orientation (well-being, settledness, contentment), to disorientation (anguish, crisis, loss of control, loss of meaning), to the joyful and unexpected surprise of reorientation or new orientation.[43]

Turning attention to God is not a one-time event but a lifelong task and discipline, and we need the help of others. As Peterson says: "Embarrassingly forgetful of the God who saves us, and easily distracted from the God who is with us, we need priests to remind us of God, to confront us with God."[44] Such a person "enables another person to recognize and respond to God in their lives."[45]

On Sunday in worship, people get oriented to God by giving praise, hearing Scriptures read and expounded, talking with God about essential things, being bonded with fellow believers, remembering we are not alone, honoring "the better part," and giving offerings to God. And whether sermons are didactic, moral exhortation, or therapeutically affective, they should always orient people toward God.[46]

On Sundays, in many different ways, we test our directions against the direction of God's reign. We see the need to readjust. Then God's reality and priorities inform us throughout the week, both in mundane life and in crises. We need ongoing orientation and reorientation in this hard work.

Faith lives in the middle, between the origins of God's good creation and the promises of God's eschaton. Pastors, as Peterson notes, accompany people of faith "'in the middle,' facing ugly details, the meaningless routines, the mocking wickedness, and all the time doggedly insisting that this unaccountable unlovely middle is connected to a splendid beginning and a glorious ending."[47] Pastors orient people to God. And whether things go well or poorly, God's people continually need to remember and be reoriented, that is, to repent.

Pastoring, then, is spiritual *orienting* or *orientation*. "Orient" itself was originally a noun that meant "east." It became a verb in the context of worship, where it meant arranging or aligning a church sanctuary to face east. *Orient* is a worship word.

Orienteering is a sport in which one finds one's way through difficult territory or wilderness by relying only on a map and compass. It is participatory. Someone (not always the most skilled or adept person) is designated to hold and consult the map or compass. It is also a team effort; the strong and the weak rely on each other and work together.

Seeing the pastor as a spiritual orienter or even orienteer holds great promise. An active, positive term, it is readily accessible. It encompasses all that a pastor does and is. In contrast to clericalism, which focuses attention on clergy, in this model the pastor's role is to point and direct attention elsewhere, i.e., to God. *Orienting* is a stronger term than *directing*. It is not enough to turn or direct one's gaze to God: one must rework, redirect, and reorient one's life and actions that way.

Pastoring as spiritual orienteering fits well with spiritual theology. The pastor is not concerned only with parishioners' intellectual assent to certain theoretical formulations. Rather, the pastor is concerned with imparting good theological doctrine (by teaching, preaching, modeling, and mentoring) so that people's lives are oriented to God's priorities. In spiritual orienting, as in spiritual theology, Christian life is not separate from reflecting on Christian life. Intellectual study and personal growth, transformation, and pilgrimage are not sundered. Spiritual orienting encourages people to respect and reverence the absolute transcendence of God and to submit or orient their lives to that reality. Spiritual orienting calls for people to integrate mind, heart, strength, and hand into a life to which God calls us.

The primary characteristics of an Anabaptist approach to spiritual theology fit well with a spiritual orientation perspective. This perspective respects faith experiences. It is about being in right relationship with God. It functions by the various spiritual disciplines and practices that keep us attuned to God's priorities. It is a corporate activity. It has the practical outcome of forming faithful disciples who live out Christian convictions. It directs us toward God's priorities of doing justice. It is a continuing challenge needing adjustments and new learnings, and thus it calls for constant humility. Being a Christian is not a one-time proposition but a lifelong process of radical change, *metanoia*, repentance, and reorientation.

The pastor as spiritual orienteer is also on the journey and also needs constant orientation and reorientation. We too need the compass and map of Scriptures, prayer, accountability, community, formation, and worship. A major part of our work is prayer, not just for the ministries or people we encounter, but so that we are richly formed to be a fruitful part of those ministries and have something to offer others. As Nouwen said: "To contemplate is to *see*, and to minister is to *make visible*; the contemplative life is a life lived with a vision, and the life of ministry is a life in which this vision is revealed to others."[48]

Conclusion

Too many pastors do their theology and ministry in ways that are not clearly thought out or articulated, often on the basis of hunches and intuition, or worse, out of reactivity. While hunches and intuition are at times the work of the Spirit, our theology and ministerial tasks are too important to be left only to such haphazard means. We have seen here the promise of working from a spiritual theology perspective to become pastors who are spiritual orienteers or spiritual orienters.

Notes

[1] Here I am adapting Robert J. Schreiter's understanding of what he calls "Wisdom Theology"; see *Constructing Local Theologies* (Maryknoll: Orbis Books, 1985), 85.

[2] Eugene H. Peterson, *Subversive Spirituality* (Grand Rapids: Eerdmans, 1997), 196.

[3] Alan Jones, *Journey into Christ* (Philadephia: Trinity Press International, 1992), 14; cf. 33, 20.

[4] Schreiter, *Constructing Local Theologies,* 86.

[5] Peterson, *Subversive Spirituality,* 196.

[6] Charles André Bernard, "The Nature of Spiritual Theology," in *Exploring Christian Spirituality: An Ecumenical Reader*, ed. Kenneth J. Collins (Grand Rapids: Baker Books, 2000), 233.

[7] Geoffrey Wainwright, "Types of Spirituality," in *The Study of Spirituality*, ed. Cheslyn Jones, Geoffrey Wainwright, and Edward Yarnold (New York: Oxford University Press, 1986), 598.

[8] John Macquarrie, "Prayer and Theological Reflection," in *The Study of Spirituality*, ed. Jones, 587.

[9] Actually, these quotes are taken from Kenneth Leech's discussion of apophatic traditions of spirituality. While apophatic traditions might be seen as a subset of spiritual theology, I argue that these particular apophatic qualities also apply to spiritual theology as a whole. See Leech's *Experiencing God: Theology As Spirituality* (San Francisco: Harper & Row, 1985), 174-75.

[10] Ibid., 344.

[11] Frederick Buechner, *The Sacred Journey* (San Francisco: Harper & Row, 1982), 1.

[12] Macquarrie, "Prayer and Theological Reflection," 587.

[13] Leech, *Experiencing God,* 344.

[14] Macquarrie, "Prayer and Theological Reflection," 587.

[15] Ibid., 586.

[16] Ibid., 110.

[17] Ibid., 31.

[18] Ibid., 31-32, 46, 379.

[19] Macquarrie, "Prayer and Theological Reflection," 587.

[20] Leech, *Experiencing God,* 323.

[21] Jones, *Journey into Christ,* 107.

[22] Jones, *Journey into Christ,* 25.

[23] Quoted in Ernesto Cardenal, *Abide in Love* (Maryknoll: Orbis Books, 1995), 64.

[24] *Confession of Faith in a Mennonite Perspective* (Scottdale, Pa.: Herald Press, 1995), 59.

[25] Ibid., 60; italics added.

[26] Everett J. Thomas, ed., *A Mennonite Polity for Ministerial Leadership* (Newton, Kans., and Winnipeg, Man.: Faith & Life Press, 1996), 14-17, 19-21, 32-35.

[27] Avery Dulles, *Models of the Church* (Garden City, N.Y.: Doubleday, 1974).

[28] Carnegie Samuel Calian, *Today's Pastor in Tomorrow's World* (New York: Hawthorn Books, 1977), 8-22, 119.

[29] Donald E. Messer, *Contemporary Images of Christian Ministry* (Nashville: Abingdon Press, 1989).

[30] William H. Willimon, *What's Right with the Church* (San Francisco: Harper & Row, 1985), 126.

[31] Stanley Hauerwas and William H. Willimon, *Resident Aliens: Life in the Christian Colony* (Nashville: Abingdon Press, 1989), 133.

[32] Willimon, *What's Right with the Church,* 129.

[33] John A. Esau, "Recovering, Rethinking, and Re-Imagining: Issues in a Mennonite Theology for Christian Ministry," in *Understanding Mennonite Leadership: Essays Contributing to a Developing Theology of Ministry,* ed. John A. Esau (Elkhart: Institute of Mennonite Studies, 1995), 11.

[34] Ibid., 1-6; also in *Understanding in Ministerial Leadership,* see Marlin E. Miller, "Some Reflections on Pastoral Ministry and Pastoral Education," 57-60; and Marcus Smucker, "An Emerging Theology of Ministry: Incarnational Presence," 100-102.

[35] Esau, "Recovering, Rethinking, and Re-Imagining," 11, 15, 21-22.

[36] Smucker, "An Emerging Theology of Ministry," 102.

[37] Henri J. M. Nouwen, *Gracias! A Latin American Journal* (San Francisco: Harper & Row, 1983), 31.

[38] Eugene H. Peterson, *Under the Unpredictable Plant: An Exploration in Vocational Holiness* (Grand Rapids: Eerdmans, 1992), 175.

[39] Ibid., 181.

[40] Hauerwas and Willimon, *Resident Aliens,* 139.

[41] Ibid., 140.

[42] William H. Willimon and Stanley Hauerwas, *Lord, Teach Us: The Lord's Prayer and the Christian Life* (Nashville: Abingdon Press, 1996), 18-19.

[43] Walter Brueggemann, *The Message of the Psalms: A Theological Commentary* (Minneapolis: Augsburg Publishing House, 1984).

[44] Eugene H. Peterson, *Leap over a Wall: Earthy Spirituality for Everyday Christians* (San Francisco: HarperCollins, 1997), 20.

[45] Eugene H. Peterson, *Subversive Spirituality* (Grand Rapids: Eerdmans, 1997), 240.

[46] This schema for preaching is from Bernhard Lang, *Sacred Games: A History of Christian Worship* (New Haven: Yale University Press, 1997), 3.

[47] Peterson, *Subversive Spirituality*, 128.

[48] Henri J. M. Nouwen, *Clowning in Rome: Reflections on Solitude, Celibacy, Prayer, and Contemplation* (Garden City, N.Y.: Image Books, 1979), 88.

13

Paying attention

The minister as listener

June Alliman Yoder

> "The Lord has given me a well-trained tongue
> that I may know how to speak to the weary
> a word that will rouse them.
> Morning by morning he wakens—
> wakens my ear to listen as those who are taught."
> (Isa. 50:4 NAB)

> "Let anyone with ears listen!"
> (Matt. 11:15)

> "What I say to you in the dark,
> tell in the light;
> and what you hear whispered,
> proclaim from the housetops."
> (Matt. 10:27)

In the very beginning, according to the Hebrew Scriptures, the voice of the Creator spoke, the cosmos listened, and the desired form came into being. A major motif in both testaments is that of God speaking and people hearing, discerning, and answering or acting.

Hearing and listening

In *The Lamb Christology of the Apocalypse of John,* Loren Johns writes that the invitation to hear is common in the Old Testament, "but the specific implication that one can have ears and still not hear draws on a well-established tradition in the Prophets about the nature of spiritual perception."[1] This idea recurs in Matthew and Mark and is repeated in Revelation: "Let those with ears listen!" Those addressed are urged to "perceive spiritually—that is, to go beyond surface interpretation or what seems obvious to the senses." They are warned that "failure to perceive spiritually is tantamount to rebellion against God."[2]

Another ancient voice, that of Socrates, also spoke to the issue of hearing and listening. He pointed out that listening for understanding or comprehension was a skill that would disappear with the spread of written language. Perhaps to some degree he was right. However, we are now moving past the printed page, and print media have lost their primacy for many people. Listening for comprehension is a skill much in demand again.

As writers need readers, so speakers need listeners. Even when the role of listeners is recognized, they are often thought of as passive, as empty vessels. But it is not enough to be merely heard when what you want is to be listened to. A parent may mistakenly assume that because he utters some words in the presence of his child, she has understood and will remember and take to heart what he said. In another familial scenario, a husband leaves the room while his wife is talking. She says, "Listen to me when I talk to you," and he answers, "I can hear you." Hearing is a natural process, and provided one's ears are not damaged and one's brain is functioning normally, one cannot help but hear sounds of certain intensities and wavelengths. But it is possible not to listen. Speakers have no guarantee that they were heard just because hearers were present, awake, and not deaf.

Active listening adds several dimensions to hearing, including understanding (taking in data), paying overt attention (attentiveness), analyzing what is heard, and acting on the basis of what was heard. Listening might be defined as hearing and paying attention. In some respects, the notion of paying attention or giving attention may be more pertinent than that of listening, because not all that we hear can be measured in decibels.

Minister as listener

Every communication model includes three elements: a *source* of the communication; a *message* of some sort, which is encoded and decoded either electronically or with words and sounds or in actions; and a *receiver* or listener or destination. Different models and different communication situations use different labels for these three elements, but they constitute the bare bones of communication theory.

Often congregations value ministers for what they say, and much discussion about communication in ministry focuses on the role of the minister as source. We tend to neglect the role the minister plays as receiver, as a partner on the other side of a communication event. Parishioners reflect on words eloquently spoken, sermons delivered with passion, and comfort gently offered, but they seldom think of all the listening that goes into making the speaker effective. I am convinced that for the pastor, listening, or paying attention, is the single most important form of ministry and the activity that most defines the pastoral role.

Listening to God

A minister begins the listening journey by attending to the invitation of God to join God's ministry team. We use the language of *call* to talk about this spiritual nudging of the Holy Spirit in the life of the one being moved into ministry. The call has an internal component, reflecting the call of God, and an external or human component, reflecting the call of the church. The minister must be willing to listen to the call, and after understanding it, paying attention to it, and discerning it, must be willing to respond positively to it. This listening and attending to the call of God and the church are often part of the seminarian's work.

When a minister has responded affirmatively to the call of God and the call of a congregation, the listening continues as the Spirit gives guidance and reveals the will of God for the ongoing work of ministry. This spiritual discernment often involves no sound waves, but in it pastors listen to a guiding word from the Lord God.

A ministry that is not rooted in relationship with God is hugely compromised. Pastors must have a confident and loyal faith in Jesus and his saving love and must regularly spend time communicating with God; their ministry must be nourished by regular encounters with God. A ministry that depends solely on the abilities of the pastor is no ministry. A preacher whose work is not rooted in relationship with God merely gives speeches on religious topics. A pastoral counselor whose spiritual core is atrophied becomes a social worker.

I cannot overemphasize this point. Pastors dare not spend all their quiet time desperately searching for something to preach or to read at a hospital bedside. If pastors are to serve as ones who represent God, they must know God. And we learn to know others by listening to them, not by talking to them.

Listening to people

Equally important to effective ministry is listening to people, hearing the concerns they communicate in words, in actions, and in silences. Listening to what people say underneath their words is an important part of ministry, which some find difficult to understand and others treat as insignificant. Significant listening may entail many things, including discerning the heart of God, noticing the nonverbal messages a parishioner communicates, and interpreting the seating arrangement at an elders meeting.

The minister must become a master of reading context as well—whether that context is the member's family, the congregation as a whole, the community, or the world. And the minister should attend carefully to the ministry situation, whether it is the sanctuary on Sunday morning, the funeral home, or the nursing home.

Preacher as listener

To illustrate the importance of listening in ministry, I turn to an analysis of a common ministry task and observe the listening that is needed to accomplish it. Because I preside where students are learning to preach, I naturally turn to the work of preaching, but I hope readers will make the connection to other ministry tasks as well.

When we think of preaching, we automatically think of the action of speaking, of delivering a message, and perhaps also about the congregation's listening. Preachers are often intensely focused on what they will say and how they will say it. They also consider how the congregation will receive what they say. I am convinced that ministers who want to improve their preaching should focus more on their own listening.

Preaching is a complex integrating task, and there is much to which the preacher must attend. The simple three-part model of communication described above quickly becomes complex when we apply it to preaching. The source, among a host of possibilities, could be God, the Bible, or the preacher. The messages are multiple, and include intended and unintended ones. The receivers can be hundreds of people all doing their own interpretations. The model is simple, but the communication that happens in preaching is complex. I want to consider some of the things to which the preacher must listen or pay attention.

Listening to the biblical text

The encounter with the biblical text is one of the first places that the preacher listens. Sometimes this listening involves frequent rereading of the text, text translations, and critical methods. But always the point is to listen to the text and hear what God is saying through it. The preacher sits quietly though not idly with the text, waiting for it to speak its truth. As Barbara Brown Taylor writes, "I cannot think of any other text that has so much authority over me, interpreting me faster than I can interpret it. It speaks to me not with the stuffy voice of some mummified sage but with the fresh, lively tones of someone who knows what happened to me an hour ago."[3]

For preachers, the Bible is the beginning place for the sermon, so they must listen carefully and accurately to the text. The preacher must learn who the writer is, to whom the passage was written, and what the intended message was in its original setting. Then the preacher should look at how that message has been translated and interpreted over the millennia.

Then the preacher considers how those readings of the text might speak to our times. The truth of long ago and far away must somehow be brought to the present congregation. Faithful reading of the text is an important way of listening to God. The written word speaks if the preacher will listen. Too often the preacher is in a hurry, and the text gets a sloppy hearing at best. Preachers should take time to participate in the slow process of sitting with the passage and waiting for it to yield its word.

Listening to the context of the congregation

The next place where the preacher listens is to the immediate context of the congregation. The preacher must be aware of the make-up and demographics of the congregation. Individual needs in the congregation and the congregation's corporate needs must both be heard. Preaching is different from other forms of ministry. Because it is a constituent of public worship, in it the needs of the whole body of the congregation must be attended to. A significant gap sometimes exists between what individuals in the congregation need or want, and what the congregation needs. Attending to both, pastors should preach toward what they perceive to be the pastoral needs of the congregation as a whole.

Having listened to the needs of the congregation, the preacher goes back to the text to receive a message for the church in this time and place. As the preacher attends both to the text and to the congregation, the Spirit offers a message for this situation. The preacher holds the congregation and the text and listens to them both, moving back and forth between them until a message emerges in which the text speaks to a need of the congregation.

Listening to the experts

In preparing the sermon, the preacher also listens to scholars and other experts who have written on the text. These voices can shed light on the chosen text. Listening to these experts helps the preacher hear the theology of the text and the history of its interpretation. Preachers do not operate in a vacuum, and they benefit from listening to the voices of those who have studied the text in depth and know the history of its interpretation. The preacher then evaluates whether any of these voices are useful to the work of this particular sermon. The Holy Spirit joins preachers as they evaluate what they hear and understand and deal with in their encounter with the work of Bible scholars writing on the biblical text.

Listening to the broader context

Another significant voice in the preparation process is the context beyond the congregation. Attending to the wider context will aid the preacher's decisions about the form, illustrations, and language of the sermon. In *Preaching As Local Theology and Folk Art,* Leonora Tubbs Tisdale writes about the task of exegeting the congregation.[4] Tisdale refers to the preacher as ethnographer. Like a cultural anthropologist with a "participant-observer" field method, the pastor listens to, watches, and analyzes the congregation, the larger society, and the world, and seeks to understand the impact of each on the congregation.

Participant-observer is a useful label for the minister who is both in the congregation and apart from the congregation. The world of the congregation is no longer just the congregation and the village. Everyone has access to world events and ideas. So exegesis must also include understanding how the particular congregation sees itself in light of the world context. For example, in the aftermath of the terrorist attacks of September 11, 2001, people heard biblical texts with different ears; the impact of these events caused them to interpret texts in new ways.

The preacher must listen to the language of the congregation, noting the pronunciation, idioms, and trigger words, before shaping the sermon. Each region has its own way of speaking and its own vocabulary. Effective preachers will listen for these words and ways and remove as many barriers to listening as they possibly can.

Listening during the delivery of the sermon

During the delivery of the sermon the preacher still needs to attend to the Spirit of God, the sermon text, and the congregation. Always the preacher must be listening to the Spirit as it ministers. Sometimes the Spirit may ask the preacher to change the prepared sermon in major or slight ways. Sometimes the Spirit may encourage the preacher, provide strength, or in other ways attend to the preacher. The Spirit and the preacher must listen to one another so that the work of the preaching ministry can be accomplished.

The preacher must also be listening to the text of the sermon. Perhaps that seems obvious, but it bears mentioning. Recently I reviewed a video of a student preaching before a congregation. At one point he stopped. Later he admitted that he got to thinking about his headache and just forgot what he was talking about. Preachers who cannot manage to pay attention to the sermon they are preaching should not be surprised to learn that their listeners are having trouble!

In *Performing the Word,* Jana Childers reflects on the importance of concentration for the preacher. She is referring to focused attention and hearing that is strong and unwavering. Concentration eliminates distractions, helps preachers stay focused on their task, and lets the task absorb them.[5] Stripped of distractions, the preacher stands in service of the sermon.

At the same time that the preacher is listening to the Spirit and paying attention to the text of the sermon, this minister of the Word needs to be paying attention to the eyes and hearts of the congregation. Sometimes my students standing in front of the class to preach see nothing in the faces of those listening. Movement is meaningful, and the effective preacher must learn to interpret signs of sleepiness, agitation, restlessness, thought, and questioning. It is part of the preacher's task to listen to the silences of the congregation.

Silence is not the absence of communication. In *The Dynamics of Human Communication,* Myers and Myers note some of the different forms of silence. Those that may apply to the preaching situation include the silence of attentive listening to an important story; the silence of bored superiority and withdrawal; the silence of completeness, when everything that needs to be said has been said; the silence of a grief too deep for words; the silence of reverence and contemplation, as when one encounters something beautiful; the silence of terrible anger, when one is tensed up so as not to let the steam out; and the silence of challenge, like that of a pouting child.[6] One of the preacher's tasks is to be able to listen to what the congregation is saying nonverbally and to understand accurately what the people are conveying. I believe that reading the text of the congregation is as important to successful communication as reading the biblical text.

Listening to oneself

Finally, preachers must listen to themselves. Part of the preacher's work is paying attention to the sleep, exercise, and food that are needed to keep body and voice in good condition. After preaching one pastor will be exhausted, another will feel elated and exhilarated, and another will need to be alone. Preachers must know and listen to the needs of their own spirits and bodies and attend to them if they are to be able to continue their work week after week into the years.

Preachers should also pay attention to their appearance in order to minimize distractions to the congregation. Anything about the preacher's self-presentation that makes it difficult for the congregation to hear must be attended to—including glittering earrings, loud ties, tattoos, untrimmed mustaches, floral prints, or rumpled shirts. In communication theory these things are called noise although they are silent. Preachers must listen for this kind of noise as well and do their part to quiet it.

Conclusion

According to Isaiah 50:4, "The Lord has given me a well-trained tongue that I may know how to speak to the weary a word that will rouse them." Often preachers are so concerned with the well-trained tongue that they forget the second part of the verse: "Morning by morning he wakens—wakens my ear to listen as those who are taught." Those who do not listen have nothing to say, for it is the Lord who wakens our ears to listen as it is the Lord who trains our tongue.

Over the years I have become deeply convinced of the importance of active, attentive listening to the effectiveness of ministry in general. If we were to apply to other ministry tasks the kind of analysis done above with respect to preaching, we would discover that other ministry tasks are also highly dependent on listening. In fact, *most ministry tasks call for significant listening time and acute listening skills.* Such analysis would also lead us to the discovery that the *listening that undergirds one ministry task aids other ministry tasks* as well. Listening in one area informs and benefits practice in others. For example, listening to Scripture is useful in preaching, spiritual direction, and pastoral care; listening to context is vital for preaching, teaching, and premarital counseling. Finally, we would discover that *listening itself is a primary ministry activity.* In some cases, all people need is for someone to listen to them. Indeed, listening is a ministry in and of itself. In contemporary North American society, many people feel alone and crave the experience of having someone listen carefully to them.

We need to redeem the word *listen.* We ought to begin to honor listening as the active and fruitful work that it is. Unfortunately, many regard listening as unproductive. They equate it with sitting around doing nothing. Our fixation on multitasking leads us to assume that the successful person does several things at once. I propose that just listening is an important and demanding task, perhaps the most important thing a minister does. I am convinced that it can be done best in a concentrated, focused way. And I believe that it connects us as ministers to God, to the biblical text, to the congregations we serve, to the world we live in, and to ourselves.

Let anyone who has ears to hear, listen!

Notes

[1] Loren L. Johns, *The Lamb Christology of the Apocalypse of John: An Investigation into Its Origins and Rhetorical Force,* Wissenschaftliche Untersuchungen zum Neuen Testament, 2nd series, no. 167 (Tübingen: Mohr Siebeck, 2003), 180.

[2] Ibid., 181.

[3] Barbara Brown Taylor, *The Preaching Life* (Cambridge: Cowley Publications, 1993), 52.

[4] Leonora Tubbs Tisdale, *Preaching As Local Theology and Folk Art* (Minneapolis: Fortress Press, 1997), 56-90.

[5] Jana Childers, *Performing the Word: Preaching As Theatre* (Nashville: Abingdon Press, 1998), 104.

[6] Gail E. Myers and Michele Tolela Myers, *The Dynamics of Human Communication: A Laboratory Approach,* 5th ed. (New York: McGraw-Hill, 1988), 146-48.

14

Pastoral ministry as improvisatory art

Rebecca Slough

When I was a seminary student, Ray was in many of my classes. Anxious to learn all he could about various aspects of ministry, he asked many questions. Nearly all of them began "How do you . . . ?" and his classmates could fill the blank with the topic at hand: "How do you talk to people who are dying?" "How do you help people plan a wedding?" "How do you run a church council meeting?"

Ray left many classes disappointed with the answers he got. He never seemed to understand that the answer to many of his questions was "It depends." None of Ray's professors could answer his questions adequately, because the people with whom Ray would minister were unknown, as were the places and circumstances of his future ministry.

It was when Ray went to his first congregation that he began learning the fine art of improvisation. Human beings improvise continuously, with varying degrees of sophistication. Our conversations are often elaborate improvisations informed by conventions of language, social structure, and communicative strategy. Games are defined by rules, but playing them requires improvisation. Problem solving is an improvisatory skill.

As in other areas of human experience, in pastoral ministry the art of improvisation is indispensable, because many situations are unpredictable and unique. Some beginning pastors, like Ray, want manuals detailing the proper way to meet every pastoral situation. Most eventually realize that they cannot compile a set of how-to instructions. Ray and his colleagues come to understand that pastoral identity is shaped by their ability to meet people in the specific places, times, and activities of each day.

This essay explores the relationship between the practices of improvisation and pastoral ministry. Part one briefly describes the art of jazz improvisation; part two demonstrates its parallels with pastoral ministry. The concluding section suggests some implications of this exploration for ministry education programs.

The art of improvisation

To improvise is to compose verse, music, story, or movement on the spur of the moment; to utter or perform extempore.[1] The artist responds to "unforeseen challenges and opportunities . . . composing a performance that fits and enhances the moment and the situation in which it takes place, perhaps by serving as the vehicle of a superhuman agent or connecting with a source of inspiration that suddenly becomes available."[2] The participants in an improvisatory event recognize that "something unique is happening in their presence at the moment of performance."[3]

To the observer, what is created in that moment may seem offhand, magical, spontaneous. But the ability to improvise rests on structures of knowledge, listening and execution skills, a deep understanding of social interaction, and a keen awareness of the nature of the moment. An improvisation is

> the creation of a musical work, or the final form of a musical work, as it is being performed. It may involve the work's immediate composition by its performers, or the elaboration or adjustment of an existing framework, or anything else in between. To some extent every performance involves elements of improvisation, although its degree varies according to period and place, and to some extent every improvisation rests on a series of conventions or implicit rules.[4]

In many cultures, artists' skills are assessed by their ability to take familiar stories and embellish them to fit specific occasions. They may create new stories based on the common experience of the people assembled for the performance. Musicians are judged by their abilities to render unique performances of familiar tunes, or they may create new melodies using familiar motifs and bending musical conventions to serve the purpose of the immediate moment.

> In its purest and most formative state improvisation is a process rather than a product; it is a series of steps using a sound, an idea, an action, an element that develops

and changes in both predicted and unexpected ways through the give and take of the performers. With rigorous attention to the moment, coupled with the free play of imagination, these sounds, ideas, actions expand to disclose what is heretofore unseen or unheard or untouched. What is born is often marked by familiarity but also surprise.[5]

Paul Berliner's *Thinking in Jazz: The Infinite Art of Improvisation* documents the development of many contemporary jazz players and singers.[6] Improvisation is a thinking activity in which the musician is continually making choices. Contrary to popular assumption, improvisation is not simply "free," "personal," "from the heart," a stream-of-consciousness approach, a matter of free association. Jazz musicians play with freedom, with a personal style that draws on present emotions, but it is far from thoughtless.

> Five factors are chiefly responsible for the outcome of the jazz player's improvisation: intuition, intellect, emotion, sense of pitch, and habit. His intuition is responsible for the bulk of his originality; his emotion determines the mood; his intellect helps him to plan the technical problems and, with intuition, to develop the melodic form; his sense of pitch transforms heard or imagined pitches into letter names and fingerings; his playing habits enable his fingers to quickly find certain established pitch patterns. Four of these elements of his thinking—intuitions, emotion, sense of pitch, and habit— are largely subconscious. Consequently, any control over his improvisation must originate in the intellect.[7]

Competent jazz musicians train themselves by listening carefully to other performers and trying to imitate the ways these artists stylize standard melodies or create interesting rhythms. They memorize a large repertoire of jazz standards and new pieces and then learn to play them all keys. They master standard chord progressions for specific genres (e.g., blues, Dixieland, bebop) and learn the chords for all the melodies they know. Many jazz musicians read music and routinely make dictations of melodies or chord progressions they hear. They work out their personal styles of melodic ornamentation and develop alternate harmonic options for melodies. They know their instruments or their voices intimately, practicing tirelessly to perfect the extremes of their technique. Some performers pursue classical and jazz studies in university or conservatory. Since jazz remains a predominantly aural/oral tradition, most listeners do not realize the knowledge structures that undergird jazz performances or the years of disciplined training most jazz players have spent in acquiring their skills.

Improvisation starts with a basic melody or theme that is developed into a satisfying unit. This motif is the paradigm or model around which improvisation unfolds. Sometimes the melody is simply ornamented or rhythmically adjusted. New variations on the basic theme are explored and extended. "Improvisation, like composition, is the product of everything heard in past experience, plus the originality of the moment. The contents of even a very accomplished improviser's solos are not all fresh and original, but are a collection of clichés, established patterns, and products of the memory, rearranged in new sequences, along with a few new ideas."[8]

The knowledge structures and skills required to play jazz are not only internalized cognitively, they are known in the muscle and bone of the players' bodies.[9] In *Ways of the Hand* David Sudnow describes how his hands learned fitting jazz sequences.[10] His narrative demonstrates how the improvisational process relies heavily on what the body knows through endless practice of complete melodies, chord progressions, and riffs.

Jazz is practiced within a network of performers who learn from and teach each other. When individual players have gained a reasonable proficiency with melodies and chord progressions, and have worked out most of their technical problems, they are ready to play with bands. In these settings a new set of skills develop. The first is the ability to listen to everything that the members of the band play. It is not enough to play your own part. Your part must be coordinated with other parts that are unfolding. Players and singers give each other ideas to incorporate in their solos or accompaniments all the time. "The background issue to keep in mind is that at any given moment in a performance, the improvising artist is always making musical choices in relationship to what everyone else is doing. These cooperative choices, moreover, have a great deal to do with achieving (or failing to achieve) a satisfying musical journey—the feeling of wholeness and exhilaration, the pleasure that accompanies a performance well done."[11]

> To be effective they listen to each other very closely, they move into the dialogue from what they hear and add their own particular take at the moment. As they absorb the sound, the emotion, tension, beauty, they notice the familiar patterns and play with the texture. They may imitate the sounds, or they may draw from them and go on. In the process the sound grows, it is a living response in the moment. The process repeats itself. More listening, more learning, more dialogue, more practicing, more risks, more conversation from within and without. . . . Once in awhile something extraordinary happens.[12]

Mature jazz players and singers continually extend their knowledge of musical structures, develop new skills for listening and managing their instruments, and fine tune their abilities to coordinate their responses with others. Good musicians are fully attentive to what is happening in the moment and bring to bear everything their minds, souls, and bodies know about creating interesting music. In jazz performance the discerning ear can hear with clarity improvisatory choices.[13] Audiences listen and watch as performers make intelligent decisions as they respond to each other.

Ministry and the art of improvisation

Like jazz performances, pastoral ministry happens in specific contexts, with particular people, in real time. It may happen on the spur of the moment as a response to "unforeseen challenges and opportunities."[14] Pastors choose a response "that fits and enhances the moment and the situation in which it takes place."[15] They do so, not for the sake of creating something artistic, but for the sake of acting on Christ's behalf toward another person or group. They serve "as the vehicle of a superhuman agent or connect with a source of inspiration"[16] that is powerfully and immediately known.

Jazz improvisation performances are usually ephemeral. Unless they are recorded, they exist in the moment and are gone forever. Many acts of ministry are ephemeral as well. Their significance may be lost to the minister and to the one ministered to. But some ministry improvisations hold the *kairos* experience of God's fullness breaking into the moment. Because the Spirit blows where it chooses, it can appear at surprising times.

> From there Jesus set out and went away to the region of Tyre. He entered a house and did not want anyone to know he was there. Yet he could not escape notice, but a woman whose little daughter had an unclean spirit immediately heard about him, and she came and bowed down at his feet. Now the woman was a Gentile, of Syrophoenician origin. She begged him to cast the demon out of her daughter. He said to her, "Let the children be fed first, for it is not fair to take the children's food and throw it to the dogs." But she answered him, "Sir, even the dogs under the table eat the children's crumbs." Then he said to her, "For saying that, you may go—the demon has left your daughter." So she went home, found the child lying on the bed, and the demon gone. (Mark 7:24-30)

Jesus' encounter with this woman incorporates improvisation. As he seeks a respite from the demands on his attention and time, out of the blue appears this cheeky Gentile woman who will not take "No" for an answer. Jesus understands from traditional Jewish sources that his ministry is primarily to his own people and not to the Gentiles, and he does not seem to take her seriously. His response lets her know that she is not one of the people he is meant to serve. Her comeback, a brilliant improvisation, turns his words around: she is content with the crumbs he can offer and stubbornly claims a small benefit of his healing power. Jesus, recognizing the truth in her repartee, sends her home with the promise that her daughter has been healed. The woman seems to have caught Jesus off guard. Yet as a result of this encounter a young child is restored to health, and Jesus realizes that Gentiles are part of his mission.

Pastors are often judged on the basis of their abilities to offer wise counsel, a gracious gesture, a heartfelt prayer, a just admonition, or a forgiving word in situations they could not have anticipated. Like Ray, new pastors do not fully trust their ability to respond appropriately. Most are busy refining technical skills in preaching, teaching, administering, and leading the congregation. The knowledge structures required for meeting the variety of ministry situations they encounter are developing in their minds, but these resources are not fully available in their bodies for action. Pastors have to practice many aspects of ministry over and over again for their bodies to know the gestures, rhythms, timings, and expressions that they have available to meet other people fully.

Like jazz improvisers, pastors use their intuition, intellect, and emotion to engage in ministry. Instead of using a sense of pitch, as jazz musicians do, they develop a sensitivity to the tenor of what is happening around them. They listen deeply to what people say, and don't say, and to how people communicate what is deep within them. Pastors sense when the Spirit of God is moving in the midst of the congregation. They notice undercurrents that spread discontent. Prayer, reading the Bible in study and devotion, examination of conscience, and nurturing relationships with family and friends are habits they bring to ministry. Intuition, intellect, emotion, tone, and habit all interact to enable the pastor to extend God's justice, grace, and salvation.

Robert Morris describes a visit to a parishioner who in a short period of time had lost her son, been in a near fatal auto accident, and endured a long recovery only to have relentless leg pain.[17] When she most needed her husband's help, he developed a severe case of shingles. She was resentful. "The inner walls of victimhood were closing in. After a quietly vitriolic tirade about every aspect of her existence . . . she blinked, looked at me, and asked tremulously, 'Don't you think I'm becoming a terrible harpy?'"

Stunned, Robert also blinked, and he swallowed, prayed, and wondered how to respond. "I followed the guidance that came back in answer to my prayer; I told her, as gently as possible, that she was headed straight for harpydom. . . . Did she really want to end up in that kind of inner hell, however good the causes for it might be?" What was she to do? she asked. "As my inner prayers for guidance intensified, I heard myself saying, 'Well, Jesus tells us to love our enemies, and bless those who curse us. The pain is now a deadly enemy of your soul, not just your body. Every time it comes, why don't you bless it instead of cursing it?' Part of me was horrified to face this poor, suffering woman with such a rigorous demand. To my everlasting surprise and relief, [she] gasped, sat up straight, dried her eyes, pursed her lips in thought for a minute and then said, matter-of-factly, 'Very well then; that's what I'll do.' And so she did."

Robert could not have anticipated the turn this pastoral visit took. Confronted with a moment of truth, he trusted his ability to listen prayerfully and his knowledge of Christ's liberating words, which were set in a new key. The pastoral wisdom he offered startled and horrified him. Yet his words presented the woman with a clear and humanizing choice that opened the way to a deeper level of healing.

The primary theme of the church's ministry in the world is God's salvation through Jesus Christ and the inauguration of his reign. Pastors create endless variations on this theme when they visit sick members, bless babies, lead Bible studies, marry couples, or work with the church elders. Their acts of ministry are not "all fresh and original, but are a collection of clichés, established patterns, and products of the memory, rearranged in new sequences, along with a few new ideas,"[18] provided through the inspiration of the Spirit. Nothing that Robert did with his complaining parishioner was new. Yet the combination of knowledge, skill, and inspiration that he brought to bear during his visit gave her new life.

Pastoral improvisation is always done in relationship with other people. In preaching, worship leading, and teaching, the pastor's improvisatory skills are on public display. But much of pastoral ministry happens in smaller settings. Here pastors continually coordinate their actions with those of other people—church staff, community neighbors, believers and nonbelievers, the congregation's youth and elderly, couples in counseling—for the sake furthering Christ's saving work in their lives. Pastors listen for the themes people present and pick them up with complementary energy or urgency. Pastors extend or alter the motif, shift the accents, change the harmonies, and then offer it back for more response. Both Jesus' and Robert's stories demonstrate the give-and-take of improvisation, through which new possibilities come into being.[19]

Implications of improvisation for educating pastors

Educating students to be pastoral improvisers does not require sweeping changes in seminary curricula and ministry training programs. Basic subject areas could remain constant, though some shifts in emphasis would be needed. The biggest changes would be in finding more effective ways to assess students' abilities to improvise with the knowledge they have acquired.

Knowledge structures

Biblical, historical, and theological studies remain essential disciplines for gaining knowledge structure with which future pastors can improvise. These studies should put students in touch with the full expanse of the biblical story so they recognize their place in the continuation of that story. Students need to learn biblical and theological understandings of the human person and human societies in all their glory and sinfulness to gain an honest and compassionate appraisal of themselves and the people they will serve.

To see their own times in the church's life realistically, they require a broad knowledge of the church's history from a pastoral perspective. It should focus on the ways pastors have worked over time, on models of pastoral reasoning, on the changing faces of the church and its practices, and on the continuities of church life in the midst of change.

Worship, nurture, and mission are functions of congregational life they must understand thoroughly. They need familiarity with the varieties of expressive practices faithful Christians have developed to engage in these practices. Throughout their studies, future pastors should be exposed to and challenged to interact with images, metaphors, symbols, and rituals related to basic themes of Christian faith (e.g., redemption, conversion, transformation, new life, death, and growth, etc.), using poetry, novels, music, the visual arts, drama, and dance. These media feed the improvising imagination.

Technical skills

Like jazz musicians, pastors must continue to refine their technical skills for ministry, but their initiation into these needed skills begins during their ministry education. To improvise effectively pastors need to be able to read the Bible competently in a variety of ways: orally for public proclamation and interpretation; prayerfully for personal and small group devotion; analytically for study, reflection, and teaching; and analogically for connecting Scripture with mundane events of daily life.

They need to be able to tell the biblical story in a myriad of ways to people of all ages, educational levels, and life experiences.

They need skills in reading the character of congregations and their social locations.

Pastors must acquire skills in listening prayerfully to what is said or not said, gestured, or implied in many different circumstances. They need to learn to look and feel below the surface of conversations, actions, and events.

People preparing for ministry also need to learn how to link their intuitive knowledge with tangible evidence. They must learn how to coordinate their actions with others—in ways that are intentionally complementary or contrasting, that promote or disrupt equilibrium.

They need a capacity to discern their effect on other people, a proficiency in talking in a variety of ways (e.g., informal conversation, discussion, debate, disagreement, conflict, preaching, teaching, and advising). They need to practice an ability to write in a variety of persuasive and pastoral forms (i.e., memos, notes, letters, summaries, reviews, essays, papers).

Pastors in training must cultivate a capacity to act playfully, spontaneously, freely, creatively, seriously, compassionately. They need to learn to pray without ceasing. They need to hone their skills in reflecting on past actions, assessing responses, determining fitting choices, and cleaning up mistakes.

Developing these skills allows pastors to bring the fullness of themselves as thinking, feeling, intuitive, physical, and spiritual beings to each moment of ministry. Having these skills "in hand," knowing them "by heart," opens innumerable avenues for responding to the varied demands pastors face. Assignments and class activities that explicitly connect these technical skills and the knowledge acquired through specific courses would help young pastors improvise with more confidence after graduation.

Community practice

Reading and writing are the primary skills emphasized in most seminary and ministry education programs. Essential as these are, an overemphasis on them may inhibit the development of improvisational skills.[20] Nearly all programs preparing people for pastoral ministry could do more to honor the class environment as a community in which improvisation is practiced. Developing improvisational skills while using knowledge structures will require that teachers and students practice a number of ways of talking with each other, ranging from joking, bantering, storytelling, and casual conversation, to serious discussion, formal debate, argumentation, persuasion, and negotiation. Theological training needs to learn to value all these expressions of knowledge competence.

Ministry students will learn to listen deeply to the words, gestures, and patterns of discourse, and coordinate their responses in ways that enlarge, illuminate, refine, vary, or shift the ideas offered for consideration. They will examine the structure of action taken by themselves, their class, and other individuals and groups, and evaluate the "fit" of various responses to difficult experiences.

They will practice reading a text by constructing a verbatim summary, an outline of central points, a fitting paraphrase, a rendering that can be understood by a nonprofessional, and a "translation" into a completely different medium appropriate to it (e.g., poetry, drama, sermon, dance, drawing, or music). They will perform bodily in ways fitting for the course (reading texts aloud, practicing the ceremonies of the church, moving in space, touching people with respect and consideration).

In this kind of ministry training, the class environment will be characterized by freedom to make honest mistakes without fear of humiliation, and it will hold the assurance that one will be kindly corrected by other learners. No doubt, many classes currently use these practices in some form. Educating pastors, like Ray, in the art of improvisation that will serve their ministry will require more attention to these skills.

Notes

[1] *Oxford English Dictionary*, 2nd ed. (Oxford: Oxford University Press, 1989).

[2] Stephen Blum, "Recognizing Improvisation," in *In the Course of Performance: Studies in the World of Musical Improvisation*, ed. Bruno Nettl (Chicago: University of Chicago Press, 1998), 27.

[3] Ibid., 27.

[4] Stanley Sadie and John Tyrrell, eds., *The New Grove Dictionary of Music and Musicians*, 2nd ed. (New York: Grove, 2001), 12:94.

[5] Janet R. Walton, "Improvisation and Imagination: Holy Play," *Worship* 75 (July 2001): 297.

[6] Paul Berliner, *Thinking in Jazz: The Infinite Art of Improvisation* (Chicago: University of Chicago Press, 1994).

[7] Jerry Coker, *Improvising Jazz* (New York: Simon & Schuster, 1987), 1.

[8] Ibid., 36.

[9] Certainly classically trained musicians internalize knowledge structures and physical skills in their bodies. However, many of these musicians do not engage in extended improvisational sequences during their performances. Their "muscle memory" serves to replicate set pieces and not to find new versions of those pieces in the midst of their performances.

[10] David Sudnow, *Ways of the Hand: The Organization of Improvised Conduct* (Cambridge: Harvard University Press, 1978).

[11] Ingrid T. Monson, *Saying Something: Jazz Improvisation and Interaction* (Chicago: University of Chicago Press, 1996), 27.

[12] Walton, "Improvisation and Imagination," 297.

[13] Drama, storytelling, dance, or particular sports could also have been the focus of our exploration of improvisation; in this piece I have briefly described its use within the domain of jazz because of literature available to me on jazz practices.

[14] Blum, "Recognizing Improvisation," 27.

[15] Ibid.

[16] Ibid.

[17] Robert C. Morris, "Suffering and the Courage of God," *Weavings*, 17, no. 5 (September-October 2002): 9-10.

[18] Coker, *Improvising Jazz*, 36.

[19] Jazz players generally learn how to improvise as part of a community of musicians; sadly, few pastors have the luxury of learning how to improvise in a community with other pastors. While ministry educational programs and conference pastoral-peer structures are addressing this problem, too many new pastors do not receive the kind of collegial support essential for practicing their improvisatory skills.

[20] In "Writing As a Spiritual Discipline," Stephanie Paulsell makes a strong case for writing as a spiritual practice for the sake of others, which has a place in the seminary curriculum. By and large I concur with her. However, the amount of writing students do in seminary programs is disproportionate to the amount and kind of writing they will do as pastors. Writing will not be the primary medium through which the ministry of most pastors will be realized. Paul Griffiths examines the limits of academic styles of reading in "Reading As a Spiritual Discipline." Both essays are found in L. Gregory Jones and Stephanie Paulsell, *The Scope of Our Art: The Vocation of the Theological Teacher* (Grand Rapids: Eerdmans, 2002), 17-31.

15

The pastor as caregiving sage

Daniel S. Schipani

One of the mixed blessings in ministerial formation and pastoral practice in the twentieth century was the development of pastoral counseling as a specialized activity, even a profession. As Donald Capps has observed, the establishment of pastoral counseling centers and the growth of a population of trained specialized pastoral counselors has placed pastors who serve congregations in a quandary with regard to this ministry art. Many pastors have found these developments daunting and have seen them as providing a rationale for leaving counseling to the "professionals."[1]

In this essay I argue in favor of reclaiming pastoral counseling as an essential task for those who minister in congregations. I do so by highlighting the unique, although by no means exclusive, role of pastors as caregiving sages. They should be able, within the larger framework of congregational care, to counsel people facing life's challenges (e.g., those confronting a vocational decision) and struggles (e.g., those grieving the death of a loved one). Indeed, pastors serving congregations are called to do such counseling, not as mental health professionals in the psychiatric sense, but as ministers of the gospel and worthy representatives of the caring, healing Christ.

In the last few years I have been working on an understanding of pastoral counseling as the practice of wisdom, with the goal of growth in wisdom—knowing how to live well—in the light of God.[2] I view pastoral counseling as a special art and form of ministry of the church, in which human emergence is uniquely sponsored by a way of walking with others—whether individuals, couples, families, or small groups— as they face life's challenges and struggles. The overall goal is that they may live wisely in the light of God. In other words, pastoral counseling focuses primarily on awakening, nurturing, and developing people's moral and spiritual intelligence.

When wisdom thus defines its overall guiding principle, this ministry art can be reenvisioned. The resulting revisioning illumines the following characteristics of pastoral counseling: it must be viewed, practiced, and taught pastorally; it must be contextualized ecclesiologically; it must be centered on Jesus Christ as the Wisdom of God; it must be grounded in Scripture; it must be viewed, practiced, and taught as a unique form of the (re)creative process guided by the Spirit; and it must be oriented toward the reign of God. In what follows we will turn our attention to each of these aspects of pastoral counseling as congregational ministry.

Pastoral counseling viewed and practiced pastorally

Pastoral counseling must be defined and carried out as part of the congregation's ministry of care rather than as an arm of the psychotherapy industry or as a mental health profession. Further, the disciplines of practical and pastoral theology should provide the context within which pastoral counseling is reflected upon both critically and constructively. These disciplines should inform the practice of pastoral counseling.

I propose that *pastoral ministers should perceive themselves as caregiving sages*. With such a vocational identity they intentionally and uniquely partake in the overall orientation and purpose of all forms of ministry, sponsoring human emergence in the light of Christ. Pastors must remain aware of this general purpose while ministering to individuals, couples, families, and other small groups who bring to counseling their particular agendas of care. Whenever they authentically focus on this purpose, pastors who counsel can collaborate with God's Spirit in the formation and transformation of the emerging human self as spirit with its threefold pattern of vision, virtue, and vocation. That is to say, the rich and complex counseling agenda with its specific objectives arising from counselees' special needs for care will seek to foster growth in the following dimensions: their way of seeing and knowing, or the *vision* of the living God; their way of being, their character or heart, or the *virtue* of Christ; and their way of living, including play, work, and service, or the *vocation* of the Spirit.[3]

It follows that *pastors who counsel must become proficiently bilingual, able to speak the languages of psychology and of faith*.[4] On the one hand, they must know the language of psychology and of counseling[5] in the dominant cultural framework, where psychology, especially in its psychotherapeutic expressions, functions as conventional and pragmatic wisdom. Hence, pastors who counsel acquaint themselves with and use psychological views and resources related to human development, personality, psychopathology, and so on. On the other hand, pastors who counsel must be proficient in the languages of faith and of theology. Therefore, they must be able to engage in pastoral diagnosis and to help people articulate and make sense of their spiritual self-assessment and discernment.

Paul Pruyser's classic treatment of pastoral diagnosis and spiritual discernment emphasizes that pastoral counselors must use their special training, knowledge, and experience to provide care from their unique pastoral and theological perspective. This approach is often neglected but nevertheless expected by those who turn to pastors. Pruyser also proposes specific guidelines focused on awareness of the holy, providence, faith, grace and gratefulness, repentance, community, and sense of vocation.[6] Pruyser's contribution has been helpfully supplemented by Nancy Ramsay in her book, *Pastoral Diagnosis: A Resource for Ministeres of Care and Counseling.*[7]

This bilingual proficiency is particularly pertinent in our time, given the prominence of psychology and psychotherapy in the dominant culture. Addressing the question of the status and the role of psychotherapy in our society, Robert Woolfolk starts with the notion that the therapeutic perspective is so endemic to contemporary life that its categories and assumptions shape our conceptions of what it is to be human: "Psychological theories now are taken for granted and have become our common sense and conventional wisdom."[8] He argues that psychotherapy will always involve wisdom as well as expertise, pedagogy as well as technology.[9] Woolfolk uses wisdom here to mean practical know-how, primarily in the realm of relationships and emotions, including the capacity to discern goals and means and to engage in adequate decision making amid the complexities of everyday life. He thus juxtaposes the (Aristotelian) notion of *phronesis*—usually translated as practical wisdom—with the contemporary concept of practical and emotional intelligence.

Vocationally and ideologically, pastors who counsel understand themselves primarily in terms of the ecclesial context and the life and work of the church. This is the case even when they are not employed by a particular congregation, conference, or church-based institution. Further, pastors as counselors explicitly represent the historical and social reality of the church and the church's call to become a sacrament of the reign and the wisdom of God, as I indicate below. Therefore, pastoral counselors are primarily, although by no means exclusively, accountable to the church.

Pastoral counseling contextualized ecclesiologically

Reframing pastoral counseling as a ministry of the church implies that we take seriously the church's call to become a living sacrament[10] of the reign and the wisdom of God in the midst of history and culture. I use the term *sacrament* intentionally, with its threefold meaning of sign, symbol, and means of grace. The church is called to become a truthful sign that points in the right direction, the direction of wholeness and the wise life. It is also called to become a symbol that faithfully re-presents—embodies in itself—the wisdom of God. It is called to become a fruitful means of grace, an instrument and agent of God's wisdom in the world and for the sake of the world. Given its commitment to the way of Jesus and to ongoing discernment for the sake of faithfulness, the church is meant to become the wisdom community par excellence. That affirmation means, among other things, that we must view the faith community as the primary focus for care, and the primary context and agent of care and counsel for the people of God. At least three implications follow.

Pastors as counselors seek to minister primarily with a communal and contextual paradigm of pastoral care.[11] Within this framework clinical and other models can be selectively and critically appropriated. In this paradigm, pastoral care is viewed as the ministry of a faith community in light of its social context. The focus is on the caring community and the various contexts of care, rather than being only on pastoral care as the work of the ordained pastor. In other words, the guiding, nurturing, sustaining, reconciling, and healing dimensions of care are seen as a function of the whole church, not only for the well-being of its own members but especially for the sake of the larger human community.[12]

Pastors as counselors and pastoral theologians acknowledge that God's call for the church is to manifest the revelatory presence and praxis of God's reign and God's wisdom. At the same time, they help the church discern the shape of this call and are themselves shaped by it. They identify and describe that call as the vocation of the church to become a good form[13] of human reality and wholeness in the light of God's reign and wisdom. I use the expression *good form* to include both an ethical (righteous, morally good) and aesthetic (harmonious, beautiful in shape) meaning. Of course, such good form always consists of a unique historical and contextualized embodiment of divine reign and wisdom. It is also clear, however, that no single faith community is capable of perfect form, of fully reflecting God's life and wisdom. The point is that faith communities are better and more beautiful to the extent that they take on the form of Christ.

It makes sense for us to speak of ministry arts precisely because all types of Christian ministry have to do with God's fashioning business, with forming and transforming people toward the Christlike, toward the good form, which can be only dimly imagined and eschatologically anticipated. Thus pastors must acknowledge the ethical and aesthetic aspects of the church's identity and character as people of God, body of Christ, and temple of the Spirit.[14] To the extent that congregations become truthful, faithful, and fruitful sacramental communities, they also become revelation. Faith communities thus can provide grace-filled glimpses of the reign and the wisdom of God.

The formation and transformation of the faith community becomes a major interest and concern. Thus the primary, although not exclusive, focus of pastoral counseling is the formation and transformation process involving the whole congregation and every aspect of congregational life. More specifically, that interest and concern can be articulated in terms of certain fundamental questions: How does the practice of pastoral counseling enhance the worship of the people of God? How does it help equip the church for building up God's family as the body of Christ? How does pastoral counseling empower the church as dwelling place of the Spirit to participate in God's mission in the world and for the sake of the world?

Pastoral counseling centered on Jesus Christ, the Wisdom of God

Reframing pastoral counseling as wisdom in the light of God implies the affirmation that Christ is the center for this practice of care. It also implies that Christ is the center of the critical and constructive (pastoral) theological reflection that stems from the practice and undergirds and evaluates the practice of care. A number of implications follow when we understand the work of pastors who counsel in this light.

Pastors who counsel seek to be guided by Christ-inspired vision of human becoming or humanization—human wholeness and fullness of life, and wholesome and wise living. Hence, they must find explicit connections between their actual ministry practice and the confession that Jesus Christ embodies the life and wisdom of God and makes known to us God's will for human conduct and destiny. It is crucial to be clear and consistent about this confession.[15] That Christ-inspired vision for human becoming must be considered together with holistic views of salvation and shalom. Pastors as counselors thus appropriate and integrate these fundamental theological convictions about the work of Christ for the re-creation of our full humanity.

Pastors who counsel are concerned with the manifold expressions of faithfulness and growth in the life of faith (discipleship). They seek to relate this longed-for faithfulness and growth to rich and complex counseling settings and agendas. Many situations make pastoral counseling desirable or necessary, in the face of existential challenges and struggles (for instance, making significant choices, dealing with interpersonal conflicts, coping with pain and death, or confronting abuse). Within these occasions for ministry, the reflection of pastoral theologians and the work of pastors as caregiving sages must establish meaningful connections between presenting issues and growth in the life of Christian faith. Spiritual growth is thus understood in light of our conviction that Christ is "the power and the wisdom of God . . . who became for us wisdom from God, and righteousness and sanctification and redemption. . . . We have the mind of Christ" (1 Cor. 1:24b, 30b; 2:16b).

As representatives of Christ, pastors who counsel long for their own growth into Christ and seek to relate and to act with a Christian character. This kind of counseling assumes several interrelated dimensions of identity and character on the part of the caregiver. These include a Christian frame of mind or way of knowing, a Christian heart or way of loving and being, and a Christian sense of vocation or way of living and working. Pastors who counsel enact that representation in the special shepherding relationship that defines counseling as pastoral in the specific sense of the term. In other words, pastoral counselors explicitly seek to establish a pastoral care relationship in the name and in the Spirit of Christ. Obviously, one might expect that something similar will occur with Christians who work in the practical human sciences such as education and applied psychology. There, too, one would hope that professing Christian practitioners practice in a Christian manner and reflect Christian character.[16] However, those pastors who counsel will represent the church explicitly. Further, they will deliberately represent the caring Christ who guides and nurtures, sustains, reconciles, and heals people in need of God's saving grace in the midst of their existential challenges and struggles.[17]

Pastoral counseling grounded in Scripture

The biblical foundation and inspiration of pastoral counseling must be reflected and expressed in a number of interrelated ways, including the four highlighted in the next paragraphs. Taken together, these guidelines help us define what it means to counsel biblically as a necessary feature of pastoral counseling.

Pastors who counsel work with a biblically informed wisdom framework and perspective. This framework will be in tune with our confessional affirmation that the Scriptures are "the fully reliable and trustworthy standard for Christian faith and life [which must be understood and interpreted in harmony with Jesus Christ—the Wisdom of God, the Word become flesh] as we are led by the Holy Spirit in the church."[18] A biblically informed framework and perspective will decisively determine their view of reality, knowing and truth; of human nature and destiny; of formation and transformation; of the nature of the good; of human wholeness and wellness; and of daily wise living, loving, and working.

When they offer counsel—as when they teach and preach—*pastors give due consideration to the teachings, narratives, poetry, prophesy, and other biblical materials, as these expressions of the written Word properly illumine and address counselees' existential challenges and struggles.* The particular setting and ministry art of pastoral counseling will condition how biblical material is considered. A variety of possibilities may be identified.[19] However, the Bible is not merely a helpful tool or resource for pastoral counseling; it contributes decisively to the very goals, process, and content of this ministry art. Thus pastors who counsel affirm the power of Scripture as an agent of disclosure and of change. Simultaneously, they need to remain aware of the specific situations encountered in counseling and be sensitive to the particular needs and growth potential of those seeking care. In any event, the Bible is not conformed to counseling or therapy goals but rather the reverse. Any psychological and psychotherapeutic theories and approaches used in pastoral counseling must be consistent with the power of the Bible to disclose wisdom in the light of God. This guideline reflects an understanding that the Bible is the one essential book of the church. It is also congruent with the normative convictions of our faith tradition concerning Scripture.[20]

Pastors who counsel give special attention to a unique hermeneutical process with the goal of wise discernment, wise decision making, and wise living.[21] They acknowledge that the counseling process, when viewed as a dynamic encounter with the living documents and narratives of people's lives, includes an inductive structure that is analogous to reading the biblical text in terms of asking (observing), assessing (judging), and applying (acting). They also acknowledge that the counseling process includes a unique form of hermeneutical circulation engaging not only counselees' personal agenda in family and sociocultural settings but also the agenda of the reign of God in dialogue with that of both church and society. Pastoral counseling using this guideline rejects the literalist, rationalist, and fundamentalist use of the Bible in counseling, as promoted by some well-known authors.[22] On the contrary, counseling pastors seek to guide a multi-way conversation which involves the story and the vision graciously revealed in Scripture and in Jesus Christ, and people's personal and family stories and visions in the midst of their social situations and life's challenges and struggles. In short, a process that is truly practical and theological must take place.

In the counseling setting, pastors play a role that is analogous to their role as teachers, preachers, and spiritual directors: they must act as grace-filled and worthy intermediaries in the interaction of the counsel of God with the counselees. I do not intend *the counsel of God* here to mean merely godly advice, instruction, or words of wisdom (although advice, instruction, and words of wisdom are normally called for in pastoral counseling). Rather, by *the counsel of God* I mean the

very reality of divine presence, grace, and power.[23] Given such a privilege and responsibility, therefore, *pastors seek to nurture their own
spirituality and to grow in their own biblically grounded ways of seeing
and knowing, loving and being, and living and working.* Their personal
journey of discipleship, their own life-walk on the way of wisdom,
must also be grounded on Scripture.

Pastoral counseling carried out as a (re)creative process guided by the Spirit

Wisdom in the light of God is a gift we can receive and mediate by
divine grace. Reframed in terms of the way of wisdom, pastoral
counseling therefore challenges pastoral theologians and counselors
to consider seeking, discerning, and appropriating authentic signs and
expressions of wisdom. Interdisciplinary exploration leads us to look
at the counseling process primarily as a special version of the creative
process, including its recreating, healing, and liberating dimensions.
Guided by the Holy Spirit, this process must be theologically
reinterpreted and practically appropriated in Christian ministry.[24] Two
related guidelines follow.

*Pastors as counselors seek to participate in God's trinitarian praxis of
guiding, nurturing, and sustaining; liberating, reconciling and healing;
and renewing and empowering.* They do so by exercising careful spiritual
discernment and theological reflection in the context of pastoral
counseling, together with their actual counseling work in specific
ministry settings. Consciously and prayerfully, pastors seek to be
inspired, sustained, and directed by the Spirit of God. Further, they
perceive their work as caregiving sages as one of partnership and collaboration with the Spirit of God.[25] In other words, they know that
by themselves they cannot effect growth in wise living and human
emergence in the light of Christ, for God alone gives healing and
growth, as Paul reminded the Corinthians (1 Cor 3:7b). Yet they also
know that, precisely in their role as counselors, they have a unique
opportunity to sponsor growth as they are present to people in ways
conducive to collaboration with the Spirit, that is, with compassionate
initiative, hospitable inclusiveness, gentle empowerment, and a gen-
erous invitation to partnership and community. They may thus counsel
fully attuned to the divine counselor and advocate who reminds us of
Jesus' way and guides us into all truth (John 14:26; 16:13).[26]

Pastoral counseling must also be viewed, practiced, and taught as fundamentally analogous to other practices of ministry such as teaching, preaching, mentoring, and spiritual guidance. In light of this principle, we discern a structural continuity among the diverse ministry art forms; these ministry arts have much in common because they all share an undergirding pattern which is essential to foster learning, conviction, formation, and transformation. The dynamics of collaboration with the Spirit include the following dimensions and movements that define the common pattern and design:[27] (a) engagement, which makes it possible to create safe spaces and contexts of rapport for discipling and caring ministries; (b) expression, which invites people to share their own stories and visions; (c) reflection and discernment, including the kind of "scanning" that allows for the creative work of the imagination; (d) explicit access to the wisdom of the faith community; (e) appropriation, which invites people to understand, judge, and make decisions; and (f) commitment, which includes guidance for acting on choices and commitments made together, with expectations of shared accountability, for the common purpose of wise living.

Pastoral counseling oriented toward the reign of God

The symbol of God's reign points to the vision and the promise of the commonwealth of freedom, justice, peace, welfare, and wholeness which is primarily a divine gift and which will ultimately be fully realized beyond history. *Pastors who counsel seek to appropriate and reflect the conviction that the ultimate context of wisdom, including wisdom in and for discernment, guidance and growth, reconciliation, healing, liberation, and wholeness, is the culture of the reign of God.*[28] I suggested above that partaking of that culture calls for and at the same time fosters wise living in the light of God. Affirmation of the biblical and theological foundations and framework that I have proposed, especially focusing on the connection between God's reign and divine wisdom,[29] suggests two final guidelines for pastors who counsel as a ministry of the church within the culture and the reign of God.

Pastors who counsel remain aware that their ministry work as caregivers always takes place within the social and cultural context of the church and the larger society. They claim that the reign of God is a social reality and a culture, a way of life that may take form in any historical culture. Further, they claim that God's reign can adapt and correct all other existing cultural forms (including, of course, the church's): relationships, systems, practices, power dynamics, values, beliefs, and ideals can be addressed, challenged, affirmed, or transformed in the light of the wisdom of God. By drawing on the threefold declaration of Jesus as the way, the truth, and the life (John 14:6), Ray Anderson highlights three components of the reign of God that serve as environment and horizon for the Christian counselor: (a) discernment that makes meaning and coherence available to the careseekers (i.e., the way that Jesus came to be and to share); (b) a righteousness embodied in the moral structures of the people of God (i.e., the truth that Jesus came to be and to create); and (c) a sense of identity communicated through a story in which each person participates, with a hope that compels faith to value life and to love community (i.e., the life that Jesus came to be and to give).[30]

Pastors who counsel become ethical agents of the culture of the reign of God. They practice as "cartographers and tour guides for a better culture."[31] Given their primary loyalty and normative commitment, they seek to give consistent and specific consideration to the ethical dimensions of their ministry. Ethical dimensions include not only professional ethics and personal values, and norms narrowly viewed, but also the communal and sociopolitical import of their ministry.[32]

Finally, actual embodiments of God's reign can take place on different levels and in diverse forms, as Alvin Dueck suggests. As an ethical culture, the story and the vision of God's reign can provide the narrative and the visional context for the counselor as ethicist. The reign of God is our recreating, liberating, and culture-creating story and vision; it provides the ethos and ethic for counseling and a critical and political perspective on our Western culture. The church as wisdom community is called to become a living sign of God's reign in its practice and its reflection on what it means to be human in the twenty-first century. Individuals and families are invited to partake of life in the light of God's reign. And the pastor's character as caregiving sage is especially to be shaped by the rituals, the narratives, and the discernment of the Christian faith community.[33]

Notes

[1] Donald Capps, *Living Stories: Pastoral Counseling in Congregational Context* (Minneapolis: Fortress Press, 1998). Capps affirms the essential role of pastoral counseling in the life of the congregation in response to "a fundamental human

need to give systematic, constructive attention to the way that individuals 'story' their lives [inspirationally, paradoxically, and miraculously] so that they may develop new, more fulfilling life stories" (viii). Capps argues for a "paradigmatic revolution" by introducing a narrative approach to counseling that integrates biblical insights and individual and family systems models of therapy.

² For the full argument that *wisdom in the light of God* is the most appropriate ground metaphor for pastoral counseling, see my book, *The Way of Wisdom in Pastoral Counseling* (Elkhart, Ind.: Institute of Mennonite Studies, 2003).

³ A detailed description of those three dimensions of the self as spirit is included in my essay, "The Purpose of Ministry: Human Emergence in the Light of Christ," to be included in another book project under way.

⁴ For a systematic and clear treatment of the question of becoming bilingual with regard to the perspectives, language, and understandings of psychology and theology, see Deborah van Deusen Hunsinger, *Theology and Pastoral Counseling: A New Interdisciplinary Approach* (Grand Rapids: Eerdmans, 1995). Hunsinger builds her case for interdisciplinary integrity and practical clarity on a Barthian approach to method.

⁵ Carl R. Rogers, possibly the single most influential psychologist in the early stages of the modern pastoral counseling movement, wrote the classic work on the difference between counseling and psychotherapy, *Counseling and Psychotherapy* (Boston: Houghton Mifflin, 1942). Normally, helping professionals view counseling as a relatively short process—one to five sessions—which tends to be problem-oriented. That is, it usually does not focus on personality structure and dynamic. A broad definition of psychotherapy includes the purpose of "amelioration of distress . . . relative to any or all of the following areas of disability or malfunction: cognitive functions (disorders of thinking), affective functions (suffering or emotional discomforts), or behavioral functions (inadequacy of behavior), with the therapist having some theory of personality's origins, development, maintenance and change along with some method of treatment logically related to the theory and professional and legal approval to act as a therapist" (Raymond J. Corsini and Danny Wedding, eds., *Current Psychotherapies*, 5ᵗʰ ed. (Itasca, Ill.: F. E. Peacock, Publishers, Inc., 1995), 1.

⁶ Paul W. Pruyser, *The Minister As Diagnostician* (Philadelphia: Westminster Press, 1976). See also George Fitchett, *Assessing Spiritual Needs: A Guide for Caregivers* (Minneapolis: Augsburg Publishing House, 1993).

⁷ Nancy J. Ramsay, *Pastoral Diagnosis: A Resource for Ministers of Care and Counseling* (Minneapolis: Fortress Press, 1998).

⁸ Robert L. Woolfolk, *The Cure of Souls: Science, Values, and Psychotherapy* (San Francisco: Jossey-Bass, 1998), 1.

⁹ Ibid., chapter 6, "Psychotherapy and Practical Knowledge."

¹⁰ In Latin America and elsewhere, the reference to the church's call to become a sacrament of the life of God in the world and for the sake of the world became more frequent after the documents stemming from Vatican II became public.

¹¹ For a helpful discussion of the communal-contextual paradigm, see John Patton, *Pastoral Care in Context* (Louisville: Westminster John Knox Press, 1993), part 1. For Patton this interpretive model supplements and corrects the traditional and the clinical paradigms in pastoral care.

¹² For a discussion of distinctive Anabaptist commitments on the question of faith community care, including understandings of wellness and illness, care and cure, suffering and death, see Graydon F. Snyder, *Health and Medicine in the Anabaptist Tradition: Care in Community* (Valley Forge: Trinity Press International, 1995). For a helpful essay on the importance of focusing on the congregation, see Don S. Browning, "Pastoral Care and the Study of the Congregation," in *Beyond Clericalism: Congregation As a Focus for Theological Education,* ed. Joseph C. Hough Jr. and Barbara Wheeler (Atlanta: Scholars Press, 1988), 103-118. And for an exploration of actual practices of and understandings of care in Mennonite congregations, see Erick J. Sawatzky, "Extending the Boundary: Pastoral Care of the Mennonite Congregation" (M.Th. thesis, Calvin Theological Seminary, 1998).

¹³ The term *good form* is used here metaphorically, that is, in a way analogous to the proposals of classic *Gestalt* psychology.

¹⁴ In the fourth chapter of the book in progress I deal with the trinitarian basis of the church's identity and character.

¹⁵ In the case of our faith tradition (Anabaptist/Mennonite), for example, normative statements about Jesus Christ are particularly pertinent. See "Jesus Christ.," Article 2 of *Confession of Faith in a Mennonite Perspective* (Scottdale, Pa.: Herald Press, 1995). The commentary accompanying this article makes the point that, in addition to identifying Jesus Christ the Messiah as prophet, priest, and king, "this confession also identifies Jesus as teacher [of divine wisdom who has made known God's will for human conduct], against the backdrop of Old Testament wisdom literature. . . . As disciples we participate in this fourfold work of Christ" (13, 15).

¹⁶ Members of the American Association of Christian Counselors and the Christian Association of Psychological Studies express the same commitment in different terms; it is also a stated principle of doctoral programs in clinical psychology such as those of Fuller Theological Seminary and Wheaton College. Mark R. McMinn puts it well in *Psychology, Theology and Spirituality in Christian Counseling* (Wheaton: Tyndale House Publishers, 1997): "The Christian counselors best prepared to help people are those who are not only highly trained in counseling theory and techniques and in theology but also personally trained to reflect Christian character inside and outside of the counseling office. This character cannot be credentialed with graduate degrees or learned in the classroom; it comes from years of faithful training in the spiritual disciplines—prayer, studying Scripture, solitude, fasting, corporate worship" (14).

¹⁷ For a classic affirmation of this position, see Wayne J. Oates, *The Christian Pastor* (Philadelphia: Westminster Press, 1951); see also Oates's *Protestant Pastoral Counseling* (Philadelphia: Westminster Press, 1962), in which he formulates his view of pastoral counseling from within a free church tradition.

[18] See "Scripture," Article 4 of *Confession of Faith in a Mennonite Perspective*, 21.

[19] See, for instance, Donald Capps, *Biblical Approaches to Pastoral Counseling* (Philadelphia: Westminster Press, 1981); *Reframing: A New Model of Pastoral Care* (Minneapolis: Fortress Press, 1990); "The Bible's Role in Pastoral Care and Counseling: Four Basic Principles," *Journal of Psychology and Christianity*, 3, no. 4 (1985): 5-14; and "Bible, Pastoral Use and Interpretation of," in *Dictionary of Pastoral Care and Counseling*, ed. Rodney J. Hunter (Nashville: Abingdon Press, 1990), 82-84. See also Edward P. Wimberly, *Using Scripture in Pastoral Counseling* (Nashville: Abingdon Press, 1994).

[20] "Scripture," Article 4 of *Confession of Faith in a Mennonite Perspective*. The guideline is also consistent with affirmations about the place and interpretation of the Bible found in the statement of philosophy of theological education at Associated Mennonite Biblical Seminary: "As teachers of the church and servants of the Word, we accept the Scripture as the primary measure of what we teach in all theological disciplines. . . . It means that we seek to have the categories of our disciplines, the history and ministries of the church, and our interpretation of the contemporary world measured and formed by Scripture." See "Ministerial Formation and Theological Education in Mennonite Perspective," reprinted as Appendix 1 in this volume (243).

[21] Discussions of hermeneutics and pastoral care and counseling, and pastoral and practical theology, can be found in Donald Capps, *Pastoral Care and Hermeneutics* (Philadelphia: Fortress Press, 1984); Charles V. Gerkin, *Re-visioning Pastoral Counseling in a Hermeneutical Mode* (Nashville: Abingdon Press, 1984); and *Prophetic Pastoral Practice: A Christian Vision of Life Together* (Nashville: Abingdon Press, 1991).

[22] See, for example, Jay E. Adams, *The Use of Scripture in Counseling* (Grand Rapids: Baker Books, 1975).

[23] On this point, see Ray S. Anderson, *Christians Who Counsel: The Vocation of Wholistic Therapy* (Grand Rapids: Zondervan Publishing House, 1990), especially chapter 6, "The Word of God As Empowerment for Change."

[24] Concerning this normative guideline I am especially indebted to James E. Loder, *The Transforming Moment*, 2nd ed. (Colorado Springs: Helmers & Howard, 1989); and *The Logic of the Spirit: Human Development in Theological Perspective* (San Francisco: Jossey-Bass, 1998). Loder's pioneering interdisciplinary work includes a proposed way to appreciate the God-initiated and -sustained collaborative endeavor engaging the Holy Spirit and the human spirit in a number of settings such a those of counseling and psychotherapy.

[25] On this point of ministry practice as collaboration with the Spirit, see June A. Yoder, "Collaborative Preaching: Persuasion and the Spirit in Close-Up" (D.Min. thesis, Bethany Theological Seminary, 1991).

[26] See "Holy Spirit," Article 3 of *Confession of Faith in a Mennonite Perspective*, 17-20. Discussions of the Holy Spirit for the field of pastoral care can be found in

Marvin G. Gilbert and Raymond T. Brock, eds. *Theology and Theory*, vol. 1 of *The Holy Spirit and Counseling* (Peabody: Hendrickson Publishers, Inc., 1985); John Kie Vining, *Spirit-Centered Counseling* (East Rockaway, N. Y.: Cummings & Hathaway, 1995); and John Kie Vining, ed., *Pentecostal Caregivers . . . Anointed to Heal* (East Rockaway, N.Y.: Cummings & Hathaway, 1995).

[27] I am intentionally connecting my own proposal with Thomas Groome's and James Loder's work at this point. See Groome, *Sharing Faith*, especially the appplications of his "shared praxis approach" to several ministry forms, in the last part of the book.

[28] For this way of articulating the normativity principle, I am indebted to Alvin C. Dueck, *Between Jerusalem and Athens: Ethical Perspectives on Culture, Religion, and Psychotherapy* (Grand Rapids: Baker Books, 1995), especially part 1. See also Anderson, *Christians Who Counsel*, chapter 5, "The Kingdom of God As Therapeutic Context."

[29] Scholars such as John Dominic Crossan suggest that the *kingdom of God* language of Jesus also can be considered in the context of the wisdom tradition and theology. *The Historical Jesus: The Life of a Mediterranean Jewish Peasant* (San Francisco: Harper San Francisco, 1991), 287-92.

[30] Anderson, *Christians Who Counsel*, especially 86-102.

[31] Dueck uses this phrase in his discussion of psychotherapists as ethicists, in *Between Jerusalem and Athens*, 13.

[32] In the field of pastoral care and counseling there have been promising developments in this regard in recent years, as documented, for example, in Pamela D. Couture and Rodney J. Hunter, eds. *Pastoral Care and Social Conflict* (Nashville: Abingdon Press, 1995); George M. Furnish, *The Social Context of Pastoral Care* (Louisville: Westminster John Knox Press, 1994); and Jeanne Stevenson Moessner, ed., *Through the Eyes of Women: Insights for Pastoral Care* (Minneapolis: Fortress Press, 1996).

[33] I deliberately add *vision* to *story* because I want to emphasize more than Dueck does the future-oriented, hope-filled, prophetic, eschatological, and utopian dimensions involved in, and elicited by, the biblical symbol of the reign of God.

16

Power and authority

Helping the church face problems
and adapt to change

J. Nelson Kraybill

During my years of working in England, I once organized a mediation
process for a deeply divided congregation of another denomination.
The minister of this traditional church had experienced a personal
charismatic renewal. Trained as a lawyer, he had an analytical and
organizational mind. But a personal encounter with the Holy Spirit
had transformed his expectations of congregational life and worship.

The minister began to teach from the pulpit on healing, spiritual
gifts, tongues, and evangelism. Feeling a call from God to see renewal
in his congregation, the rejuvenated minister prayed and coached
some members of his flock into euphoric worship and deeper awareness
of God. Music changed, and worship services became unpredictable
in structure and format. Some worshipers fell to the floor in a trance,
and new believers started to come to the church.

One day, on personal retreat, the minister received a vision of
how God wanted that congregation to change and extend itself through
evangelism. The minister wrote out the plan and convinced church
council members of its merits during a leadership retreat. With the
apparent backing of the church council, the minister presented this
vision to the congregation and began to implement the plan.

A rebellion ensued. Older members of the congregation missed
traditional hymns and did not like popular chorus songs. Some people
felt manipulated into worship expressions that seemed unnatural to
them. But the most common complaint was that basic patterns of
congregational life and witness were being decided by the pastor and
by his supporters on the church council. A large portion of the congregation was grateful for strong leadership, but a substantial minority
felt disempowered and out of the loop. They withdrew support from
the minister. The resulting crisis paralyzed and nearly destroyed the
congregation.

Paradox of power at the heart of the gospel

At the heart of the gospel lies this paradox: the Lamb of God, who came with such vulnerability that he died on a Roman cross, also is the Lion of the tribe of Judah. This Lamb-Lion acted with such authority and power that he was able to transform the lives of his followers and of millions in subsequent generations who believed in his name.

It has been the ongoing challenge of the Christian church, seeking to be faithful to a Lord of such paradox, to engage the issues of power and authority in ways that are true to the gospel. This challenge is unavoidable, because power and authority are integral factors of any functioning group, organization, or society. Either the church will embrace the responsibility for using power and authority wisely, or the church will be on the receiving end of internal and external forces that may use power and authority for less than noble ends.

The Gospel of Mark vividly illustrates the paradox of authority in the life of Jesus. On one hand, the evangelist portrays Jesus exercising awesome power by calming the sea, exorcising demons, forgiving sins, healing the sick, and silencing powerful opponents. On the other hand, Mark presents Jesus as one willing to serve—even to the extent of laying down his life. The paradox of power and authority in Mark is captured in the teaching of Jesus, "You know that among the Gentiles those whom they recognize as their rulers lord it over them, and their great ones are tyrants over them. But it is not so among you; but whoever wishes to become great among you must be your servant, and whoever wishes to be first among you must be slave to all" (Mark 10:42-44).

The paradox of authority and servanthood in Mark, according to a recent interpreter, "is intended to persuade Jesus' followers to balance these two motifs in their own discipleship role within the community of believers. One cannot exist without the other."[1]

Power and authority are not intrinsically good or evil

Believers in the early church were keenly aware of the pervasiveness of power and authority, and they recognized the potential for great evil or great good in these forces. The gospel entered a first-century political and economic world in which the power of the Roman imperial government was massively and often oppressively visible. From the perspective of New Testament authors, Rome ruled all the known world and was a constant backdrop for the story of Jesus and the early church. We see textual evidence of imperial power in everything from the decree of Emperor Augustus at the time of Jesus' birth (Luke 2:1), to the house arrest of Paul at Rome at the end of his missionary career (Acts 28), to a late first-century admonition to "honor the emperor" (1 Pet. 2:17).

Christian theological assessment of such overwhelming political power ranged from Paul's cautiously optimistic view of earthly rulers to the virulent rejection of Roman authority expressed by John of Patmos. What these two early leaders share, however, is a conviction that authority exercised by humans is derivative. Human authority and power either come from God (Rom. 13:1: "There is no authority except from God, and those authorities that exist have been instituted by God"), or they come from Satan (Rev. 13:2: "And the dragon gave [the beast] his power and his throne and great authority"). Even in the case of Revelation 13, in which the beast seems to represent idolatrous and blasphemous Rome, the ultimate source of power is God: Satan, who vests the beast with power, had usurped that power from God (Rev. 12:7-9).

The New Testament generally reserves positive use of the word "authority" (*exousia*)[2] for references to God or Jesus. When the word refers to others (such as disciples, Paul, or congregational leaders), typically an accompanying phrase reminds the reader that such authority is derived from God, Jesus, or the Scriptures.[3]

Early Christians confessed that God was the only legitimate source of power (Rom. 13:1). Because Christians view the Son of God as divine, their loyalty to Jesus Christ is above all other allegiances. This radical commitment is reflected in the political accusation against Christian missionaries at Thessalonica: "These people . . . have been turning the world upside down. . . . They are all acting contrary to the decrees of the emperor, saying that there is another king named Jesus" (Acts 17:6-7).

The book of Revelation is full of liturgical praise to God—and specifically to Jesus—who alone is "worthy . . . to receive power and wealth and wisdom and might and honor and glory and blessing" (Rev. 5:12; cf. 4:11). Throughout Revelation, honorary titles and gestures of allegiance are lavished on Yahweh God and his Messiah.

These expressions of allegiance seem to parallel and directly compete with expressions of loyalty commonly showered on the Roman emperor and his minions.

Power in the church is radically different from power in pagan society

The above citations are among many indications in the New Testament that early Christians understood the claims of the gospel to radically relativize earthly political powers. Yet the primary concern of the early church seems to have been the nature of power and authority within the new faith community of those who called Jesus *kurios* ("Lord," the title commonly given to the emperor).

Throughout the New Testament runs a theme that believers are to adopt attitudes toward power, authority, and servanthood that mirror the life of Jesus. That is, followers of Jesus embody and wrestle with the same paradox of power/authority and servanthood that the Gospel writers portray in Jesus. The author of the fourth Gospel records Jesus washing his disciples' feet and saying, "I have set you an example, that you also should do as I have done to you" (John 13:15). Paul writes, "Let the same mind be in you that was in Christ Jesus, who . . . emptied himself, taking the form of a slave" (Phil. 2:5-7).

The emphasis on servanthood in the early church is striking because the dominant (Roman imperial) culture was highly stratified and class-conscious. Imperial society was a power pyramid, with the all-powerful emperor at the apex and powerless slaves at the broad base. Class stratification was as follows:[4]

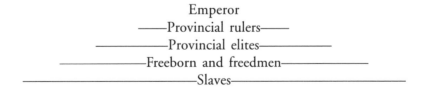

Roman imperial society functioned on a patronage system, with most individuals being both patron to someone below them and client to someone above them. Patron-client relationships in the first century were formalized and ubiquitous, with well-recognized terminology and rituals. Patrons gave benefits to clients, such as employment, business loans, or access to economic and political influence. In exchange, clients gave loyalty, praise, and service to their patrons. Patrons wanted to be recognized—publicly, if possible—as "benefactors."[5] Clients wanted to be recognized—publicly, if possible—as "friends" of their more-powerful patrons.[6] People in the middle of the power pyramid were typically both client and patron, relating in those respective roles to people above and below their social level.

Jesus rejected the familiar power pyramid and patronage systems of his day: "The kings of the Gentiles lord it over them; and those in authority over them are called benefactors. But not so with you" (Luke 22:25-26). In other words, Jesus recognized that pagan society had a pyramid of power relationships, and he intended for his followers to structure their own group relationships according to a different pattern. Even in relations with pagan society, Jesus admonished his disciples to avoid any striving for upward mobility. At banquets, where social position usually dictated seating position, Jesus instructed his followers to take the lowliest place at the table (Luke 14:7-11).

Many people in the early church would have been influenced by Roman imperial understandings of power and authority. Corinth, from which we have an abundance of early church evidence through the writings of Paul, was a relatively young city with fluid social strata and political structures. Corinth was a crossroads urban area, filled with immigrants and people seeking upward mobility.

Paul writes to the church at Corinth, "Not many of you . . . were powerful, not many were of noble birth. . . . But God chose what is weak in the world to shame the strong" (1 Cor. 1:26-27).[7] After alluding to the social/political/economic weakness of believers at Corinth, Paul continues with the underlying principle of his own ministry: "I decided to know nothing among you except Jesus Christ, and him crucified" (1 Cor. 2:2). The power of Paul's leadership rested in the Holy Spirit, not in Paul himself.

Contrast of power *praxis* in pagan and Christian settings

The late first-century letter of 1 Peter gives a striking profile of the contrast between pagan and Christian engagement of power structures. A large portion of this document falls into two major sections:

1 Pet. 2:11–4:11   Directions for how believers relate to power structures that do not recognize the lordship of Jesus Christ.

1 Pet. 4:12–5:11   Directions for how believers handle power within the faith community that recognizes the lordship of Jesus Christ.

These two major sections are apparent because of their parallel structure: each section begins with the word "Beloved" and ends with a doxology. [8]

The first section (2:11–4:11) focuses on relationships with a pagan world. It says that Christians should "accept the authority of" political rulers, that believing slaves should "accept the authority of" (non-Christian) masters, and believing wives should "accept the authority of" (non-Christian) husbands. At the structural center of this section is a hymn fragment that refers to Jesus: "He committed no sin. . . . When he was abused, he did not return abuse" (1 Pet. 2:22-23). The experience of Christians relating to pagan power structures will be suffering and apparent powerlessness, toward a redemptive and missiological end (2:24; 3:1-2).

The second section (4:12–5:11) deals with power relationships within the Christian church. Instead of speaking to the party that society would normally deem to be the subservient one in a power relationship (as was the case in the first section), the author now addresses the person holding power—the congregational elders. The structural center again is a hymn fragment: "God opposes the proud, but gives grace to the humble" (5:5). Clustered around this hymn fragment are exhortations for leaders to "tend the flock . . . exercising oversight" (5:2). Elders should "not lord it over those in your charge, but be examples" (5:3). To all readers the author says, "Humble yourselves" (5:6). The experience of leadership within the faith community will be one of unpretentious, attentive modeling, mentoring, and overseeing. This way of exercising power will receive divine blessing and validation when Christ returns (5:6).

Church leadership is vested with Holy Spirit power

Along with all the above evidence of servanthood and humility in church leadership comes abundant evidence that both Jesus and early church leaders were vested with power, particularly in the context of mission.

The synoptic Gospels emphasize that Jesus acted and spoke "as one having authority" (Mark 1:22, par.); the fourth Gospel underscores the notion that Jesus' authority was granted to him by God (John 12:49). Jesus sent out his followers on a preaching assignment, and "gave them authority over unclean spirits, to cast them out, and to cure every disease" (Matt. 10:1). The first Gospel concludes with Jesus' words, "All authority (*exousia*) in heaven and on earth has been given to me. Go therefore and make disciples of all nations . . . " (Matt. 28:18-19).

Luke begins his narrative of the early church after the resurrection with Jesus' assurance to his followers, "You will receive power (*dunamis*) when the Holy Spirit has come upon you; and you will be my witnesses . . . to the ends of the earth" (Acts 1:8). These and other references in a missiological context suggest that power and authority ultimately enable the church to cross barriers of taboo, class, race, and nation to reconcile people to God.

Acts 15: Leadership addressing conflict

Any group or society that survives and remains vital will encounter constant change. Change comes because of new factors in the environment or from new needs or personalities within the group, and it nearly always generates conflict. Effective exercise of power and authority in such a changing environment is measured to a large extent by the leaders' ability to direct the process and outcome of conflict in a way that strengthens the group.

The New Testament model of leadership, with emphasis on humility, rejects authoritarian or coercive approaches that were common in the ancient world. There is abundant evidence that early church leaders acted with authority, despite vigorous rejection of *hubris* and coercion in the Christian community. The very fact that the New Testament letters and books ever got written is, in each case, an assertive expression of power and authority.

Most early Christian literature was generated by conflict, and perhaps no issue was more volatile than the question of whether Gentiles needed to adhere to the full Jewish law in order to be part of the church. This strategic matter had far-reaching implications for the mission, identity, and character of the entire Christian movement. Without assertive and wise leadership, this matter could have seriously divided the church.

The book of Acts gives a succinct narrative of a process the early church used to address the question of relationships between Jews and Gentiles. The following steps are evident:

1. There was a big disagreement. "Certain individuals" differed with Paul and Barnabas on the question of circumcision, and "no small dissension and debate" arose (Acts 15:1-2).
2. The church sought out a forum in which all parties could be heard. The local faith community in Antioch took action and appointed "Paul and Barnabas and some of the others . . . to go up to Jerusalem to discuss this question with the apostles and the elders" (15:2).
3. People in conflict had opportunity to tell their stories. The delegation of disputants arrived at Jerusalem and "reported all that God had done with them" (15:4).
4. There was enough time to air convictions, feelings, and perspectives. There was "much debate" (15:7).
5. Leaders, after careful listening, proposed a way forward that took into account concerns raised on both sides of the issue. "After they finished speaking, James replied, 'My brothers, . . . I have reached the decision that we should not trouble [with circumcision] those Gentiles who are turning to God, . . . but we should write to them to abstain only from things polluted by idols and from fornication . . . ' " (15:13-21).
6. The proposed solution was ratified by consensus. With the "consent of the whole church" the leaders at Jerusalem sent a delegation to Antioch to convey the agreements reached (15:22-25).

Far more than a mere facilitator, Paul was bringing visionary agenda and issues to the church. When new realities of the mission enterprise generated conflict, Paul and others involved in debate looked to three places for decision-making cues: (1) up-to-date evidence from a real ministry situation, (2) the witness of Scripture, and (3) guidance of the Holy Spirit as experienced by the gathered faith community.

There is some indication that the dispute recorded in Acts 15 was not resolved as neatly as Luke would have us believe (cf. Gal. 2:1-14). There also may have been more of an authoritarian spirit to the role of James (Acts 15:13) than my interpretation would suggest.

Nevertheless, Acts 15 provides one example of leaders moving the faith community through change in a way that involved vigorous and appropriate exercise of power and authority.

Leaders with courage
to differentiate *and* stay in relationship

One decisive and positive element in the Acts 15 story is that leaders had the courage both to differentiate and to stay in meaningful relationship with others in the church community. This theme is developed by Edwin H. Friedman in his book *Generation to Generation.*[9] Friedman notes that churches and synagogues function much like families. He writes: "What is vital to changing any kind of 'family' is not knowledge of technique or even of pathology but, rather, the capacity of the family leader to define his or her own goals and values while trying to maintain a nonanxious presence within the system."[10]

In family systems therapy, "the criterion of whom to counsel is no longer who has the symptom, but *who has the greatest capacity to bring change to the system.*"[11] It may not be the "identified patient" with whom the therapist works, but someone in the family who appears to be functioning well and is in a position to influence the patient. Applied to problems and challenges in the church, this principle suggests that it often will be the leader who has the greatest capacity to change the system.

This principle does not mean that leaders take personal responsibility for everything the group does. To do so would indicate that they have not differentiated their personalities from that of the group (and that they will absorb a dangerous amount of stress). Nor will effective leaders manipulate or coerce the group, as that would keep others from maturity. Nor do these leaders simply go their own way and ignore the group's desires, because the result will be loss of trust. Friedman concludes, "It is the maintaining of self-differentiation while remaining a part of the family that optimizes the opportunities for fundamental change."[12]

Friedman depicts leadership in a group as falling somewhere on a continuum between charisma and consensus.[13] Charismatic leadership depends on the sheer energy, brilliance, and persuasiveness of the leader. This type of power tends to make members of the group into dependent followers and creates serious instability when the leader dies or leaves. Consensus-oriented groups abhor polarization, and they discourage the individualism or assertiveness of any leader. Such groups will usually be less imaginative and are apt to be derailed by extremists or dysfunctional members.

A family systems understanding of group dynamics calls for leadership through self-differentiation of the leaders themselves. "The basic concept of leadership through self-differentiation is this: If a leader will take primary responsibility for his or her own goals and self, while *staying in touch* with the rest of the organism, there is more than a reasonable chance that the body will follow. . . . Any leader can stay in touch if he or she does not try to stand out. The trick . . . is to be able to differentiate self and still remain in touch in spite of the body's effort's to counter such differentiation."[14] These leaders do not try to define their followers but only themselves.

The apostle Paul's authority at Corinth and Philippi

The apostle Paul apparently did not always adequately differentiate himself from the congregations with which he worked as a leader. See, for example, his solicitous and agonized response to the Christians at Corinth when they rejected his authority, and his jubilation when the congregation again affirmed him (2 Cor. 7:2-16). But Paul's candor about his inner emotional response as a leader is valuable because it reveals his human struggle to place responsibility for the direction of a congregation with Christ and with the church members, not with himself as a leader.

Paul's view of authority pivots on his understanding of the cross as the power of the gospel. "I decided to know nothing among you except Jesus Christ, and him crucified," is how Paul summarizes his message and his ministry at Corinth (1 Cor. 2:2). He speaks of coming to Corinth "in weakness and in fear and in much trembling" (2:3). He identifies as fully as possible with the person of his Lord: "But we have the mind of Christ" (2:16); "we take every thought captive to obey Christ" (2 Cor. 10:5). The way Paul differentiates as a leader is by subsuming his ego and personality into the character and presence of the risen Christ. Such a self-conscious blending of personality in leaders could spin off into delusions of grandeur if they begin to think of themselves as divine. But what Paul incorporates from Christ is the paradoxical power of the cross—not coercion but suffering love, respect even for the enemy, and clear expression of personal conviction.

In 2 Corinthians 11–13, the apostle indulges in some self-defense, pleading, sarcasm, and boasting. But even in the midst of this outburst there is evidence that Paul still has his theology of leadership rooted in the cross. Paul "boasts" of his weakness and vulnerability, and he reports that the Lord told him, "My grace is sufficient for you, for power is made perfect in weakness" (2 Cor. 12:9). This phrase captures the paradox of noncoercive leadership that is both full of conviction and self-differentiated: leaders who love and care enough to stay in touch even with those who disagree or oppose have astounding power.

The object of good leadership is both to bring individual members of the community to maturity and to help the group move toward corporate objectives. Paul tells readers at Corinth, "We rejoice when we are weak and you are strong. This is what we pray for, that you may become perfect" (2 Cor. 13:9). To believers at Philippi he says, "Work out your own salvation with fear and trembling; for it is God who is at work in you" (Phil. 2:12-13). The author of Ephesians wants leaders in the church "to equip the saints for the work of ministry" until all members come "to maturity, to the measure of the full stature of Christ" (Eph. 4:12-13).

Although Paul himself does not always exhibit nonanxious presence as a leader, he periodically seems to catch himself owning too much as an apostle. Throughout his letters, he turns responsibility for the outcome of a congregational crisis or decision over either to the faith community in question, or to God. Paul differentiates, asserts, makes himself vulnerable, provides leadership—and then usually insists that ownership for the direction of the church lies entirely in the hands of his readers under the lordship of Christ. His power and authority rest more in the clarity of his convictions and message than in his office as a missionary, apostle, or church planter.

Leadership without easy answers

In a recent book entitled *Leadership without Easy Answers,* Ronald Heifetz gives a paradigm of group decision making that emphasizes the role of the leader in helping groups face their own problems.[15] "Imagine the differences in behavior when people operate with the idea that 'leadership means influencing the community to follow the leaders vision' versus 'leadership means influencing the community to face its problems.'"[16]

Heifetz decisively advocates the latter view, and he maintains leadership is more an activity than a position of authority or a set of personal characteristics.[17] The primary task of leadership is to help groups address conflicts in values, and to diminish the gap between the values people stand for and the reality they face. Most groups will have competing values, and a number of these may need to be included within the group for it to function. Good leadership, Heifetz says, "places emphasis on the act of giving clarity and articulation to a community's guiding values. Neither providing a map for the future that disregards value conflicts nor providing an easy way out that neglects the facts will suffice for leadership."

Healthy group process will positively encourage conflict, in the sense of eliciting a full range of perspectives and convictions from within (or even from beyond) the group. Heterogeneity is a valuable resource for social learning, but leaders must help steer a group toward agenda that is worth sustained attention. Groups facing difficult problems are tempted to seize upon a distracting issue that feels manageable rather than to face straight into complex, foundational matters that might be more pressing.[18] It is possible, for example, that current North American Mennonite preoccupation with homosexuality is such a distracting issue. Underlying this lightning-rod issue may be more foundational questions of Bible interpretation, sources of authority, acculturation, urban-rural tension, or understanding of the meaning of covenant.

When groups become highly conflicted or agitated, members often look to authoritarian or charismatic figures who will decide on behalf of the group and impose solutions. These leader-focused strategies ultimately disable the group, diminishing personal and collective resources for accomplishing adaptive work in the future.[19]

Conflict management as a powerful leadership tool

Because group adaptation always means dealing with conflict, it is noteworthy that the New Testament has specific counsel on steps to be taken when disputes arise. Parties in conflict must be in direct conversation with each other, and they should go to a third party only as a last resort (Matt. 18:15-19). The church is a place where members speak the truth in love (Eph. 4:15) and do not let the sun go down on anger (Eph. 4:26). These basic rules of conflict management are indispensable for effective leadership and will help shape the ethos of a faith community. Churches can be reassured by the fact that the New Testament reflects communities that were rife with conflict and diversity. For example, the fact that the New Testament includes four Gospels is evidence that the early church found it necessary to embrace diversity.

The function of good leadership is not only to help the group identify the important issues that merit sustained attention, but also to help regulate the intensity and format for group processing. Heifetz compares this task to that of a cook adjusting heat under a pressure cooker. "If the pressure goes beyond the carrying capacity of the vessel, the pressure cooker can blow up. On the other hand, with no heat nothing cooks."[20] Leaders must help set the pace and flow of information to the group and must help organize the process of group decision making. They must help the group do reality testing, thinking through the practical implications of various options. And they must be willing to self-differentiate, stating their own convictions and insights in a nonthreatening way that invites others to do the same.

Finally, it should be noted that in exceptional circumstances leaders may need to act decisively in autocratic ways, either because the time is too short for group process or because the group is not resilient enough to cope with the stress of decision making. In normal group life, however, it is a sign of good leadership to "give the work back to the people" when important corporate agenda must be decided.[21]

Vision setting as a way to empower the church

Helping the church articulate and own a vision is perhaps the most empowering task leaders can perform. Underlying most vision in the early church was a firm conviction that the end of history was near. God was about to redeem a fractured creation and make all things new in Jesus Christ. Virtually all major innovations or costly changes of behavior in the early church—communal economy, the mission effort, and love of enemies—were rooted in this Christian eschatology.

Implications of Christian eschatology are not limited to the future; the church starts living now the way all of humanity someday will live in the reign of God. The central task of leaders in the early church was to articulate where history was headed because of Jesus Christ, and to call believers to embody that future now by leading lives "worthy of the Lord" (Col. 1:10).

Leading worthy lives requires a variety of short-term steps, and here effective leaders must help the church shape vision. Phillip Lewis describes a vision-creating process that oscillates between a congregational leader setting out vision and seeking insights or response from the congregation.[22] Transformational leaders become "communications champions," consistently and repeatedly setting out group objectives in ways that inspire and energize.

Summary

Effective church leaders are more than facilitators; they are initiators who remain accountable to God, to the Scriptures, and to members of the church. They are visionaries who constantly compare what *is* with what *could be* by the grace of God. They are conflict managers who build so much trust and respect into group decision making that church members are free to express any idea or concern.

Authority for this kind of leadership comes from Christ himself, which means leaders will act with the apparent powerlessness of the cross. There will be no coercion or manipulation, just the grace-filled example of leaders who speak their own convictions with clarity and love. There will be no paralysis of interminable search for artificial consensus, nor the atrophy of imagination that comes with authoritarianism. Rather, leaders will skillfully help the church face problems, hear diverse perspectives, and seek Holy Spirit guidance to plot a course that is faithful to the Scriptures and responsive to a breadth of concerns in the faith community.

Notes

[1] Narry F. Santos, "The Paradox of Authority and Servanthood in the Gospel of Mark," *Bibliotheca Sacra* 154 (October-December 1997): 460.

[2] The lexical scope of this common word for authority in the New Testament is considerable, so the exact meaning must be interpreted from context. Possibilities include "freedom of choice, right to act, ability to do something, capability, might,

power, authority, absolute power, warrant, ruling power, official power." Walter Bauer, William F. Arndt, F. Wilbur Gingrich, *A Greek-English Lexicon of the New Testament and Other Early Christian Literature* (Chicago: University of Chicago Press, 1979), 277-79.

[3] E.g., Luke 9:1; 1 Cor. 9:8. When Paul ventured an opinion that was not so derived, he understood that he no longer spoke with the same level of authority (1 Cor. 7:25; 2 Cor. 11:17).

[4] The following diagram and discussion of patronage are adapted from my book, *Imperial Cult and Commerce in John's Apocalypse* (Sheffield: Sheffield Academic Press, 1996), 72-80.

[5] At Ephesus, for example, archeologists have found hundreds of inscriptions and plaques put in public places, in which clients honor or thank their patrons. This practice was pervasive in the first-century Roman world.

[6] The *friend* language for client-patron relationship is evident at the appearance of Jesus before Pilate, when accusers reminded Pilate of his patronage obligations: "If you release this man, you are no *friend* of the emperor" (John 19:12).

[7] The fact that "not many" believers at Corinth came from socially or politically prominent backgrounds suggests that at least some did. One such case might be Erastus, who was "city treasurer" (Rom. 16:23).

[8] For insights on the structure of 1 Peter, and the implications for power relationships, I am indebted to Mary H. Schertz, "Nonretaliation and the Haustafeln in 1 Peter," in *The Love of Enemy and Nonretaliation in the New Testament*, ed. Willard M. Swartley (Louisville: Westminster John Knox Press, 1992), 258-86.

[9] Edwin H. Friedman, *Generation to Generation: Family Process in Church and Synagogue* (New York: Guilford Press, 1985).

[10] Ibid., 2-3. Friedman is not the first to draw a parallel between family systems and leadership in the faith community. Several New Testament authors note that qualified leaders in the church likely will be those who have functioned well in their own marriage and family systems (1 Tim. 3:4-5, 12-13; cf. Titus 1:6).

[11] Ibid., 22.

[12] Ibid., 29.

[13] Ibid., 225-28.

[14] Ibid., 229.

[15] Ronald A. Heifetz, *Leadership without Easy Answers* (Cambridge, Mass.: Belknap Press of Harvard University Press, 1994).

[16] Ibid., 14.

[17] Ibid., 20-23.

[18] Ibid., 37.

[19] Ibid., 73.

[20] Ibid., 106.

[21] Ibid., 121.

[22] Phillip V. Lewis, *Transformational Leadership: A New Model for Total Church Involvement* (Nashville: Broadman & Holman, 1996), 93-102.

17

What is at the heart of pastoral ministry?

Erick Sawatzky

As a result of developments in the last half of the twentieth century, pastors and congregations are now experiencing a tentativeness and an ambivalence regarding both pastoral ministry and ordination itself that is relatively new in the history of Christianity. What does the pastor do? What does ordination mean? Who ordains? Who should be ordained? Where does the pastor fit? These are among the questions at the heart of the matter.

Answering these questions requires that we reenvision or reconceive the office of pastoral ministry, which is unique because of the particular confluence of location, leadership, authority, and professionalization embodied in the pastor. In this essay, I will seek to identify these four factors that converge in the office of pastor, in the hope that by again embracing this ministry in the life of the church, we will glorify God, and God's church will be strengthened.

Location

The pastor and pastoral ministry are searching for a location. In many denominations these days the emphasis in ministry is on the unordained members of the congregation rather than on the ordained clergy. Congregations stress that all have a gift from God, that every member is in some kind of ministry. In some cases this emphasis is the result of a shortage of ordained clergy, and in others it was prompted by the theological realization that ministry belongs to all God's people.

In the (Old) Mennonite Church fifty years ago, the ministry belonged to the ordained clergy. Bishops, preachers, and deacons, all ordained for life, were in charge of congregations and districts. The congregation's leadership model looked something like this:

Ordained	*Not ordained*
Bishops	Trustees
Pastors	Sunday school superintendent
Deacons	Sunday evening
	Literary society
	Mennonite youth fellowship
	Sewing circle

Then came reaction and change. Rebellion against authority characterized much of North American society, and that trend influenced the church.[1] Church members and society became more educated and professional. The visibility of the social sciences increased. Church councils came into vogue. The clergy moved over and in some cases were displaced.[2] In the 1960s and 1970s, congregational organization looked more like this:

Not ordained	*Ordained*
Congregation	Pastors
Church council	
Deacons committee	
Elders	
Lay ministers	

Still later, in the 1980s and 1990s, in some settings congregational ministry divided itself into two parts: spiritual ministry and program ministry. What is most interesting about the congregational leadership model of this period is that the ordained clergy appear nowhere on the chart. Pastors were presumably called to something and were located somewhere in congregational life, but what they were called for and where they fit are not evident. The lines of accountability and authority are not apparent.

Executive

Ministry group	Administration
Spiritual ministry	Program ministry

Leadership

In addition to lack of clarity about the location of pastoral ministry in congregational life, churches and pastors experience profound confusion and ambivalence about leadership, and about whether and how the pastor exercises it.

The last several decades have produced many books on how to be a leader. Workshops and seminars abound that claim to make one an expert at church leadership and church growth. Pastors and church workers flock to these events and emerge sighing, "If I could only be like [_____], our church would prosper."

Many of us are accustomed to identifying a particular office with leadership. We consider the president or prime minister the leader of the country. The captain of a team is normally thought of as the team's leader. Similarly, the pastor of a church is often thought of as the leader of that congregation. This assumption leads pastors to expect that people will follow them, and that people should do so. Sometimes congregations do. Sometimes they do for a little while, and then they gradually cease to do so.

It is often true that the person holding a particular position is in fact a leader. In many situations it is people of credibility, competence, congruity, and sterling character who rise to positions of prominence and places of leadership. When they do, the leadership qualities ascribed to them are reinforced by their performance. People respect competent performance and follow, at least some of the time.

But, sadly, people who hold leadership positions are not always people of credibility, competence, congruity, and sterling character. They evoke no new admiration or trust by who they are and by what they do. The trust which had been granted to them by virtue of their office, they lose through irresponsible conduct or gross misconduct. They cannot lead because they have no followers.

Leadership is more than position and performance. Leadership, understood positively, is essentially a matter of the heart. It is a relationship. It hinges on the ability to attract people to follow a vision, a program, a course of action, or a plan of action. And that is, fundamentally, a matter of the heart. It is the heart, metaphorically speaking, that must communicate wholeness, maturity, a degree of wisdom, and depth. It is the heart that attracts people, inviting them to follow.

Vaclav Havel, playwright, dissident, prisoner, president of Czechoslovakia, said it well when he addressed the Congress of the United States in 1990: "Consciousness precedes being, and not the other way around. . . . Salvation of this human world lies nowhere else than in the human heart, in this human power to reflect, in human meekness and in human responsibility."[3] Parker Palmer, reflecting on these words in March 1990 in an address given for the Indiana office for campus ministries, goes on to say, "I don't know if there has ever been, from a more remarkable source, a stronger affirmation of the work of religion and higher education than Havel's words. . . . Matter, he is trying to tell us, is not the fundamental factor in the movement of history. Spirit is. Consciousness is. Human awareness is. Thought is. Spirituality is. Those are the deep sources of freedom and power with which people have been able to move boulders and create change."

Until recently, not much has been written or spoken about the spiritual foundations of leadership. We were far too preoccupied with the mechanics of it all. Perhaps we assumed a level of maturity and spirituality present in most people, and with that as a given, believed that anyone could be a leader if they had the right tools.

We have learned the hard way. American industry and the church have slowly come to see that information, tools, and position alone do not make a leader. Relationships make a leader! People do not follow for long those who offer only information or gimmicks. People follow character, credibility, and congruency. In their 1991 research, James M. Kouzes and Barry Z. Posner found that the characteristics people admired most in leaders, and which ranked far ahead of many other factors, were honesty, the capacity to look forward, the ability to inspire others, and competence.[4] Strong character inspires trust and confidence. Hence, in leadership training much of American business now stresses partnerships, collegiality, cooperation, and collaboration.

We in the Christian tradition have known that such qualities of character matter in leaders, not because such leadership works, or because it produces profits. We understand that the power of such leadership derives from creation itself. Human beings are made in the image of God. God is relational. It is in the quality of our relationships that we express our conformity to the way of God.

The fact that qualities of relationship are important for Christian leaders rules out arguments over position and place. It rules out operating in a hierarchical fashion, lording it over others. It invites participation, collaboration, and creativity.

Paradoxically, this relational style of leadership, which gives away power, does not deplete leaders' power supply nor diminish their capacity and authority to lead. Rather, leaders' authority and capacity to inspire and lead grow. Competence, relationships, and credibility are another part of the heart of the matter.

Authority

Leadership and authority are closely related. No one can lead without authority, and no leader is without authority.

But what kind of authority? In what does true authority consist? As noted above, society and church members rebelled against authority decades ago, especially against perceived and real authoritarianism. They replaced authoritarianism with process and plural leadership, but the issue of authority did not go away. Authoritarianism in the plural is still authoritarianism.

In what does pastoral authority consist? How is it to be exercised? I believe that pastoral authority is a matter of three related but separate phenomena: person, position, and performance.[5]

The pastor as person

We often refer to someone as a teacher, a physician, or an attorney. Sometimes we add a value judgment by saying she is a good teacher, an excellent physician, or a sensitive attorney. Occasionally, we will address the first category and speak of someone's person or character by saying he is "whole," "spiritual," "congruent," "deep," or "sophisticated." While first impressions and judgments about people are often made on the basis of positions they fill and on how well they perform in these roles, our long-term loyalties and judgments are usually based on their character, on essential qualities of their being.

Some vocations draw and depend upon the resources of character more than others. Being a pastor is one of these. While competence in preaching, teaching, and other pastoral tasks is important, it is the character, self-concept, and spiritual core of pastors that sustain them and support their long-term ministry. At the same time, it must be said that people of sound character must also be capable of doing the tasks they are given.

United Church of Christ pastor Karen Lebacqz, an author in the field of pastoral ethics, tells of searching for years for the clue that would unlock some of the mysteries around pastoral sexual ethics. Against her will, and against great personal resistance, she finally accepted the reality that what made the pastor different had to do with "the numinous."[6] This difference accounted for the fact that the sexual indiscretions of pastors were more devastating to congregations than the sexual indiscretions of others. It made sense of the fact that congregations expect more from their pastors and treat them differently than other people.

It may be helpful to draw some analogies. We may ask about what constitutes a painting. Is it merely a collection and arrangement of colors? Hardly! A painting speaks. A painting emanates something. Or we might ask about what constitutes a symphony. Is it merely a collection and arrangement of notes? Again, hardly! A symphony is more. It communicates a message. Similarly, a pastor is more than what she does. A pastor is more than the sum of the pastoral tasks to be performed—preaching, teaching, administration, counseling, visiting, and public service. The "more" has to do with an expectation that the pastor represents and embodies the sacred, the spiritual, and the holy in a particularly blended way. This embodiment accompanies the pastor whatever task he may be doing, whether he is enriching, empowering, and facilitating the spiritual life of the body, or discipling those in his care. If that embodiment of the sacred is missing, a major piece of what it means to be a pastor is missing.

The pastor's position

Normally, a person without a call to a position and place cannot be a pastor. An exception may be the person who is temporarily between position and place. The itinerant pastor also has a call and a place, even if it is not permanent. Both call and location are essential. It is vitally important for a pastor to have a position from which to function, both when the call is sensed internally, as coming from God, and when the call is confirmed by a congregation. There is little place for the "pastor at large." It is through the position, the office, that the pastor has access to information, to chosen leaders, boards, and committees, and to channels of formal and informal power. And this access is part of what makes a pastor.

Using the language of *office* is a way of speaking about the representational role that a pastor fulfills on behalf of the church. The office of ministry is owned by the church and given to the position, not to the person, at the time of credentialing. Hence, somewhat paradoxically, while the office belongs to the position, it is the pastor as a person who carries, tends, and embodies it. The authority that comes with it must be continually earned. As noted above, the concept of office also comes into play when one is temporarily between calls, is itinerant, or is retired. I prefer the language of *ministerial leadership* to *leadership ministries,* because ministerial leadership points to a state of being captured by the office, while leadership ministries points in a functional direction.

When we introduce someone by saying "This is our pastor," we often mean something more than "This is the person who has this job." Often this introduction implies a vocation, a calling, and quality of person, not merely a job. The meaning is mysteriously deeper and fuller.

The pastor's performance

One whose competence in executing the tasks of pastoral ministry is combined with integrity of character continually earns the right to tend the office of ministry. Incompetence and breaches of ethics are grounds for the church to suspend or remove this right. In the absence of call, one occupying the office should suspend one's rights.

Competence means ability to perform certain tasks well. No one can be a pastor without carrying out pastoral tasks such as preaching, teaching, and officiating at communion and weddings and funerals. It is through the performance of these tasks that identity is gained and competence is demonstrated.

One need not be competent in everything. Few pastors can do everything well, and congregations do not expect excellence across the board. What is important is that one does well enough the tasks that one's congregation determines to be essential.

It is difficult to speak of essentials and nonessentials in pastoral ministry. However, the essentials usually include the various public ministries, the more private person-to-person ministries, and the tasks we include under management. If these tasks are accomplished, the pastor is often judged positively in her pastoral role, and a common vision is frequently identifiable.

We have come full circle, for we are dealing once again with the central core and the central commitments of the person. Does this person have a call from God and the church? Does he have the depth of commitment and the wholeness of character to project a vision for a congregation and win their trust?

The reader may wonder: Are there any people alive who can meet the criteria just presented? And must they do so for life or just for a designated period of time? May one not just do pastoral work, such as visiting people, leading worship, and preaching occasionally? May we not just be faithful workers in the church faithfully exercising our gifts?

This matter is not a simple one. We are all called to ministry, and sometimes for lay people that call includes performing the tasks that pastors usually perform. This subject brings us to the question of professionalization.

Professionalization

Location, leadership, and authority are not the only issues for pastoral ministry. The professionalization of the pastor is another. The shift from the plural ministry of "the bench" to the ministry of the solo pastor who was educated and sometimes "did it all" was rapid and often abrupt. An added difficulty was that this transition ran counter to the ideas of some scholars engaged in recovering the Anabaptist Vision. Some Mennonite scholarship of the 1960s and 1970s emphasized the universal ministry of all baptized believers, interpreting the Reformation concept of "the priesthood of all believers" as an idea that meant, in effect, "the pastorhood of all believers."

The impact of these ideas on Mennonite pastors and congregations was profound and continues to the present. Congregations called a pastor and tended to expect him to accept "a pastorate," not merely to be a pastoring person. In instances where the pastor could not make the adjustment to these expectations, the result was confusion. The location and the identity of the pastor were thrown into crisis.

On the positive side, this change opened up the possibility of pastoral ministry to competent, called women, and in general to many more people. The emphasis on gifts has made it much easier to be a pastoring person. On the negative side, serving as a pastoring person is not the same as being a pastor who accepts the responsibility and authority of a pastorate. The change and confusion has sometimes made it more difficult for people to accept ordination and assume the role of pastor.

Doing the tasks of ministry that a pastor usually does meets only one of the criteria for being a pastor; the other criteria include having a call from God and from the church, holding a position, and competence. When all these are present, one's consciousness and identity change from doing something to being someone. The regularity and frequency with which one does something also contribute to shaping identity.

Who is this "someone"? Certainly, a pastor is not a person who "runs the church." Rather, the pastor is a person called by God and the congregation to be their spiritual guide, their primary representative to the universal church and to the world, and their leader. The Scriptures assume and support leadership for God's people. Our culture looks for and supports a particular form of pastoral leadership.

I tend to believe that when one has become a pastor, one is a pastor for life, although one's location in ministry may change. When God and the church have spoken, the call is not easily revoked or suspended. One does not put on or take off a role for certain times and occasions. Something of the mysterious is lost when pastoral ministry is specific to time and location, understood as controlled entirely by humans. Pastors are not and need not be perfect human beings; they should be people who are competent and whose character is congruent with the role they fill. These qualities are at the heart of the matter, vital aspects of the pastor's authority and professionalism.

Summary

Each of these factors—location, leadership, authority, and professionalization—contributes to the unique office of pastor. Although the location of the pastor has often been understood by way of analogy with other leadership positions, such analogies ultimately fail, because the position of pastor is unique. And while leadership has been understood in many different ways, pastoral leadership gives particular attention to competence, relationships, and credibility. Authority must continually be earned by a pastor in the integration of person, position, and performance. And while the professionalization of the ministry has served to demystify it and open it up to women, some remystifying of the office may be warranted as we recover a healthy sense of pastoral ministry as God's calling to what is finally more than the sum of human being and doing.

Notes

[1] When I use the word *rebellion,* I mean a change in the thinking of society and the church regarding authority. In some cases, members had seen bishops and other authority figures abuse or misuse power. In general, as people became professionals in their chosen fields, they reacted against and resisted the authority of people in other fields.

[2] In the General Conference Mennonite Church the clergy did not move over as readily or as far. In the U.S., GC clergy had a longer history of being professionals.

[3] Quoted by Parker Palmer in "Leading from Within"; http://www.teacherformation.org/html/rr/intro-f.cfm

[4] James M. Kouzes and Barry Z. Posner, *Credibility: How Leaders Gain and Lose It, Why People Demand It* (San Francisco: Jossey-Bass Publishers, 1993), 14.

[5] John Esau, retired director of Ministerial Leadership Services for the General Conference Mennonite Church, first introduced me to these categories. At times in our history Mennonites have chosen to emphasize one or another of these three, disturbing the delicate balance among them. A functional emphasis, highlighting competent practice, developed in the 1960s and 1970s largely because of a perceived or real overemphasis on position and positional authority in the earlier years of the twentieth century. In the latter years of the twentieth century the call to recover the importance of position (office) came about because the personal, representational, and numinous dimensions were missing in the emphasis on doing. Doing pastoral tasks—preaching, facilitating, administrating programs competently, and enabling and equipping the ministry of others—was not adequate for effective pastoral ministry.

[6] The numinous is that mysterious quality ascribed to a person who represents the holy or sacred.

Introduction to appendixes

Loren L. Johns and Ben C. Ollenburger

Appendix 1 addresses how pastors and other church leaders are formed and educated in the free church tradition. Conversations on these matters among faculty of Associated Mennonite Biblical Seminary originally centered in the Dean's Seminar[1] and eventuated in "Theological Education in the Free Church Tradition," a statement that articulated an egalitarian, nonhierarchical view of pastoral ministry, deemphasizing the offices of pastor and teacher in the church. In the late 1980s new faculty and new thinking by president Marlin Miller began to emphasize the office and special requirements of pastoral ministry. These changes led to intense discussions in the early 1990s about what kind of curriculum best serves this understanding.

Appendix 1 thus originated in a specific historical and theological context. Nevertheless, it deals with issues fundamental to any understanding of theological leadership and pastoral ministry in the free church tradition. It also addresses the education and formation that best prepare people for those ministries. Behind the matters dealt with in the document are the functionalism vs. office debate and care to avoid the tendency in some traditions to organize theological education narrowly around the tasks of ministry. It speaks to the limited but crucial role of a seminary in passing on traditions that have proved to be carriers of faithful witness to God's reign, in helping Christian communities make good judgments about normative Christian beliefs, and in articulating the church's beliefs in ways that nurture Christian life and faith. As such, Appendix 1 serves as a brief Mennonite theology of ministry and of the theological education and preparation that serve that theology.

Appendix 2 was written by AMBS dean Gayle Gerber Koontz in 1994. It addresses the implications of the previous document for the design of AMBS's curriculum. Its primary significance lies in its concise and clear delineation of the practical pedagogical implications of the longer document. Particularly noteworthy is its description of the seminary's "commitment to a missional orientation and perspective"—long before "missional church" became a priority of the denomination.

Note

[1] For more on the Dean's Seminar, see "Introduction" above (2); "That Some Would Be Pastors" (15-23); "Mennonite Ministry and Christian History" (53); and Ross T. Bender, ed., *The People of God* (Scottdale, Pa.: Herald Press, 1971).

238

Appendix 1

Ministerial formation and theological education
in Mennonite perspective

Associated Mennonite Biblical Seminary is an educational community established and commissioned by the General Conference Mennonite Church and the Mennonite Church in North America to educate Christian ministers and to provide theological leadership in the churches' teaching ministry.

In carrying out this twofold vocation, the seminary draws particularly on the resources of the Mennonite heritage which has its origins in the Radical Reformation. At the same time, the seminary faculty seeks to articulate and communicate understanding and practice of Christian faith and ministry that are ruled and corrected by Scripture. Further, the seminary community strives to sustain an educational ethos that inspires commitment to the Christian church's local and global mission in today's world.

Ministerial formation

Christian ministry finds its highest purpose in serving the church's calling to be the community of faith that witnesses in the world to God's reign as revealed in and through Jesus Christ. We believe that God calls the church to proclaim the kingdom of God and to be a sign of God's reign on earth[1] through the enabling presence and power of the Holy Spirit in the name of Jesus Christ.

Through the guidance of the Holy Spirit, the church's institutional resources can be a means of witnessing to God's reign in the world. Through the movement of the Holy Spirit, local congregations can be participants in the global mission and ministry of the church. Through the transforming presence of the Holy Spirit, ethnic, racial, class, and other divisions can be relativized and remolded into a new humanity in the body of Christ. Through the inspiration of the Holy Spirit, the church can invite others to faith in Christ and to a life of discipleship. Through the regenerating power of the Holy Spirit, the church as the community of faith can be preserved as a people among all nations without depending on any nation for its security, or blessing the rule of any nation over other nations.

We acknowledge that churches in the United States and Canada frequently settle for something less or something different. Christians in North America are frequently tempted to measure success by calculating institutional resources and influence. We sometimes limit our care and concern to our immediate surroundings while neglecting the church's broader mission and ministry in the world. Not infrequently we identify the community of faith with one ethnic group or race or class of people. Some depreciate evangelization; others emphasize a form of evangelization devoid of discipleship. Sometimes we also confuse the reign of God in this world with the domination of our particular nation over other nations. When churches thus lose sight of their calling in these or other ways, Christian ministry is also subverted and made to serve lesser ends.

While we recognize that Christian ministry has frequently fallen short of its highest purpose, we gratefully acknowledge that, through the grace of God, Christian ministry has also served well the church's calling to proclaim and signify the reign of God. As a seminary faculty we seek to learn from both the shortcomings and the accomplishments of Christian ministry in our time and throughout the history of the Christian church. And as a Mennonite seminary faculty, we devote particular attention to discerning the shortcomings and strengths in the Radical Reformation and Mennonite views and practices of ministry in the light of the church's calling.

Ministerial formation therefore begins with repentance, commitment, and confidence: repentance for accepting lesser purposes for ministry, commitment to serving the church's primary calling of being the community of God's kingdom in the world, and confidence in the sustaining and transforming power of the Holy Spirit.

We believe that all believers are called to participate in Christian ministry. The Holy Spirit distributes gifts to each member of the church for the common good of all and for their shared mission of witnessing to Jesus Christ in the world. As the ministering community called to proclaim and signify the kingdom of God, the church is a "royal priesthood, a holy nation."[2] All believers are called to lead lives wholly dedicated to praising God and to serving God among all peoples. All believers are called to participate in the worship, the mutual care and discipline, and the mission and service of the church.

Throughout church history, Christian ministry has frequently been limited to a body of clergy who alone minister to and mediate God's grace to the body of lay members of the church. The Radical Reformation and other renewal movements in the past and present have rejected the division of the church into lay and clerical classes. In a Mennonite perspective, God's grace comes to every believer through faith, through the community of faith as a whole, and through the gifts of the Holy Spirit to each member of the body of Christ. In this sense, all believers are priests; the church is a priesthood of all believers.

However, in the modern North American context the priesthood of all believers has sometimes been misunderstood in ways that undermine the particular ministries of pastors, missionaries, teachers, evangelists, and other church leaders.

The influence of individualism has, on occasion, made Christians reluctant to seek and accept the counsel of pastors and teachers within the body of Christ. Pastors and teachers have in turn been tempted to see their particular ministries more in terms of individual careers than as representative ministries of the church. Further, the influence of egalitarianism in Western culture has led some Christians to diminish the distinctive roles of pastors and other church leaders in the community of faith. Pastors, missionaries, and other church leaders have in turn depreciated their particular vocations within the common ministry and mission of the church.

As North American Mennonites we have at times adopted a form of clericalism that restricted Christian ministry to the few. At other times we have emphasized the ministry of all believers in ways that have undermined the particular and distinctive ministries of pastors and other church leaders. We acknowledge that neither tendency builds the church or undergirds its mission to proclaim and signify the reign of God in the world. The church is strengthened for its mission when believers are nurtured and guided by faithful pastors and other church leaders. As a seminary faculty, we are therefore committed to educating pastors and other church leaders to exercise their distinctive ministries, to equip other believers for their ministries, and to provide guidance for the church as a priestly, prophetic, and missionary community.

Pastoral and other church leadership ministries each have a set of common characteristics and carry a cluster of specific responsibilities. The term *office* refers to the common characteristics and specific responsibilities of a particular ministry and to the way it is ordered in relation to other ministries in the church.[3] For example, the office of pastoral ministry will normally include particular responsibility for leading congregational worship, preaching and teaching, providing pastoral care, administration (in the sense of giving guidance in the congregation's ministry and mission as a whole), helping to call forth and nurture the ministries of others in the congregation, and cultivating good relations with other congregational and conference bodies. With the responsibilities of the office also come appropriate authority and standards of accountability. Many congregations will have one pastor who gives primary attention to these responsibilities in cooperation with other congregational leaders. Other congregations will have two or more pastors who collaborate with each other and with other congregational members to fulfill the responsibilities of the pastoral office.

The Mennonite heritage and vision of Christian ministry has insisted on congruity between ministerial office and the ministering person. The personal and spiritual qualifications of people called to ministerial office are as important as their abilities to carry out the responsibilities of their role. Such qualifications for every ministerial office include a strong faith commitment nurtured by prayer; continuing study of the Scripture and participation in the life of the community of faith; discriminating appropriation of Mennonite and broader Christian belief and tradition; the church's discernment and call; a continuing sense of call and God's presence in one's life;[4] love for the church and the willingness to serve others without an excessive need for personal recognition; the willingness to receive and give counsel; and moral integrity in both personal and public life.

Specific expressions of pastoral and other ministerial offices may vary according to the personal characteristics of the minister and the context of ministry. For example, a pastor may be a particularly gifted and capable preacher while less gifted and skilled in providing administrative leadership. In such instances, the congregation should provide a pastor with opportunity for developing administrative abilities, or call other ministers to help carry out the administrative responsibilities of the pastoral office. The priorities of pastoral ministry may also vary from time to time and from congregation to congregation, depending on such things as the history of a given congregation, its membership, the moral and financial support it provides a pastor, and its relationship to other congregations. Similar variations may apply for the offices of missionaries, teachers, evangelists, and other church leaders.

Throughout church history, Christians have been tempted to depreciate the importance of ministerial office at the expense of ministerial character, or to overemphasize the personal qualifications of ministry while playing down the importance of ministerial office. As Mennonites, we also have sometimes erred on the one side or the other in seeking to live out the heritage of the Radical Reformation or to correct what we have perceived to be less than helpful directions in other Christian traditions. Nevertheless, both the heritage of the Radical Reformation and the Christian church's calling to proclaim and signify the reign of God in the world underscore the importance of both person and office.

The education of pastors, missionaries, teachers, evangelists, and other church leaders thus includes character formation, the acquisition of knowledge, and the cultivation of the requisite abilities to guide the church in carrying out its mission. Ministerial formation in this comprehensive sense begins in the congregation well before people enter seminary. The seminary devotes focused and concentrated attention to continuing and deepening the formation of ministerial character, to the disciplined study of the church's heritage and mission, and to supervised practice in the responsibilities of ministerial office.

Theological education

Just as the seminary has a particular role to exercise in ministerial formation, so the seminary faculty has been called to be a center of scholarly inquiry and to provide theological leadership in the church's teaching ministry.

The responsibilities of the church's teaching and scholarly ministry are at least threefold. They include passing on traditions that have proved to be carriers of faithful witness to God's reign, providing guidance to help bodies of believers in diverse cultural settings make good judgments about normative Christian beliefs and practices, and articulating the church's message in ways that nurture Christian life and faith in the contemporary world.

Each of these responsibilities has a critical and a constructive task. In the critical task, the churches' present and past beliefs and practices are examined for the purpose of discerning the church's faithfulness and need for renewal. In the constructive task, proposals are made for shaping the church's practices and beliefs in ways that are intended to be faithful to its calling. These critical and constructive tasks of evaluating past beliefs and practices and shaping present ones need to take the social and cultural environment as well as the internal life of the church into account. Because the church is called to proclaim and signify the kingdom of God by being light and salt in the world,[5] its mission includes critique of the systems of thought and conduct that undermine or oppose faith in Jesus Christ. At the same time, its mission includes discerning and using those elements of human wisdom and conduct that can become helpful instruments of the church's witness to the reign of God as revealed in and through Jesus Christ.

Theology and theological education are closely related to the church's teaching ministry. As a disciplined body of knowledge and a disciplined way of thinking, theology grows out of and informs the church's teaching ministry. As a disciplined body of knowledge, theology includes the study and appropriation of the church's normative traditions, the criteria for making judgments about faithful beliefs and practices, and the language in which the church best articulates its message. As a disciplined way of thinking, theology seeks to bring coherence, consistency, insight, and intellectual rigor to both the critical and constructive tasks of the church's teaching ministry.

As participants in the church's teaching ministry and as theological educators, we believe that faithful belief and practice are to be measured above all by consonance with Scripture. According to a Radical Reformation perspective, Scripture as interpreted in the community of believers should take precedence over the legitimate but relative claims of traditions, the contemporary experience of believers, and human reason for assessing the faithfulness of Christian beliefs and practices. During several periods of Mennonite history, this primacy of Scripture has been reflected by referring to teachers and pastors as "servants of the Word."

As teachers of the church and servants of the Word, we accept the Scripture as the primary measure of what we teach in all theological disciplines. This does not mean that we seek to limit theological education to biblical studies or to ignore the questions those disciplines raise for interpretation of Scripture. Rather, it means that we seek to have the categories of our disciplines, the history and ministries of the church, and our interpretation of the contemporary world measured and formed by Scripture. We endeavor to interpret the modern world and the church's teaching within the biblical framework.

In North American Protestant seminary education, the role and place of the Bible is usually seen in one of two major ways. According to the one representative view, the Bible is perceived and studied primarily in terms of its formation and its formative role in the earliest stage of the developing Christian traditions. Further, the Bible is seen as a collection of many and diverse materials that have been fundamentally shaped by particular historical and cultural contexts which differ from each other, but even more greatly from the settings in which churches find themselves in the modern Western world. This view usually accompanies the broader judgment that no one church or doctrinal tradition provides the bridge that guarantees continuity of meaning between the biblical materials and contemporary Christian teaching. Where the Bible is thus perceived and studied, it is no longer understood as the normative foundation for a unified and coherent body of theology that constitutes the seminary curriculum and encompasses the biblical, historical, systematic, and practical disciplines.[6] According to the other major view, the Bible constitutes the normative foundation for doctrinal orthodoxy and evangelical piety, which in turn are seen as standing in basic continuity with Scripture. This view emphasizes the authority of the Bible by making a doctrine of the inspiration of Scripture the governing criterion for right belief and biblical interpretation. In some cases the view of inspiration permits only literal interpretation of Scripture. In other cases the understanding of God's inspiration of the text encourages other levels of interpretation as well. But in either case, those who subscribe to this general position tend to emphasize the fundamental unity of the Bible as God's Word. This view generally assumes a basic continuity in meaning between scriptural teaching and contemporary doctrine. Where the Bible is thus perceived and studied, it is assumed to be the normative foundation for theology and the entire range of theological disciplines in some fashion.[7] While both of these approaches to Scripture have influenced and can be found among Mennonites, in its response to Scripture AMBS seeks to resemble and differ from each of these major Protestant views. That is to say, we have learned from both of these perspectives.

Like the second approach, we accept the Bible as the normative standard for faithfulness of life and thought rather than primarily as the earliest stage of multiple and disparate Christian traditions. However, we would emphasize the authority of Scripture more by calling for a persistent practice of studying and interpreting the biblical texts in the community of faith, than by requiring adherence to a particular doctrine of biblical inspiration.

Like the first approach, we are committed to the disciplined study of the biblical texts themselves, with appropriate attention to their uniqueness, to the differences between the Scripture and the churches' traditions, and to the differences between the contexts of the biblical texts and the modern world. However, we would emphasize that Scripture, with all its internal diversity, and with its differences from the contemporary world, remains the one foundational and trustworthy resource for measuring our faithfulness to God's Word today. And it is precisely these differences between the Bible and our contemporary convictions and values that provide an opening for us to critically assess the faithfulness of the churches' beliefs and practices; through them God reorients us to proclaim the church's message and mission in today's world.

Further, the theology and ethics associated with these two representative approaches to Scripture tend to neglect or play down several of the core convictions about Christian faith and life which, we believe, are grounded in the Bible and therefore remain normative for the Christian church in all times and places. Specifically, the church's calling to proclaim and signify the kingdom of God has included several characteristic emphases in a Mennonite perspective: the creative and transforming as well as the forgiving quality of God's grace; the significance of Jesus' life and teaching as well as of his death and resurrection for our salvation; the church as a community of believers whose voluntary covenant is symbolized by believers' baptism, congregational discipline, and mutual care; Christian faith expressed by living as disciples of Jesus Christ in all of life; nonparticipation in violence and war and commitment to the way of peace even as a way of confronting evil; serving others by seeking what makes for genuine peace and by inviting unbelievers to faith in Jesus Christ; and simplicity in worship, ritual, and lifestyle.

None of these core convictions taken alone is unique to the historical Mennonite traditions. Nevertheless, the claim that all of them are essential though not exclusive parts of what constitutes Christian faithfulness today, precisely because they are grounded in Scripture as appropriated by the church through the leading of the Holy Spirit, remains relatively distinctive. And the claim that these core convictions should figure prominently in the practice and understanding of theological education belongs at the heart of a biblical seminary in the Mennonite tradition.

We confess that as Mennonites in the North American context we have often been willing to settle for something less or something other than theological discernment and a teaching ministry informed by these core convictions. At times we have been tempted to think and act as if these core convictions constituted all that matters for Christians, rather than seeing them as essential parts of a larger theological vision. We have sometimes been hesitant to offer these convictions as instruments of witness in the world and as matters for serious conversation with other Christians. And we have sometimes been tempted to rationalize the discrepancies between presumed convictions and practiced realities among us, rather than seeing such differences as challenges for theological discernment and church renewal. Theological education in a Mennonite seminary therefore includes both a critical and a constructive appropriation of a particular heritage in discerning conversation with other Christian traditions and their contemporary expressions.

We readily acknowledge that we have not yet succeeded in articulating a well-rounded and shared account of theological education in which "the categories of our disciplines," our understandings of "the history and ministries of the church, our interpretation of the contemporary world," and the church's mission would be clearly "measured and formed by Scripture."[8] Nevertheless, we commit ourselves to work toward that goal in the coming years. Working toward such an integrated and comprehensive account may in any case represent a continuing task and a directional orientation rather than a fixed habitat in which to house theological education.

In the meantime, we agree that theological education so oriented does not mean depreciating but cultivating theological disciplines other than biblical studies. We are not convinced that the higher the number of Bible courses, the more biblical the theological education. Rather we call faculty members in all disciplines to refer their teaching to the world of Scripture.

We also agree that theological education in a Mennonite biblical seminary means that faculty members and students maintain regular personal and corporate disciplines of studying Scripture and cultivating familiarity with it. It means that class bibliographies and library holdings include literature representing both of the approaches to the Bible described above. And it means that the seminary maintains conversations with representatives of both of these major Protestant views through lectureships and other ways. It means that we value teaching and learning the biblical languages and that the biblical languages will be taught in ways that undergird students' seminary studies and the ministries for which they are preparing. It means that all faculty members are expected to refer what we teach to Scripture understood as a canonical whole centered on Jesus Christ. Although we are not yet in a position to spell out all this means for theology and theological education, we are committed, as a seminary faculty, to make working out the implications of this orientation a high priority in the coming years.

As participants in the church's teaching ministry and as theological educators we further believe that Scripture witnesses to a God whose saving work encompasses both personal and social dimensions. And we believe that response to the gospel of Jesus Christ issues both in missionary love and commitment to the way of peace.

As has been true for views on ministry office and character and for the two approaches to Scripture noted above, North American Christians have been tempted to emphasize one aspect of God's saving work or our response to it to the diminution or exclusion of the other. Thus theological education might emphasize God's liberating acts and peace and justice concerns, but neglect personal healing, missionary leadership, and inviting others to faith in Christ. On the other hand a seminary might carry on the tradition of God's gracious forgiveness and the restoration of sinners, of healing and welcoming individuals to faith, but miss the economic or political dimensions of God's good news in Christ or the way Christian peacemaking is rooted in that gospel. In both of these cases, the role of the church—as a sign of God's new social order or as a community of forgiven disciples—may be played down.

As a seminary faculty we seek to understand, value, and teach Christian commitment to both mission and peace, both individual and social salvation, both peace and justice. As faculty members continue to modify the seminary curriculum and contribute to the ethos of theological education at AMBS, we commit ourselves to communicate a whole gospel, to correct our own failures in doing so, and to renew our efforts to engender a vision of the church that both proclaims this gospel and serves as a sign of God's coming rule.

Guidelines for theological education: A church-based design

The twofold vocation of AMBS—to educate Christian ministers and to provide theological leadership for the teaching ministry of the churches—calls for a vision of theological education focused on the church and its mission in the light of the reign of God. It calls for AMBS to be a center of the church's teaching ministry committed to the task of theological education as both a graduate and professional school.[9]

The approach to theological education that undergirds curriculum design at AMBS centers on the church's identity, purpose, life, and ministry. Alternative approaches to theological education tend to start either with the nature of theology or with the nature of professional ministry.[10] A focus on the church and its mission in light of the reign of God requires that contributions from these other theological approaches be critically and creatively appropriated. A church-based or ecclesial paradigm[11] for theological education suggests the following principles for curriculum design:

First, the curriculum is approached primarily from the perspective of the nature and the purpose of the church. The different dimensions of the curriculum will, therefore, keep that concern in focus. Second, theological education is oriented toward the formation and transformation of the faithful church in the world, in response to God's gracious rule. The overall task of theological education is for the sake of supporting and renewing the church's worship, community, and mission.

It is significant to claim that a church-based pattern inspires and orients our philosophy of theological education, first of all, because it underlines the fact that the mission of AMBS is derived from the church's mission. Second, theological education is viewed as a special dimension and setting of the educational ministry of the church and is at the service of that ministry. Third, we view the church (especially in its concrete, historical manifestations as local congregations, but also in its denominational and interdenominational expressions in the form of church institutions, agencies, and programs) as the main partner, the primary public, and the principal beneficiary of theological education. Fourth, we consider the life and ministry of living and historical faith communities—including the work of church institutions and programs—as important foci for curricular content and scholarly research. Finally, we consider congregations and other church-related programs as significant contexts for seminary accredited learning.

The following considerations shaped our statement of guidelines for theological education at AMBS: (a) the guidelines apply to all programs of study; (b) they connect explicitly the school's mission statement with the overall curriculum, and serve as a *blueprint* that orients and helps to evaluate our educational task; (c) while the guidelines have a certain normative character in pointing the way to relevant, faithful, and effective theological education, they are not to be exclusively prescriptive, for instance prescribing too specific teaching strategies or learning tasks; (d) the guidelines should be articulated as clearly as possible so they can be communicated, discussed, and evaluated, and otherwise used as an educational tool; (e) the guidelines should remain relatively open-ended in light of ongoing discussion concerning programs of study and core curriculum requirements; that is to say, we affirm interplay between the stated educational philosophy and curricular assessment.

Goals and objectives of theological education and ministerial formation

The curriculum of theological education at AMBS is designed in relation to the comprehensive aim presented in the mission statement. That aim is to prepare pastors, missionaries, teachers, evangelists, and other church leaders to both proclaim and live according to the gospel of reconciliation, to minister effectively, and to equip other believers for their ministries.

The curriculum focuses on four general objectives of growth through the enabling power of the Holy Spirit. People seeking to minister in the name of Jesus Christ will be assisted to grow toward spiritual maturity, theological depth and discernment, wise ministering practice, and personal commitment to God's reign of peace and righteousness. These four general objectives are interrelated and apply to all students in all programs of study:

Spiritual maturity

Expressions as well as criteria of growth in this area include:
- deepened commitment to the person of Christ, the Word of God, and the tradition of the church
- openness to conversion, healing, and growth
- disposition to share one's faith freely as well as respectfully
- moral sensitivity and integrity in personal and public life

Theological depth and discernment

Expressions as well as criteria of growth in this area include:
- ability to interpret Scripture faithfully
- development of theological vision and discernment in light of a historical perspective and in relation to contemporary realities
- learning the habit and practice of theological inquiry

Wise practice of ministry

Expressions as well as criteria of growth in this area include:
- affirmation of a clear sense of call to serve God and others
- capacity to minister with spiritual authority in the tradition of Jesus and the power of the Holy Spirit
- disposition to carry out pertinent modes and tasks of ministry in a reflective way
- willingness to give and receive counsel

Personal commitment to God's reign of peace and righteousness

Expressions as well as criteria of growth in this area include:
- understanding of and commitment to the biblical vision of mission, peace, and justice, rooted in God's gracious love
- development of ethical discernment at the personal, social, and political levels, in light of the inbreaking reign of God and the church's mission in the world
- disposition to call people to be healed and forgiven through God's saving work, to join the community of believers, to share the vision of shalom, and to follow the way of Christ

The context of theological education and ministerial formation

Several dimensions and understandings of context are significant for the AMBS educational task.

Community context

AMBS seeks first of all to be a community of education. Not only the curriculum but also the broader ethos of the seminary community are to serve the church's calling to be the community that proclaims and signifies the kingdom of God. The seminary's entire ethos, that is, its distinguishing characteristics, habits, and practices, should be shaped by and inspire commitment to the church's calling. We believe "that not only the content but also the context of the curriculum must be shaped by our theological convictions."[12]

Or to put the matter in slightly different terms, because teaching and learning depend to a significant degree on modeling, the seminary should provide, in ways appropriate to a church educational institution, a model of the kind of community whose ethos as well as message and mission is a sign of God's reign in the world. Theological education and ministerial formation in this perspective thus deserve more than a smorgasbord of courses and a set of supervised experiences in ministry. They depend also on a community ethos that is created and sustained by formal as well as informal and by institutional as well as personal means.

1. *A seminary shaped by the church's calling is committed to growth as a worshiping community.* The community gathers for chapel services three times a week and sponsors other times for prayer and worship. Both students and faculty are encouraged to regularly participate in and lead in worship and to practice spiritual disciplines.

2. *A seminary shaped by the church's calling is committed to remaining an international community that reflects the changing transnational character of the Christian church.* AMBS is especially committed to maintaining a Canadian American character as well as a global perspective on church and world. At the beginning of the twentieth century, almost 90 percent of all Christians as well as most Mennonites lived in Europe and North America. As of 1990, fewer than 60 percent of all Christians and fewer than 50 percent of all Mennonites lived in North America and Europe. While the majority of students and faculty are from the U.S. and Canada, some students each year come from outside North America and numerous students and faculty have had experiences of ministry and service in various countries. The seminary seeks to regularly invite guests from outside North America and encourages international lecturers and student and faculty exchanges.

3. *A seminary shaped by the church's calling is a ministering community committed to value a diversity of congregational, extra congregational, and scholarly ministries.* Through the Theological Center Guest program, Teaching and Research Seminars, recognition dinners and teas, and in other ways, we seek to celebrate excellence in the various types of ministries of faculty, students, seminary alumni, and others. Currently we likely do better at celebrating scholarly than pastoral ministry, and at recognizing peace and service than evangelistic and missionary ministries. We thus plan to work for a better balance in these regards.

4. *A seminary shaped by the church's calling is committed to foster community discernment and decision making.* Students participate in most faculty committees and sit on the AMBS Board. The advising process involves both faculty and peers in vocational discernment and assessment of strengths and weaknesses for ministry. Community assemblies, hearings, and special consultations address critical issues for community and church life, (e.g., the Gulf War, homosexuality, religion and the media, violence against women and peace theology, bondage and deliverance ministry, etc.).

5. *A seminary shaped by the church's calling is committed to be a community of mutual care and accountability.* This takes shape in seminary formed koinonia groups for interested students and faculty; mutual aid funds and actions among students, faculty, and staff; and cultivating the practice of direct address when there is offense or hurt in the community. Students and faculty address each other by first names as a reminder that the academic relationship of teachers and learners is grounded in a Christian relationship in which adults are sisters and brothers in Christ and partners in sharing the gospel of the reign of God.

Church context

The context of seminary education also includes the church—both the sponsoring Mennonite denominations and the broader Christian church. Faculty and students are expected to be involved in local congregations. The concrete, ongoing experience of church life and ministry is assumed to be foundational for teaching and learning. Participation in other church-related agencies, institutions, programs, and special projects is also encouraged for the sake of learning, service, and research. While the seminary curriculum and ethos has a distinctly Anabaptist Mennonite flavor, faculty encourage discriminating appropriation of both Mennonite and broader Christian traditions and value opportunities to converse and work with Christians from other church confessions.

Historical context

Further, we acknowledge that the church that gave rise to, inspires, and informs our theological education is a historical community. The church context that influences our learning and teaching is not only the contemporary church but a communion that has taken numerous institutional forms stretching back to the early house churches depicted in the New Testament. In our teaching and research we value the witness of the historical church and attempt to remember and learn from its persistent faithfulness and its frequent failures to fully love God and neighbors.

Sociocultural and religious contexts

AMBS and its educational mission are viewed also within the wider sociocultural and religious contexts of Elkhart, the United States and Canada, and our planet, each of which shapes educational and theological tasks. Through personal contacts, some continuing education events, the Chapel Chamber series, sharing of community information with new students, and Community Day work projects, we are beginning to take new steps to build relationships in the Elkhart community. We particularly recognize the structures of poverty and racism that have impact on our immediate environment.

National context

Because of our status as a binational Mennonite seminary located in the United States, and given the international experience and perspective of many of our faculty and students, we are especially aware of the ways in which national location shapes the issues the church faces. We recognize that culture and politics deeply affect the life of the church, often in subtle ways, and we seek to be responsive to the diversity that characterizes our educational community.

Critical discernment and faithful practice in light of these various contexts of theological education at AMBS are pervasive curricular concerns.

Content and process of theological education and ministerial formation

The educational questions concerning content ("what") and process ("how") are closely associated. Further, these two major questions in our philosophy of education are considered together with that of people in context ("who" and "where") presented above.

The overall curriculum content derives from AMBS's commitment to support and renew the church's worship, community life, and witness. Thus, the primary focus of the curricular agenda is attention to the reality of the church's life and its mission in North America and the world, in the light of the reign of God.

Theological education dedicated to preparing people to guide the church in proclaiming and signifying the reign of God is concerned with growth in the intellectual and practical abilities essential for such ministry. But it also recognizes the importance of nurturing personal and spiritual qualities crucial for such leadership. These include a strong Christian faith commitment nurtured by prayer; continuing study of the Scripture; participation in the life of the community of faith; love for the church and willingness to serve others; the willingness to receive and give counsel; and moral integrity in both personal and public life. Faculty believe spiritual growth and deepened commitment to the mind and way of Christ occur with the nudging of the Holy Spirit through a variety of means, such as study, sermon preparation, interpretation of Scripture, reflection on acts of ministry, corporate worship, receiving pastoral care and counseling or spiritual guidance, individual and group prayer.

Scripture plays a foundational role in all dimensions of the curriculum. Therefore, a major goal is to cultivate appreciation and appropriation of the Bible as well as to equip students to interpret and communicate biblical content in their lives and ministries.

The faculty is committed to work at relating Scripture as the primary normative standard for faithful life and thought to the various fields and courses of study that constitute the curriculum. Such a process involves a Spirit-led consideration of the claims of the Bible, the church's heritage and its current agenda, and the situation and challenges of society and the world. It must take into account relevant epistemological issues as well as the integrity of the disciplines.

In numerous cases the content and/or methodology of courses is influenced by the conviction that understanding of and respect for the Bible is central to faithful thought and practice. The curricular structure itself signals the importance allocated to Scripture study; the study of the Bible is not subsumed under historical studies but retains a distinct disciplinary status.

The denominational identity of the school and its commitment to the Anabaptist Mennonite heritage is reflected in the overall curriculum. Such an identity and commitment are evident in ongoing support for the Master of Arts in

Peace Studies. This identity and commitment also inform the substantive content of the courses of study in all programs by attending to recurring themes of Christian faithfulness and distinctive tenets and contributions of that heritage, including implications for ministry in today's world.

The disciplines with which the faculty has been entrusted and the mission and needs of the church call for a variety of learning tasks. Those learning tasks need to be considered together with students' personal learning styles and vocational goals.

The faculty is committed to pursue excellence in teaching while seeking to employ a variety of teaching models and approaches.[13] Methodological issues and practice are deliberately connected to the teacher's philosophy of theological education and teaching style as well as to consideration of the student's situation and learning modes and goals, subject matter, and curricular objectives.[14]

The educational philosophies and teaching styles of the faculty contribute to a student-focused overall approach to theological education and ministerial formation. Such an educational approach is distinctly mediated by the teacher's personal and professional profile, the particular nature of different fields, and specific curricular agenda. The main features of a student-focused overall approach can be characterized as follows: (a) the student's needs, interests, and potential are assessed and taken into account; (b) a climate of trust important for learning is fostered and cultivated; (c) student-centered activities and a collaborative mode for the teaching-learning process are facilitated as much as possible; (d) the unique situation of each student is addressed by way of personalized advising and instruction when feasible, and curricular content is meaningfully related to the student's world of experience; and (e) the student's involvement as an active agent in setting learning goals as well as in the evaluation of teaching and learning is encouraged.

Notes

[1] The relation between the church and the reign of God has been and continues to be a matter of considerable debate. The term "sign of God's reign," or "to signify God's reign" as used in this statement, assumes that the church is called to represent the reign of God in a particular way, without reducing the kingdom to the church. "As the community of the Kingdom in the midst of the world, the church is called to live by hope in the coming Kingdom and, by the power of the Holy Spirit, to be a foretaste of the kind of peace and justice now which God shall one day establish in all its fullness. As the community of the Kingdom in the midst of the world, the church is called to live as a forgiven and forgiving people, as a reconciled and reconciling people, as a justified and justice making people, and as a peaceful and peacemaking people, in practice as well as in attitude—because that both is and will be the reality of God's Kingdom" (Marlin E. Miller, "The Church in the World As the Community of the Kingdom: A Radical Reformation Perspective," *Brethren Life and Thought* 35 [winter 1990]: 67).

² 1 Peter 2:9.

³ Anabaptist and Mennonite confessional statements have adapted the concept of ministerial "office" to both "lay" and "full-time" ministries. See the Schleitheim articles of 1527, Article 5; Dordrecht of 1632, Article 9; Ris 1766/1895, Article 24; General Conference in Canada, 1930, Article 8; MC Confession of Faith 1963, Article 10 (less prominently than in other statements); see *One Lord, One Church, One Hope, and One God: Mennonite Confessions of Faith in North America,* edited by Howard John Loewen (Elkhart, Ind.: Institute of Mennonite Studies, 1985). See also the current draft of the GCMC and MC Joint Polity Statement.

⁴ Stanley Hauerwas suggests that the most necessary virtue for ministry today is "constancy" in the sense of "steadfastness to self and to one's task. . . ." According to Hauerwas, "A minister must live and act believing God is present in the church creating, through word and sacrament, a new people capable of witnessing to God's Kingdom. The minister must be filled with hope that God will act through word and sacrament to renew the church, but he or she must be patient, knowing that how God works is God's business. From the crucible of patience and hope comes the fidelity to task that makes the ministry not a burden but a joy. So finally we must ask of those in ministry whether they are capable of joy; if they are not they lack a character sufficient to their calling." See "Clerical Character," in *Christian Existence Today: Essays on Church, World and Living in Between* (Durham: Labyrinth Press, 1988), 143. From a Mennonite perspective, the Holy Spirit is present and acts in the church not only through "word and sacrament," but also through community relationships characterized by mutual forgiveness and discipline. For another contemporary discussion of "Theological Education As the Formation of Character," see *Theological Education,* Supplement 1, 1988. Early Anabaptist and Mennonite writers also emphasized the kinds of qualities we are here summarizing by the term "ministerial character." For example: Menno Simons, "The Vocation of the Preachers," in "Foundation of Christian Doctrine, " in *The Complete Writings of Menno Simons, c. 1496-1561,* trans. Leonard Verduin, ed. John C. Wenger (Scottdale, Pa.: Herald Press, 1986), 159-64; Pilgram Marpeck, "The Servants and Service of the Church," in *The Writings of Pilgram Marpeck,* trans. and ed. William Klassen and Walter Klaassen (Kitchener, Ont., and Scottdale, Pa.: Herald Press, 1978), 549-54; and references under "Church Order," in *Anabaptism in Outline,* trans. and ed. Walter Klaassen (Kitchener, Ont., and Scottdale, Pa.: Herald Press, 1981), 118-39.

⁵ Matthew 5:13-14.

⁶ Joseph C. Hough Jr. and John B. Cobb Jr. seem to assume this approach to Scripture and its significance for theological education in their *Christian Identity and Theological Education* (Chico, Calif.: Scholars Press, 1985). Their guiding question for theological education is couched in terms of a "world historical approach to understanding the church," which they claim "is essentially biblical" in the sense that "the idea of world history is itself a product of biblical belief in God" (20). This approach to theological education incorporates biblical studies into a historical description of Christian identity from the beginnings of the Jewish faith to

contemporary North American religious history. Hough and Cobb make little or no claim for Scripture as the primary norm for theology in a way that qualitatively differentiates it from the rest of the Christian "heritage." In similar fashion, Charles Wood incorporates biblical studies into "historical" theology in his proposal for theological education as consisting of historical, philosophical, practical, systematic, and ethical "disciplines." He favors departing from the "old Protestant" custom of considering biblical theology as "the proper locus for the pursuit of the question of what is normatively Christian," in part because historical theology should test the traditional presupposition that "the Bible is the criterion by which the representativeness of Christian witness is to be judged" (43). See also chapter 4 of Max Stackhouse's *Apologia: Contextualization, Globalization, and Mission in Theological Education,* especially the section "So Long, Sola Scriptura" (Grand Rapids: Eerdmans, 1988), 50-52.

[7] See, for example, the unpublished 1991 essay by Richard J. Mouw, "Evangelical Reflections on the 'Aims and Purposes' Literature." In this essay, Mouw does not defend a particular doctrinal formulation of biblical authority. He does however speak for a "Bible centered" curriculum. Mouw even criticizes "conservative Protestants" for often failing to distinguish between "our notions of what God is telling us in the Bible" and "what God is really telling us" (9). Simultaneously he insists that "the Bible is indeed God's written Word" for evangelicals (10). On this basis he insists on a clear distinction between biblical theology and historical theology. And on this basis he criticizes Charles Wood's view of the relation between biblical and historical theology. In his *Vision and Discernment* (Atlanta: Scholars Press, 1985), Wood acknowledges that the church has "ordinarily" presumed "that the Bible is the criterion by which the representativeness of Christian witness is to be judged." However, he goes on to contend that whether "the church has acted rightly" in making this assumption "is always open to question" (*Vision and Discernment,* 43). To that Mouw responds: "We are convinced that it is not open to serious question. . . . The primacy of the Bible is not, for us, itself open to question" (17). On these grounds, Mouw also criticizes both the view of biblical authority and the curricular place given the study of Scripture in the Hough and Cobb proposals for theological education (in *Christian Identity and Theological Education*).

[8] See above, page 244.

[9] Other centers of the teaching ministry are, first of all, local congregations, where theological education happens at the foundational level and on an ongoing basis. Second, denominational bodies, agencies, and programs are often centers of theological reflection and teaching at another level, broadening and supporting congregational perspectives. AMBS is committed to maintaining active dialogue and partnership with these different "centers" for the teaching ministry of the church.

[10] Francis Schüssler Fiorenza presents a useful study of these three approaches to theological education, including an analysis of the advantages and limitations of each, in "Thinking Theologically about Theological Education," *Theological Education* 24, Supplement 2 (1988): 89-119. The first approach moves from an

analysis of theological inquiry and the nature of theology to the nature and reform of theological education; the second approach starts its analysis of theological education with the question of the church's identity and mission; the third approach places a theological vision of ministry—or a professional view of ministry—at the center of its analysis of theological education.

[11] Among the diverse meanings and connotations of the term "ecclesial paradigm" we underscore the following two: (a) "ecclesial" as an alternative to "academic" (especially in the sense of university-focused or -oriented) thus affirming the continuity with the strong emphasis on the church context of theological education in the previous philosophy statement, "Theological Education in the Free Church Tradition"; and (b) "ecclesial paradigm" as connoting the features of a theological education model that is church based, in the senses indicated in the following paragraphs; also, a model that creatively integrates contributions stemming from both the "theological" and the "ministerial" paradigms in theological education.

[12] Ross T. Bender, *The People of God, A Mennonite Interpretation of the Free Church Tradition* (Scottdale, Pa.: Herald Press 1971), 166.

[13] Teaching methods and techniques can be seen in terms of such categories as information processing (e.g., lectures, group discussion), personal and social types (e.g., journaling), as well as those appropriate for specific skills training.

[14] Teachers seek to: (a) encourage student-managed learning as complementary to teacher-facilitated learning; (b) establish links between learning that takes place in the classroom and that which takes place through cocurricular events or in other settings and activities; (c) encourage integration of reflection and action as well as of practice and theory; (d) foster completion of learning circles involving the steps of experience, observation, conceptualization, and experimentation; (e) affirm the student's preferred learning modes and styles in the wider framework of our responsibility for theological education and ministerial formation.

Appendix 2
Theological education and curricular design at AMBS

Christian ministry finds its highest purpose in serving the church's calling to proclaim and signify God's reign on earth through the enabling presence and power of the Holy Spirit in the name of Jesus Christ. Central to preparation for Christian ministry in its variety of forms is empathic understanding of the unique vocation, the failings, and the grace-filled life of the Christian church. Thus the church, its calling, and its reality serve as the orienting point for theological education and curricular development at Associated Mennonite Biblical Seminary.

Theological education and curricular design start with the church's identity, mission, and reality rather than with an analysis of the nature of theological inquiry or a professional vision of ministry. The document *Ministerial Formation and Theological Education in Mennonite Perspective,* adopted by the seminary in 1992, outlines this approach to pastoral and theological education.[1] Identifying the church within God's reign as an orienting point for theological education suggests the following:

1. The overall task of theological education is to support and renew the church in its mission.
2. Theological education in a seminary context is a dimension of the broader educational ministry of the church and is at the service of that ministry.
3. The theology and practice of Christian ministry find their roots in the nature and purpose of the church.
4. The church, local and international, denominational and interdenominational, serves as a partner in theological education. Congregations and other church-related programs are significant contexts for seminary-accredited learning.
5. The faith and ministry of living and historical Christian communities and organizations are valued "texts" for curricular content and scholarly research.

While the three-year Master of Divinity program most fully reflects a church-focused curricular design, commitment to theological education and scholarly inquiry that takes seriously the identity, calling, and reality of the church permeates the character of all degree programs at AMBS.

Some longstanding commitments in approach to theological education at AMBS as well as some shifts in approach that have been developing at AMBS during the past decade are brought into focus when the church and its calling are taken as an orienting point. The more important of these longer-term commitments and shifts that find expression in the academic programs described in this catalog include:

1. Commitment to a missional orientation and perspective

Implicit in the calling of the church to "proclaim and signify the reign of God on earth" is a vision of the church as a missionary community. The interdepartmental course Mission and Peace: The Church's Ministry in the World, the only course required in all degree programs, seeks to elicit personal commitment to proclaim a whole gospel. The course is designed to help students understand how the inseparable ministries of evangelization and peace- and justice-making emerge from the gospel of Jesus Christ and to provide basic practical preparation for mission-oriented church leadership.

2. Renewed emphasis on leadership ministries in relation to the ministry of all believers

AMBS faculty and board members firmly believe that all Christians are called and gifted "to participate in the ministries of the church, sharing the mission to witness to Jesus Christ in the world." At the same time, the 1992 theological education statement records the conviction that "the church is strengthened for its mission when believers are nurtured and guided by faithful pastors and other church leaders."

The seminary is therefore committed to educating people who have been or may be called "to exercise distinctive leadership ministries" and who at the same time "understand the importance of equipping other believers for their ministries and are prepared to do so."

To underline the distinctive character of pastoral and other church leadership ministries, seminary faculty have adopted the language of *office*. When one is called to hold an office in ministry—whether expressed in the role of pastoral minister, evangelist, pastoral counselor, or a teacher of the church—the church assigns not only particular responsibilities, but appropriate authority and standards of accountability in relation to other ministries in the church. The Formation in Ministry course explores understandings of leadership ministries. An interdepartmental course, Theology of the Church, examines the nature and purpose of the church, Christian traditions, and contemporary cultural influences.

3. New attention to personal and pastoral formation

Theological education dedicated to preparing people to guide the church in proclaiming and signifying the reign of God must be concerned with growth in the intellectual and practical abilities essential for such ministry. But it also recognizes the importance of nurturing personal and spiritual qualities critical for such leadership.

These include among others: a strong faith commitment nurtured by prayer; continuing study of the Scripture; participation in the life of the community of faith; love for the church and willingness to serve others without an excessive need for personal recognition; the willingness to receive and give counsel; and moral integrity in both personal and public life.

Overall educational objectives at AMBS thus include growth toward personal and spiritual maturity as well as development of theological depth and wise practice in ministry. Faculty believe spiritual growth and deepened commitment to the mind and way of Christ occur with the nudging of the Holy Spirit through a variety of means—study, sermon preparation, interpretation of Scripture, reflection on acts of ministry, corporate worship in chapel services, receiving pastoral counseling, and individual and group prayer, among others. In addition, the seminary offers seminars, retreats, mentoring, and courses that deal specifically with aspects of spiritual formation.

Intentional concern in a variety of courses to deepen students' understanding of the work of the Holy Spirit in biblical and theological interpretation, in congregational decision making, and in the practice of ministries such as evangelism, pastoral care and counseling, education, and worship leadership also contributes to this dimension of pastoral formation at AMBS.

The Master of Divinity curriculum provides special structure for monitoring personal and pastoral formation through seminars, faculty advising, and a concluding ministry evaluation and interview.

4. Reaffirmation of the importance of theological depth and discernment for those who guide the church

Theology and theological education are closely related to the church's teaching and preaching ministries. As a disciplined body of knowledge, theology includes the study, reception, and transmission of the church's traditions, weighing criteria for making judgments about faithful beliefs and practices, and finding the language in which the church best shares its message. As a disciplined way of thinking, theology seeks to bring coherence, consistency, and insight to the church's teaching ministry.

Faculty seek to enable theological depth and discernment in at least three ways:

- by passing on traditions that have proved to be carriers of faithful witness to God's reign;
- by helping students learn to make good judgments about faithful belief and practice in diverse cultural settings; and
- by helping students articulate the church's message in ways that nurture Christian life and faith in the contemporary world.

Those who guide the church need to be able to discern the church's faithfulness and need for renewal. They must be able to propose ways to shape the church's practices and beliefs that are faithful to its calling. Because the church is called to be light and salt in the world, its mission includes critique of the systems of thought and conduct that undermine or oppose faith in Jesus Christ. At the same time, its mission includes using those elements of human wisdom that can witness to the reign of God as revealed in and through Jesus Christ.

AMBS faculty offer strong resources in biblical theology. They teach systematic theology from a believers church perspective, emphasize links between theology and ethics, and are interested in exploring further ways for pastors and others to assist theological discernment in congregational settings.

5. Acknowledgment of Scripture as the primary standard in theological discernment and education

Maintaining a strong seminary tradition, AMBS faculty are deeply committed to the disciplined study of biblical texts while holding that Scripture remains the one foundational and trustworthy resource for measuring the faithfulness of the church to God's Word. Interpretation of Scripture is essential for understanding the work of God in Christ and the church's identity and mission. Scripture also serves as the standard for faithful Christian life and practice. Therefore a major curricular goal for all degree programs is to cultivate respect for and thoughtful and faithful interaction with the Bible.

Faculty also are committed to relating Scripture—as the primary standard for faithful life and thought—to the various fields that make up the curriculum. They envision a theological education in which the categories of these disciplinary fields—understandings of the history, ministries, and mission of the church, and interpretation of the contemporary world—are measured and formed by Scripture.

As teachers of the church and servants of the Word, faculty have also agreed to maintain regular personal and corporate disciplines of Scripture study and to cultivate familiarity with Scripture.

6. Valuing of the seminary's Anabaptist-Mennonite heritage

The church's calling to proclaim and signify the kingdom of God has included several characteristic emphases in Mennonite perspective. While none of these convictions taken alone is unique to the historical Mennonite traditions, the constellation they represent helps to define the seminary's heritage and identity. These emphases include: the creative and transforming as well as the forgiving quality of God's grace; the significance of Jesus' life and teaching as well as of his death and resurrection for our salvation; the church as a community of believers whose voluntary covenant is symbolized by believers baptism, congregational discipline, and mutual care; Christian faith expressed by living as disciples of Jesus Christ in all of life; nonparticipation in violence and war and commitment to the way of peace even as a way of confronting evil; the dismantling of racism; the serving of others by seeking what makes for genuine peace and by inviting unbelievers to faith in Jesus Christ; and simplicity in worship and lifestyle.

Special attention in the curriculum is given to the theology, history, and experience of Anabaptist-Mennonite Christians—both in the offering of specialized courses, such as Anabaptist History and Theology, and in making references to Mennonite church life and practice in a variety of courses across the curriculum. In their teaching, faculty encourage thoughtful appropriation of both Mennonite and broader Christian traditions.

7. Recognition of the church as both content and context for learning

In building understanding and appreciation for the church and its calling, seminary programs encourage students to interact with both the biblical witness to God's reign and the ensuing life and practice of the church of Jesus Christ in the world.

The church that gave rise to, inspires, and informs theological education is first of all a historical community. In teaching and research, faculty value the witness of the historical church and attempt to remember and learn from its persistent faithfulness and frequent failures.

Particular aspects of the identity, mission, and reality of the church are explored from various angles throughout the curriculum. For example, the Pastoral Ministry and Leadership course required for most Master of Divinity students attempts realistic and loving appraisal of congregational life in relation to pastoral leadership issues and church polities. The Anabaptist History and Theology course highlights understandings of the church emerging from the sixteenth-century Radical Reformation. The Luke-Acts: Mission Perspectives course explores the vision and struggles of the New Testament church.

The Institute of Mennonite Studies, an organization devoted to scholarly inquiry and sponsored by AMBS, has given increased attention in the past several years to the development of projects in ministry studies, such as Christian initiation of new believers in Mennonite churches, congregational studies, and mutual aid. Faculty and students draw on such material to enrich their understandings of the calling and reality of the contemporary church.

The living church serves not only as a subject but also as a context for teaching and learning. Congregational and community-based internships and practica connect students to realities the church faces in contemporary North American settings. Congregationally based internships in the Master of Divinity program increase fruitful interaction between campus-based and congregationally based education.

Apart from supervised work in churches, faculty and students are expected to be involved in local congregations and to draw on this experience in their teaching and learning.

The seminary campus ethos and curricular offerings also promote deepening awareness of the global character of the church. Many students, faculty, and campus guests have lived and worked outside North America. Given the local and national loyalties of many Christians and congregations, increased understanding of and connection to the worldwide church are significant components of theological and pastoral education.

8. *Awareness that the calling of the church shapes the character of the educational community in which teaching and learning occur*

AMBS is a community of theological education. Faculty hope that the seminary's entire ethos—its distinguishing characteristics, habits, and practices—will be shaped by and inspire commitment to the church's calling. The document on theological education reiterates a statement from a former guiding document that "not only the content but also the context of the curriculum must be shaped by our theological convictions." A seminary shaped by the church's calling:

a. is committed to growth as a worshiping community.
b. is committed to remain an international community that reflects the changing transnational character and multicultural dimensions of the Christian church.
c. is a ministering community committed to value a diversity of ministries.
d. is committed to foster community discernment and decision making.
e. is committed to be a community of mutual care and accountability.

Given the high calling of the church and the related high expectations for Christian ministers and seminaries who desire to follow this calling, theological education and pastoral formation must begin and end with repentance, commitment, and confidence: repentance for accepting lesser purposes for ministry, education, and community life; commitment to serving the church's primary calling of being the community of God's reign in the world; and confidence in the sustaining and transforming power of the Holy Spirit.

Note

[1] See Appendix 1 in this volume (239-56).

Index of Scripture references

Genesis
1:1   124

Exodus
15:26   156
20   79
21   79
21:1-6   77
21:7-11   77
28:41   107, 112
29:9, 29, 39   112
29:22   107
29:26   107
29:27   107
29:29   107
29:31   107
29:33   107
29:34   107
29:35   107
32:29   108

Leviticus
7:37   108
8:22   108
8:28   108
8:29   108
8:31   108
8:33   108, 112
16:32   108, 112
21:10   108

Numbers
3:3   108, 112
28:6   107, 108

Deuteronomy
5   79
6   76
6:4-25   75
6:7-9   76

6:10-19   75
10:20   80
12:32   78
15   79
15:12   77
15:12-18   77
18:20   127
18:22   78
19:14   77
21:10-14   77
23:15-16   77
24   80

1 Samuel
19:24   122

2 Samuel
17:14   108

1 Kings
1:36   108
12:32   107
13:33   112
18:40   122

2 Kings
19:25   108
23:5   107, 108
22:8-20   122

1 Chronicles
9:22   107
17:9   107
25:1, 3   127

2 Chronicles
2:4   108
11:15   107
22:7   108
23:18   107

29:27   107

Ezra
7:10-12   79

Nehemiah
8   79

Esther
9:27   107

Job
28   84

Psalms
6   156
7:13   107
8:2   107, 108
8:3   107
30   156, 157
30:2, 8-10   157
30:3, 10-12   157
30:6   157
39   156
39:4b, 12b   156
65:9   108
68:18   124
81:5   107
88   156
90   156
103   156
111:9   108
132:17   107
133:3   108
139:16   108

Proverbs
15:25   77
22:28   77
23:10   77

Isaiah

1:10-31	122
2:6-9	122
5:1-9	122
7:1-17	122
22:8b-14	122
26:12	107, 108
30:33	107
37:24	108
48:5	108
50:4	176, 183
51	123

Jeremiah

1:5	107
7:9-11	122
8:8	76
18:18	76
22:15-16	167
28:1-12	78
28:9	78

Lamentations

2:17	108
3:37	108

Ezekiel

18:30-32	123
28:13	109
34	40, 54
36:25-28	123

Daniel

2:24	107

Hosea

11:8-9	123

Habakkuk

1:12	107, 109

Zechariah

1–8	123, 128
1:7-15	124
4:14	123
6:1-8	124
6:13	124
7–8	123
7:4	124
8:10, 12, 16, 19	124

Matthew

4:24	161
5:13-14	254
6:9-10	166
9:35–10:1	150
10:1	219
10:16	32
10:27	176
11:15	176
13	32
13:52	2, 84
18:15-19	225
22:37-40	163
28:18-19	219
28:19-20	164
28:20	150

Mark

1:22	219
1:32-34	161
1:45	161
3:14	109
3:14-15	150
4:40	157
5:34-36	158
6:1-6	157, 158
6:7-13	150
7:24-30	191
10:42-44	214

Luke

2:1	215
7:18-23	150
9:1	227
9:1-6	150
10:5-11, 17	150
14:7-11	217
22:25-26	217

John

10	32
10:12	37
12:49	219
13:15	216
14:26	206
15:16	109
16:13	206
17:14	32
17:20-21	56
19:12	227
20:21	31

Acts

1:8	219
1:22	109
3–4	150
6:2-5	72
8	151
8:7	151
10:36-38	150
10:42	109
11:21	170
11:26	124
13	151
13:1	124
13:48	109
14:15	170
14:23	110
15	57, 62, 69, 220, 221
15:1-2	220
15:2	220
15:4	220
15:7	220
15:13	220
15:13-21	220
15:22-25	220
15:22-23, 32	126
16	151
16:4	110
17:6-7	215
17:31	110
19	151
20	21
26:26	141
28	215

Romans

1:1	97
7:10	109, 110
8:18-23	158
10:8	126
12:1	103
12:1-2	170
12:3-8	15, 17, 19
12:4-5a	17
12:6	125
12:6b	126
12:8	103
13:1	110, 215
13:4	104
15:8	104
16:1-2	98
16:2	103

16:3-16	98
16:23	227

1 Corinthians

1:4-9	103
1:17	127
1:18	127
1:24b, 30b	203
1:26-27	217
2:1-5	97
2:2	217, 222
2:3	222
2:7	110
2:16	222
2:16b	203
3:7b	206
4:8-13	97
4:14-21	97
7:17	110
7:25	227
9:8	227
12	124, 125
12:3	125
12:4-31	15, 17, 19
12:8-10	151
12:28	124
12:28-30	151
14	25, 125
14:3, 4, 5, 12, 17, 26	125
14:14	125
14:15	125
14:19	125
14:20	125
14:23	125
14:29	125
15:26, 57-58	158
16:15	98
16:16-18	98

2 Corinthians

2:14-17	97
4:7-12	97
6:3-10	97
7:2-16	222
10:5	222
11–13	223
11:17	227
12:7-9	151
12:9	223
13:9	223

Galatians

1:6	103
1:23	126
2:1-14	220
3:19	110
4:19	97

Ephesians

1:10, 20-22	124
1:20-22	124
2:10	111
2:20	46
4	7, 19, 124, 125
4:3-5	125
4:3-7	124
4:8	124
4:11	124, 125
4:11-13	15, 17, 19
4:12	126
4:12-13	125, 223
4:14	125
4:15	225
4:26	225

Philippians

1:1	7, 97, 103
1:27	126
2:5-7	216
2:12-13	223
2:22	97
2:25	97
2:25-27	151

Colossians

1:10	226

1 Thessalonians

1:1	96
1:4	96
2	96
2:1, 9, 14, 17	96
2:7	96
2:7-8	96
2:9-10	96
2:11	96
2:11-12	96
2:17	96
5:12	98, 103
5:27	103

1 Timothy

3:1-13	18

3:2	103
3:4-5, 12	103
3:4-5, 12-13	227
5:1-2, 17, 19	103

2 Timothy

2:24-26	73
4:22	109, 111

Titus

1:5	18, 103, 111
1:6	227
1:6-9	73
1:7	103
3:15	109, 111

Hebrews

5:1	111
8:3	111
9:6	111

James

5:14-15	152

1 Peter

2:9	254
2:11–4:11	218
2:17	215
2:22-23	218
2:24	218
3:1-2	218
4:12–5:11	218
5	140
5:2	218
5:3	218
5:5	218
5:6	218

1 John

1:1	169
4:1	127

Jude

4	112

Revelation

1:3	126
4:11	215
5:12	215
12:7-9	215
13	215
13:2	215

Subject index

Abraham • 123

Adams, Jay E. • 211

administrators, administration • 10, 20-
21, 47, 49, 51, 58, 63, 69, 73, 85,
88, 120, 128, 168, 170, 191, 233,
237, 241

Agrippa, King • 141

Ältester • 16, 48–49, 51, 58, 85

Anabaptist, Anabaptism (see also radical
reformers, Radical Reformation) • 2-5,
17-18, 23-26, 28-30, 32-37, 39-40,
42, 44-45, 47-48, 50, 53-54, 57-58,
60, 62-65, 70-73, 100, 115-17, 129,
141, 144, 165-69, 172, 210, 235,
251, 253-54, 260-61

Anabaptist Vision • 44, 235

Anderson, Ray S. • 208, 211-12

Anglican • 47, 55

Anselm • 166

anthropology, cultural • 181

anticlericalism • 3-4, 13, 24, 26-30, 32-
37, 42, 45, 53, 57, 65, 105, 116, 168

anti-laicism • 35

apostasy • 40-41

apostles, apostolate • 4, 15, 19, 41, 46,
50-51, 57, 61, 72, 88, 90-100, 103-
4, 106, 110-11, 124-25, 150-52,
220, 222-23

Apostles' Creed • 45

apostolic succession • 50, 61

Aquinas, Thomas • 154, 161

archbishop • 29, 37

Arminianism • 50, 158

Arndt, William F. • 227

Artaxerxes • 79

Associated Mennonite Biblical Seminary •
vii, ix-xi, 1-3, 15-17, 20-24, 52-53,
58, 85-88, 100, 116, 128, 138-40,
162, 211, 239, 245-62

Auburn Seminary's Center for the Study of
Theological Education • 139-40

Augsburg Confession • 45

Augustine • 6, 153, 160, 164, 166–67

authority or authoritarianism • viii, 1-6,
12-13, 18-20, 22, 24, 27, 30, 33, 40-
43, 45-47, 49-53, 56-57, 59-73, 78-
81, 83, 87-88, 90-93, 95, 97, 101-2,
106, 113-14, 116, 119-20, 122, 128,
149, 169, 180, 213-29, 232, 234-37,
241, 244-45, 249, 255, 258

Baker, J. A. • 101

baptism • 29-30, 32, 48, 55-56, 64-65,
72-73, 89, 91, 109, 125, 153, 158,
161, 245, 260

Baptists • 46-47, 50, 55, 101

Barker, Amy L. • 128

Barnabas • 220

Barrett, Lois • 142-43, 148

Barsom, Murad S. • 161

Bartlett, David L. • 102

Basil • 153

Bauer, Walter • 227

Baylor, Michael G. • 35

Beachy, Alvin J. • 35

Beck, Duane • 155

Beker, J. Christiaan • 159, 161

believers church (see also free church) • 64,
72-73, 260

Belmont Mennonite Church • 155

bench, the • 16, 23, 235

Bender, Harold S. • 44, 52-54

Bender, Ross T. • ix, 2-3, 15, 17, 23, 34,
53, 58, 100, 256

Benjamin • 81

Bennett, David W. • 102

Bergthaler Mennonite Church • 85, 100

Berliner, Paul • 188, 196

266

Bernard, Charles A. • 173
Berry, Malinda • 139, 143, 148
Bethel College • 52, 59
bishops and episcopate • 4, 16, 18, 26, 41-44, 46-52, 55, 57-58, 65, 73, 88-91, 98, 103, 111, 149, 153, 228-29, 237
Blum, Stephen • 196-97
Body of Christ: see church as body
Boers, Arthur Paul • ix, 10, 162
Bolt, Peter • 104
Borg, Marcus • 157, 161
Bornhäuser, Christoph • 34
Bowden, John • 101
Brazil • 44
Brethren in Christ • 34
Broadway Evangelical Brethren Church • 86
Brock, Raymond T. • 212
Brown, Peter • 153, 160
Browning, Don S. • 210
Brueggemann, Walter • 170, 175
Brunk I, George • 52
Brunk II, George • 52
Brunk III, George • 52
Buechner, Frederick • 165, 173
Bultmann, Rudolf • 92, 101-2
Burrell, David • 62, 72
Burtchaell, David Tunstead • 93, 101
business • 4, 39, 43, 45, 134, 167, 217, 231

Calian, Carnegie S. • 168, 174
calling: see vocation
Calvinism • 50, 158
Campenhausen, Hans van • 91-92, 101, 125, 128
Campbell, R. Alistair • 93-94, 101-2
Canada • x, 4, 23, 42, 44, 47, 52, 58, 66, 120, 130, 132, 136, 239, 250-51, 254
Canadian Council of Churches • 66
Canadian Mennonite Bible College • 52
Canadian Mennonite University • x
canon • 2, 6, 76, 80-83, 122-24, 126-28, 246
capital punishment • 121
capitalism • 120
Capps, Donald • 198, 208-9, 211
Cardenal, Ernesto • 174
Carroll, John T. • 103
Cascadia Publishing House • viii

Catholics and Catholicism • 4-5, 7, 33, 41-42, 46-47, 50-51, 55, 57-58, 60-64, 68, 73, 91, 101, 119, 141, 146, 154
change agency • 12, 20, 39, 49, 162, 167, 172, 188, 205, 209, 211, 213, 219, 221, 225, 231, 235
chaplain, chaplaincy • vii, x, 138, 147-48, 159, 164
Chapman, Stephen B. • 82
charismata • 4, 6-7, 13, 19-20, 41, 46, 50-51, 53-56, 64, 72-73, 87-95, 120, 151, 154, 168, 213, 221, 224
Childers, Jana • 182, 185
Chirban, John T. • 160
Christendom • 26-27, 35, 91, 131, 161
Christian Century • 46, 58
Christian education: see teacher, teaching ministry
church and state • 30, 32, 48-50, 58, 60, 62-67, 78, 104, 113-14, 120-21, 124, 129, 132, 135, 137, 139, 142-44, 148, 214
church as body • 2, 9, 13, 15, 17-18, 20-23, 31, 40–41, 72, 90, 96, 125-26, 129, 140, 144, 166, 180, 202, 222, 233, 239-40
Church of England • 7, 106, 112-13, 115
Civil Rights Movement • 139-40
Clarke, Andrew D. • 94, 102-4
clergy • 4, 18, 23-24, 26-27, 35, 40, 42, 44-45, 47-50, 53-55, 58, 63-65, 73, 117, 139, 168, 172, 228-29, 237, 240
Cobb Jr., John B. • 254-55
Coker, Jerry • 197
Collins, Kenneth J. • 173
Cologne • 28-30
commissioning • 65, 73, 116, 121, 150, 164, 239
communion • 30, 42, 46, 51, 72, 85-86, 91, 159, 163, 165, 168, 234, 251
community • 6-8, 10-12, 18, 21, 24-25, 33-34, 43, 46, 48-49, 51-52, 59, 62, 65, 72, 75-76, 78-80, 82-83, 88-96, 98-104, 121-22, 126, 128, 130, 134-35, 138-39, 141-42, 145-47, 152-53, 155, 166-67, 172, 179, 193, 195, 197, 200-202, 206-8, 210, 214, 216, 218-21, 223-27, 239-41, 243, 247, 249-54, 257-62

confession of faith • 4, 26, 30-33, 37-38, 41, 45, 47-48, 63, 65, 71-73, 124-25, 168, 174, 203-4, 210-11, 251, 254

Confession of Faith in a Mennonite Perspective • 71, 168, 174, 210-11

conflict, conflict management • 12, 49, 154, 195, 203, 212, 219-20, 224-26

congregationalism • 4, 47, 54-55

Conrad Grebel University College • 52, 117

Consultation on Church Union • 56

Cornies, Johann • 51

Corsini, Raymond J. • 209

counseling, pastoral: see pastoral counseling

Couture, Pamela D. • 212

Crossan, John Dominic • 212

Culbertson, Philip L. • 160

Czechoslovakia • 230

Danzig • 49

Davies, Philip R. • 82

Davis, Steph • 148

deacon • 16, 18, 42, 47-49, 57, 73, 93, 98, 103, 228-29

deaconess • 103

Dean's Seminar • 2, 6, 15-16, 19-20, 22-24, 53, 58, 87, 100

democracy • 28, 39, 42, 45, 47, 60, 65-67, 69, 71

demonic power • 151-53, 157, 160-61, 191, 214

Denck, Hans • 166

Dillenger, John • 35

Dirk Philips • 29, 35, 37

Dirks, Heinrich • 51

disciples • 2, 21, 150, 152, 157, 164, 172, 210, 215-17, 219, 244, 246, 260

discipleship • x, 9-10, 64, 72, 92, 161, 166, 203, 206, 214, 239-40

discipline • 10, 45, 64-65, 73, 125, 129, 149, 163-64, 166, 171-72, 189, 194, 199, 206-7, 209-11, 233, 240, 242-46, 250, 252, 254, 259-60

discipling: see discipline

Djilas • 35, 47

Doell, Leonard • 100

Doohan, Helen • 102, 104

Dordrecht Confession • 48, 72, 254

Dort, Synod of • 45

Dueck, Alvin C. • 208, 212

Duisburg • 29

Dulles, Avery • 168, 174

Durnbaugh, Donald F. • 64, 73

Düsseldorf • 29

Dutch Anabaptists, Dutch Mennonites • 25, 29-30, 34, 36-37, 45, 48, 56, 58-59, 64, 136

Dutchersmith, Teresa • 138

Dyck, Cornelius J. • 17, 34-35, 37, 53

Dykema, Peter • 34-35

Early Catholicism • 7, 91

early church • 7, 40, 57, 61, 73, 88-91, 93-95, 101-2, 127-28, 149-55, 160-61, 214-20, 225-26

ecclesiology • 5, 9, 12, 55, 60, 65, 70, 89, 115, 117, 139-41, 199, 201

ecumenism • 4, 42, 55-57, 66, 72, 89, 146

education, theological (see also teacher, teaching ministry) • 2-3, 15, 17, 23, 52-53, 119, 127, 139, 148, 210-11, 238-62

egalitarianism • 2, 7, 12, 18, 24, 28, 91-92, 102, 125, 169, 241

Eifelgebergte • 29

elder • 18, 21, 29, 43, 46, 48-52, 58, 65, 73, 85, 88–89, 91-94, 98-99, 104, 110-11, 152, 155, 179, 193, 218, 220

Elkhart City Church of the Brethren • 86

Elias, Jacob W. • ix, 6-7, 85, 103

Elias, Lillian • ix

Ellis, E. Earle • 102

Elymas • 151

Emden • 30

Engels, Friedrich • 39

Engen, John van • 26, 28, 35-36

Enlightenment • 26, 42, 154

Ens, Adolf • 24, 34

Epaphroditus • 97, 151

Ephesus • 21, 99, 151, 227

Episcopalian (see also Anglican) • 90

episcopate: see bishops and episcopate

Epp, Frank H. • 58

Epp-Tiessen, Esther • 57

Erastus • 227

Esau, John A. • viii, 3, 15, 18, 23, 36, 169, 174, 237

eschatology • 90, 145, 171, 202, 212, 225-26

ethics • ix, 11, 17, 57, 64, 81-82, 83, 85,
92, 97, 104, 128, 133, 136-37, 142-
43, 165, 202, 208, 212, 232-34, 245,
249, 255, 260
ethnography • 181
Evangelical Fellowship of Canada • 66
Evangelicalism, Evangelicals • 31, 66, 154,
166, 244, 255
evangelists • 15, 19-20, 22, 73, 87, 92,
97, 102, 124-25, 144, 214, 240, 242,
248, 260
Ewert, H. H. • 52
exorcism • 150-54, 157, 160-61, 214
Ezra • 78-81, 83

Faith Mennonite Church • 138
family systems • 209, 221-22, 227
Fast, Heinhold • 36
Ferguson, Everett • 153, 160
Feuerbach, Ludwig • 41
First Mennonite Church (Saskatoon) • 65
Fischer, Norbert • 36
Fitschett, George • 209
formation in ministry • 119, 127-28, 141,
149-50, 159, 172, 198-99, 202, 204,
207, 211, 238-43, 245, 247-49, 251-
53, 255-59, 262
Franconia Mennonite Conference • 43, 51
free church (see also believers church) • 8,
15, 17, 23, 34, 42, 44, 55, 58, 87,
100, 115, 210, 238, 256
Freedman, David Noel • 116
Friedman, Edward H. • 221
Friends (Quakers) • 47
Friesen, Ivan • x, 128
Frost, Evelyn • 160
functionalism • 2-3, 6-7, 13, 15, 57, 69,
73, 86-89, 115, 234, 237
Fund for Peoplehood Education • viii
Funk, John F. • 52
Furnish, George M. • 212
Furnish, Victor Paul • 104

Garrett, Susan • 160
Gaventa, Beverly Roberts • 103
Gemeinde: see community
General Conference Mennonite Church (or
tradition) • viii, 1, 16, 23, 43, 53, 57,
65, 73, 85, 101, 121, 237-38, 254
Geneva Bible • 112, 114
Georg of Kempen • 30
Gerkin, Charles V. • 211

German • 6, 29, 35, 49-51, 58, 64-65,
115
Germany • 26-27, 30, 35, 42-43, 48-51,
58, 63-65, 136
gifts: see charismata
Gilbert, Marvin G. • 212
Giles, Kevin • 94, 102, 104
Gillespie, Thomas W. • 126
Gingerich, Barbara Nelson • viii
Gingrich, F. Wilbur • 227
Gladbach • 29
Gnadenfeld • 51
gnostics, Gnosticism • 152
Goch • 29
Goertz, Hans-Jürgen • 34-36
Goeters, J. F. G. • 29-30, 36-38
Goshen College • 16
Goshen College Biblical Seminary • 16
Gouldner, Alvin W. • 39, 57
Great Commission • 150, 164
Grebel, Conrad • 27, 37
Gregory of Nyssa • 153, 167
Gregory I • 149
Grieser, D. Jonathan • 57
Griffiths, Paul • 197
Grobel, Kendrick • 101
Groome, Thomas • 212
Gros, Jeffrey • 57
Gross, Leonard • 36
Grote, Geert • 26-28
Günther, Franz • 27

Halivni, David W. • 79, 83
Hamilton, Alistair • 58
Hananiah • 78
Harakas, Stanley S. • 160
Hardenberg, Albert • 29
Harder, Keith • viii
Harder, Leland • 17, 24, 34
Hauerwas, Stanley • 128, 168, 170, 174-
75, 254
Havel, Vaclav • 230-31
healing • 9-10, 14, 124, 150-61, 191,
193, 198, 201, 206-7, 213-14, 247,
250
health and health care (see also mental
health) • 8, 44, 133-34, 142, 152,
156, 159-60, 191, 198-99, 210
Heifetz, Ronald • 223-25, 227
Hellenistic Judaism • 92, 94, 102
Helvetica, Confessio • 45

hermeneutics, hermeneutical community • 24-25, 34, 71, 81, 92, 205, 211
Hertzke, Allen D. • 137
hierarchy • 7, 25, 42, 73, 91, 114, 168, 231
Hilkiah • 77
Hochstetler, Clair • 138, 147
Hoekema, Alle • 56, 59
Holmberg, Bengt • 102
Holmes, Urban • 168
homosexuality • xi, 66, 71, 131, 163, 224, 250
Hooker, Morna D. • 104
Hough Jr., Joseph C. • 210, 254-55
Huebner, Harry • 34
Huldah • 122-23
humility • 9-10, 27, 132, 158, 167, 172, 218-19
Hunsinger, Deborah van Deusen • 209
Hunter, Rodney J. • 211-12
Hutterites • 25

immigration: see migration, immigration
improvising, improvisation • 11, 14, 186-97
incarnation, ministry of • 5, 30, 56, 79, 83, 97, 169, 174
Indonesia • 56, 59
Institute of Mennonite Studies • viii, x, 261
Iraq • 130
Irenaeus • 38, 152-53, 160
Isaiah • 83, 123, 157

James • 220
James I: see King James I
Janz, B. B. • 52
Janz, Denis R. • 35
jazz • 11, 186, 188-90, 192, 194, 196-97
Jeremiah • 76-78
Jerusalem • 21, 57, 62, 110, 151, 212, 220
Jesus • 2, 4, 6-7, 10, 12, 21-22, 31-32, 40-41, 54, 56-57, 61-62, 72, 75, 80-81, 83-84, 87-88, 91-92, 94-100, 102, 109, 111-12, 124-25, 136, 138, 143, 145, 147, 150-53, 157-61, 164, 167, 178, 191-93, 199, 201-6, 208, 210, 212, 214, 215-19, 222, 225-27, 239-40, 243, 245-46, 248-49, 257-58, 260-61
John the Baptist • 150

Johns, Loren L. • viii, x, 1, 105, 176, 184
Johnson, E. Elizabeth • 103
Johnson, Trevor • 35
Jones, Alan • 173-74
Jones, Cheslyn • 173
Jones, L. Gregory • 197
Josiah • 77, 82
Joyce, Paul • 128
Jüchen, Theunis van • 29-30
Juhnke, James C. • 58-59
justice, injustice • 10, 27, 99, 120-22, 126, 135, 146-47, 166-67, 172, 191-92, 207, 246-47, 249, 253, 258
Jüterbog • 27

Kauffman, Daniel • 52
Kauffman, J. Howard • 24, 34
Kauffman, Richard A. • 34
Kaufman, Edmund G. • 52, 59
Keeney, William E. • 34-35, 37
Kelly, Henry A. • 161
Kelsey, Morton • 160
Kempen Confession • 4, 26, 29-33, 37, 48
Kempis, Thomas à • 27
King, Michael A. • viii
King James I • 8, 112-14
King James Version • 7, 105-7, 109-10, 112, 114-16
kingdom of God: see reign of God
Klaassen, Walter • 58, 254
Klassen, William • 17, 53, 59, 254
Kleve • 29
Kobelt-Groch, Marion • 36
Konrád, György • 57
Koolman, Jacobus ten Dornkaat • 29, 37
Koontz, Gayle Gerber • ix, 5, 34, 60, 72, 238
Koontz, Ted • ix, 8-9, 129
Koop, Karl • ix, 3, 24, 73, 116
Kouzes, James M. • 231, 237
Krahn, Cornelius • 36-37
Kraybill, Donald B. • 116
Kraybill, J. Nelson • viii, x, 12, 213
Krefeld • 29
Krehbiel, H. P. • 52
Kreider, Alan • 153, 161
Kreider, Heidi Regier • viii
Kruse, Colin G. • 104
Küng, Hans • 40-42, 57
Kydd, Ronald A. N. • 160

Lancaster Mennonite Conference • 43, 51
Lang, Bernard • 175
Lapp, John E. • 51
Lasco, Johannes à • 30
laity, lay ministry (see also priesthood of all
    believers) • 3, 13, 16, 18, 24-28, 32-
    33, 47, 53, 55, 73, 81, 117, 229
laying on of hands • 47, 56, 83, 110-11,
    115, 152
Lebacqz, Karen • 232
leaders, leadership (see also servant
    leadership) • vii, 1, 3-4, 6-7, 9, 12-13,
    15-16, 18-26, 28-33, 36, 39-59, 65-
    67, 69-70, 72-73, 75, 83-95, 98-102,
    104-6, 114, 116-17, 119, 124-25,
    127, 130, 133-35, 139-40, 142-43,
    145-46, 148-50, 152, 154-55, 168-
    69, 174, 213, 215, 217-42, 246-48,
    252, 258-59, 261
Leech, Kenneth • 165, 173-74
Leitgen • 29
Lewis, C. S. • 156-57
Lewis, Jack P. • 113, 116
Lewis, Phillip V. • 226-27
Lind, Millard C. • 17
Linnich • 29
listening • 10-11, 14, 30, 54, 76, 135,
    176-84, 187-90, 192-93, 195-96,
    220
Littell, Franklin • 24, 34
location • 13, 195, 228-29, 233, 235-36,
    251
Loder, James E. • 211-12
Loewen, Howard J. • 72-73, 254
Lord's Supper: see communion
lot, the • 65, 73
Lovering, Eugene H. • 104
Luther, Martin • 5, 25, 27, 35, 39, 63-64
Lutheran • 31, 45, 47, 50, 63-64, 118-
    19, 141
Luz, Ulrich • 144, 148
Lynn, Elizabeth • 148

Maastricht • 29
MacDonald, Margaret Y. • 94, 102
Macquarrie, John • 164-67, 173-74
magic • 150-51, 160
Maler, Jörg • 35
Marpeck, Pilgram • 257
marks of the true church • 46, 152-53
Martin, Dennis D. • 34
Martin of Tours • 153

Marty, Martin • 46, 58
martyrs, martyrdom • 25, 37, 58, 153
Marx, Marxism • 39-41, 162
Master of Divinity • 44, 159, 257, 259,
    261
McGrath, Alister • 114, 116
McKane, William • 82
McMinn, Mark R. • 210
McMullen, Ramsay • 153
medieval church: see Middle Ages
Melanchthon • 64
Mellink, A. F. • 36
Menno Simons • 6, 25, 29-32, 34, 37,
    72, 254
Mennonite Biblical Seminary • 16, 52
Mennonite Brethren Bible College • 52
Mennonite Brethren Biblical Seminary • 52
Mennonite Central Committee • 51, 142
Mennonite Church (or tradition), (Old) •
    1, 16, 23, 51, 53, 57, 101, 105-6,
    116, 228, 238, 254
Mennonite Church Canada • 66
Mennonite Church USA • 43
Mennonite Disaster Service • 130, 140,
    142
Mennonite Education Agency • viii
mental health • 134, 142, 198-99
Messer, Donald E. • 168, 174
Meyer, Paul W. • 103
Methodist: see United Methodist
Middle Ages • 3, 21, 25-28, 31, 34-36,
    154, 160, 164
migration, immigration • 4, 43, 52, 130-
    31
Miller, Ernest • 52
Miller, Keith Graber • 137
Miller, Marlin • 3, 25, 34, 52, 100, 128,
    169, 174, 254
Miller, Orie O. • 51-52
Miller, Paul M. • 105, 116
Miriam • 122, 127
Mishler, David E. • 116
mission • 2, 29, 42, 44, 48, 50-52, 55-
    57, 62, 68, 70, 74, 83, 87, 89, 100,
    120, 140-41, 144, 150-54, 159, 161,
    164, 191, 194, 202, 215, 218-20,
    223, 225, 238-43, 245-53, 255-61
missional church • 56, 258
Moessner, Jeanne Stevenson • 212
Moingt, Joseph • 60-62, 71-72
Molotschna colony • 51
Monson, Ingrid T. • 197

Morgan, Donn • 83
Morris, Robert C. • 192, 197
Moses • 75, 80
Mountainview Mennonite Church • 86
Münster • 29, 30, 36, 64
Müntzer, Thomas • 27, 35
music • 187–188, 190, 194, 196, 213
Myers, Gail E. • 183, 185
Myers, Michele Tolela • 183, 185

Nardin, Terry • 137
National Association of Evangelicals • 66
National Council of Churches • 45, 66
navigator, pastor as: see orienteer, pastor as
    spiritual
Neuhaus, Richard John • 128
Neff, David • 116
Nehemiah • 76, 78
Nero • 111
Nettl, Bruno • 196
Nicene Creed • 45
Niebuhr, H. Richard • 8, 136
Niederstift • 29
nonconformity • 9, 141, 145
nonresistance • 64, 121, 146
nonviolence, violence • xi, 27, 73, 143,
    146, 245, 250, 260
Nouwen, Henri J. M. • 168-69, 173-75

Oates, Wayne J. • 210
Obbes, Nittert • 58
Oberman, Heiko A. • 34-35
Odenkirchen • 29
office • 2-3, 6-8, 13, 18-22, 26-30, 32-
    33, 36, 51, 55-57, 61, 64-69, 72-73,
    86-87, 89-91, 93-95, 98-101, 105-6,
    114-15, 118-21, 126-28, 130, 136,
    149, 153, 169, 210, 223, 228, 230-
    31, 233-34, 236-38, 241-42, 246,
    254, 258
Oistwart, Michiel • 29
Ollenburger, Ben C. • x, 8, 118, 137
ordination, ordained ministry • 3-4, 6-8,
    27, 36, 38, 43-45, 47-49, 51, 55-56,
    58, 60, 63, 65, 69, 72-73, 85-86, 89,
    98, 105-17, 119-20, 127, 143, 201,
    228-29, 236
orienteer, pastor as spiritual • 10, 14, 20-
    22, 69, 71, 142, 162, 169-73, 246,
    249-50, 261-62
Origen • 152, 154
Orthodox Judaism • 83

Orthodoxy (Eastern) • 41, 47, 154, 160-
    61, 164
orthodoxy (theological) • 61, 244
Oyer, John S. • 36
Ozment, Steven • 35

Packull, Werner O. • 25, 34, 36
Palmer, Parker • 231, 237
papacy: see pope
Paraguay • 44
Parkview Mennonite Church • ix
pastor (see also shepherd) • vii, x, 2, 5-6,
    8-13, 16, 18-20, 22, 30, 40, 45-46,
    65, 67-70, 74, 81, 85-88, 118-21,
    127-28, 133-38, 140-41, 145, 147,
    149, 154-55, 160, 162-65, 167-68,
    170, 172, 174, 178, 181, 183, 192,
    198, 201, 210, 213, 228, 230, 232–
    36, 240-43, 248
pastoral care • 6, 33, 43, 96, 120, 138,
    159, 170, 184, 201, 204, 210-12,
    241, 252, 259
pastoral counseling • x-xi, 10-12, 14, 22,
    103, 150, 155, 159, 167-68, 170,
    178, 184, 193, 198-212, 221, 233,
    252, 258-59
pastoral epistles • 18, 20, 92, 94-95
pastoral identity • vii, 3, 10, 24, 28, 30,
    33, 47, 69, 86, 149-50, 154-55, 159,
    186, 199, 203, 208, 234-36
pastoral ministry • vii-viii, x, 1-4, 6-14,
    16, 18-21, 23, 30, 36, 40-41, 44, 50,
    53-54, 56-57, 61, 63-69, 72, 85-88,
    90-91, 94-96, 98-105, 115-17, 119-
    21, 138-39, 141-44, 148-49, 152,
    159-60, 162, 167-70, 173-74, 177-
    79, 184, 186-87, 190, 192-209, 211,
    228-29, 232, 234-42, 250, 252, 258-
    59, 261-62
Patton, John • 210
Paul, Apostle • 2, 7, 21, 25, 34, 72, 92,
    94-100, 102, 104, 111, 124-26, 141,
    151, 206, 215-17, 220, 222-23, 227
Paul, Rule of: see Rule of Paul
Paulsell, Stephanie • 197
peace, peacemaking (see also nonviolence,
    violence) • ix-xi, 48, 56, 99, 113, 125,
    128, 131, 137, 146-47, 150, 159,
    162, 207, 245-50, 253, 258, 260-61
Pelikan, Jaroslav • 50-51, 58
persecution • 9, 31, 37, 50, 64, 129
Peterson, Eugene • 164, 169, 171, 173-75

Philip • 83, 151
Philips, Dirk: see Dirk Philips
Phillips, Leanne • 148
Phoebe • 98, 103
Piper, Reynar • 30
Pipkin, H. Wayne • 34
plural ministry • 16, 18-19, 23, 87-88, 232, 235
Poettcker, Henry • 3, 58
Poland (see also Prussia, Prussian) • 49-50
polity • 4, 24, 33-34, 42, 47-49, 65, 72, 88, 90, 95, 101, 115-16, 119, 127-28, 137, 174, 254
pope • 26-27, 53, 55, 114
Posner, Barry Z. • 231, 237
postmodernism • vii, 42, 55, 165
power • 3, 5, 11-13, 18-19, 23, 26, 28, 31-32, 39-42, 49, 52-57, 59, 61-65, 83, 91, 93-94, 99-102, 110, 112, 114, 117, 123-25, 127-29, 132, 135, 150-53, 158-59, 191, 202-3, 205-6, 208, 211-27, 231-33, 237-40, 248-49, 253, 262
Praetorius, Johannes • 37
Prague • 27, 35
prayer • vii, 56, 73, 89, 110, 152, 155-59, 164-66, 168, 170, 172-75, 191-95, 206, 210, 213, 223, 241, 250, 252, 259
preacher, preaching • 4, 8, 10-11, 14, 16, 21, 24, 28, 30-33, 35, 43, 48-49, 51, 57, 63-65, 71, 85-86, 92, 96, 98-99, 109-11, 116, 120, 126, 133, 147, 150, 160, 167-68, 170, 172, 175, 178-85, 191, 193, 195, 204-5, 207, 211, 219, 228, 232-35, 237, 241-42, 254, 259
Prediger • 48-49, 51, 65
presbyter, presbyterianism • 4, 44, 46-47, 57, 90-91, 103
Presbyterian • 50, 58, 90
priest • 26-28, 47, 55, 58, 76-77, 79, 91, 111, 118-19, 168, 171, 210, 241
priesthood of all believers (see also laity, lay ministry) • 3, 13, 25, 34, 55, 73, 86, 91, 100, 105, 116, 118, 235, 240
professionalism in the ministry • 2, 11, 13, 16, 18-19, 23, 43-45, 50, 53-54, 57, 83-84, 198, 208-9, 228-29, 235-37, 247, 253, 256-57
prophet, prophesying • 5, 8-9, 14-15, 19, 46, 54, 62, 69, 71-73, 76-78, 82-83, 93-94, 102, 118-28, 133-35, 137, 163, 168, 176, 204, 210-12, 241
Protestants and Protestantism • 4, 6-7, 18, 30, 33-39, 42, 44, 47, 51, 55, 57-58, 61, 63-64, 73, 87, 115, 118, 154, 210, 244, 246, 255
Prussia, Prussian (see also Poland) • 42, 49-50
Pruyser, Paul W. • 200, 209
psychology • 160, 163, 199-200, 204-5, 209-11
psychotherapy • 11-12, 199-200, 205, 209, 211-12
public leadership, ministry • 9, 26, 60, 76, 101, 130, 135, 137, 139-48, 217, 227, 233-34, 242, 247-48, 252, 259

Quakers: see Friends (Quakers)
Queen Elisabeth I • 113

race, racism • 148, 219, 240, 251, 260
radical reformers, Radical Reformation (see also Anabaptist, Anabaptism) • 27, 31, 35, 45, 53, 64, 67, 239-40, 242-43, 253, 261
Ramsay, Nancy J. • 200, 209
Rauschenbusch, Walter • 120
Reformation • 5, 25, 27-29, 31, 34-37, 42, 44-45, 47, 50, 53, 63-64, 67, 101, 118, 154
Reformed tradition • 37, 45, 47, 50, 62, 144
regeneration • 31, 157, 171, 193-94, 213, 225, 240
reign of God • 2, 9, 12, 84, 96, 128-29, 142, 144-45, 147-48, 151, 158, 166, 199, 205, 207-8, 212, 226, 240-43, 247, 249-53, 258, 260
Rennenberg, Wilhelm von • 37
reverend • 18, 46
Rheims New Testament • 112
Rheydt • 29
Rhine, Lower • 3, 24, 26, 28-30, 33, 116
Ries, Hans de • 58
Ris Confession • 65, 72, 254
ritual • 4, 47, 56, 161, 208, 216, 245
Robinson, Lindsey • 142-43, 148
Roer River • 29
Roeschley, Jane Thorley • viii
Rogers, Carl R. • 209
Rol, Heinrich • 29

Rome • 27, 63, 95, 97-99, 111, 149, 154, 175, 215
Roth, John D. • 3, 25, 34, 71-73
Rubsam, Tewes • 30
Rule of Paul • 25, 72
Rumscheidt, Barbara • 102
Rumscheidt, Martin • 102
Russia, Russian • 4, 42-44, 49-52, 59, 136

sacramentarianism • 29, 36, 47, 56, 115, 117
Sadie, Stanley • 196
sage • 76-77, 82-83, 180, 198-99, 203, 206, 208
salaried, unsalaried ministry • 16, 18, 23, 31, 43-45, 49
Samuel • 122
Samuel, Athanasius Y. • 161
Santos, Narry F. • 226
Sarah • 123
Sasserath • 29
Sattler, Michael • 38
Saul • 122
Sawatsky, Rodney • 3, 52-53, 59
Sawatsky, Walter • x, 4-5, 39, 59
Sawatzky, Erick • x, 3, 12, 40, 103, 169, 210, 228
Sawatzky, Beverley • viii
Schertz, Mary H. • viii, x-xi, 9, 73, 128, 138, 227
Schilling, Heinz • 35
Schipani, Daniel S. • viii, x, 11-12, 198
Schleitheim • 38, 72, 254
Schloneger, Weldon • 105, 116
scholasticism • 164
Schottroff, Luise • 102
Schreiter, Robert J. • 173
Schrijver, George De • 60, 71
Schroeder, David • 34
Schulz, Ray R. • 103
Schüssler Fiorenza, Elisabeth • 92, 102
Schüssler Fiorenza, Francis • 255
Scriven, Charles • 136
seminary: see theological education
servant leadership • 7, 12, 40, 46, 53, 83, 100, 103-4, 116, 168, 211, 214, 216-18, 226, 254
Shaphan • 77
shepherd • 4, 24, 28, 30, 32-33, 38-40, 54, 72, 75, 116, 119, 124, 140, 145, 168, 204

Shippee, Bradford • 160
Silvanus • 96
Simon Magus • 151
Ska, Jean Louis • 83
Slough, Rebecca • xi
Smucker, Marcus • 169, 174
Snyder, C. Arnold • 37, 65, 73
Snyder, Graydon F. • 210
social justice: see justice, injustice
sociology • 4, 17, 24, 39-40, 53, 60, 89, 94, 102, 129, 139, 169
Socrates • 177
Sohm, Rudolf • 91, 101
sorcery • 151, 153, 160
Spirit, Holy • 3, 5, 11-13, 15, 17-20, 22, 25, 31, 55, 61-62, 64-65, 67, 71-72, 90-93, 95, 99, 124-25, 138, 151-52, 158-61, 173, 178, 181-82, 191-93, 199, 202, 204, 206-7, 211-13, 217-20, 226, 231, 239-40, 245, 248-49, 252-54, 257, 259, 262
spiritual direction • 164, 169-70, 172, 184, 205
St. John's University • 146
Stassen, Glen H. • 136
state church(es) • 50, 58, 64
Stephanas • 98
Strasbourg • 36
Streeter, B. H. • 90, 101
Stuckey, Anne • viii
Sudnow, David • 189, 197
Sullivan, Francis A. • 57
Sumney, Jerry L. • 104
Swartley, Willard M. • xi
Swidler, Leonard • 60, 71
Swiss, Switzerland • 25, 29, 38, 42, 48, 50, 64-65, 136
Switzer, David • 168
Szelényi, Iván • 57

Tasch, Peter • 36
Taylor, Barbara Brown • 180, 184
teacher, teaching ministry • vii, ix, 1, 5-6, 8-10, 14-15, 17, 19-22, 29, 31-32, 35, 43, 45, 50, 52, 54, 60-62, 65, 68-72, 74-85, 87-88, 92, 94, 111, 120, 124-26, 133, 143, 149, 164, 168-70, 172, 184, 189, 191, 193-95, 197, 204-5, 207, 210-11, 213-14, 232-34, 239-51, 253, 255-56, 258-62
ten commandments • 75, 79
Thaumaturgus, Gregory • 153

Theissen, Gerd • 92, 102
theological education: see education, theological
theology, spiritual • 10, 163-67, 170, 172-73
theology, systematic • 73, 164-65, 263
Thiessen, J. J. • 52, 57, 85-86
Thomas, Everett J. • 72, 101, 116, 127-28, 174
Thompson, Mark • 104
Timothy • 96-98, 111
Tisdale, Leonora Tubbs • 181, 184
Titus • 111
Toews, David • 52
Toews, John E. • 115, 117
torah, Torah • 76-81, 83
Trinity, Trinitarian theology • 27, 45, 59, 169, 206, 210
Troeltsch, Ernst • 136
two-kingdom theology • 141-43
Tyndale Bible • 112
Tyrrell, John • 196
Tyson, John R. • 38

United Methodist • 46, 50, 58, 168
United States • 4, 23, 45, 66, 130, 132, 230, 239, 251
Uruguay • 44

Vatican II • 53, 209
Verduin, Leonard • 37, 254
Vietnam • 4, 19, 45
Vining, John Kie • 212
violence: see nonviolence, violence
Virginia Mennonite Church • 43, 52
Visschersweert • 29
Visser, Piet • 58
vocation • vii, 6, 13-14, 37, 55, 86-87, 97-98, 100, 118-21, 127, 133, 149, 174, 197-200, 202-3, 211, 232, 234, 239, 241, 247, 250, 253-54, 257
Volf, Miroslav • 55, 59
Volz, Carl • 149, 160
Vollebier, Dietrich • 37
Voolstra, Sjouke • 58

Wainwright, Geoffrey • 173
Waite, Gary K. • 25, 34
Waltner, Erland • xi, 23, 52, 88-89, 106
Walton, Janet R. • 196-97
war • 5, 58, 77, 97, 130-31, 137, 143, 146, 245, 250, 260

Watts, James W. • 82-83
Weaver, J. Denny • 57
Wedding, Danny • 209
Wedel, Cornelius H. • 52, 59
Weinfeld, Moshe • 82
Wenger, John C. • 17, 37, 52, 254
Wesel • 29
Westerberg, Gerhard • 29
Westerhoff, John • 168
Westminster Confession • 45
Wheeler, Barbara G. • 148, 210
Wiebe, Orlando • 106, 116
Wied, Herman von • 29, 36
Wilkinson, John • 161
Williams, Stuart Murray • 24, 34
Willimon, William H. • 168, 170, 174-75
Wimberly, Edward P. • 211
wisdom, biblical wisdom traditions • xi, 5-6, 12, 27, 62, 69-72, 77, 83-84, 110, 127, 133, 164, 173, 193, 198-210, 212, 215, 230, 243, 260
wise person: see sage
Wissman, Robert • 138
women in ministry; women, ordination of • 47, 53, 55, 66, 93, 98, 100, 212, 235-36
Wood, Charles • 257-58
Woolfolk, Robert L. • 200, 209
Woolley, Reginald M. • 160
worship, worship leading • 21, 33, 48, 72, 74, 85, 100, 120, 122, 125, 145, 155, 157, 170-72, 180, 193, 202, 210, 213, 235, 240-41, 245, 247, 250, 252, 259, 261-62
Wright, N. T. • 154, 161

Yarnold, Edward • 173
Yeager, D. M. • 136
Yoder, John H. • ix, 17, 24-25, 34, 38, 52-54, 72, 87-89, 100-101, 105, 116, 136, 143,
Yoder, June Alliman • xi, 10, 176, 211
Yoder, Perry B. • xi, 6, 74

Zell, Heinrich • 37
Zurich • 27, 37
Zwingli, Ulrich • 25, 27, 35, 37
Zyl, Hermie C. van • 101